ALAN MOOREHEAD

ALAN MOOREHEAD

Tom Pocock

THE BODLEY HEAD
LONDON

A CIP catalogue record for this book is available from the British Library

ISBN 0 370 31261 9

© 1990 by Tom Pocock

Printed in Great Britain for
The Bodley Head Ltd
20 Vauxhall Bridge Road
London SW1V 2SA
by Mackays of Chatham PLC

First published in 1990

For Owen Casson, my godson,
of Melbourne, Australia

Books by Alan Moorehead

Contents

List of Illustrations and Credits

[1] Moorehead family collections
[2] Clifford collection
[3] National Library of Australia
[4] Imperial War Museum
[5] Hulton Deutsch Collection
[6] Official US Navy photograph

Introduction
& Acknowledgements

Alan Moorehead made his impact both through his writing and his presence. I was among those aware of both at the end of the Second World War when he was the most famous of war correspondents and I, at the age of nineteen, the youngest and least experienced. He seemed to make a royal progress between the liberated capitals of Europe and the battlefields, visiting the most senior Allied commanders when so inclined; it was even rumoured that he had brought his own Neapolitan chef from the Italian front. There was some substance in this reputation for he had reached the summit of his calling.

In peace, further triumphs followed; effortlessly, it seemed. He was reported living in splendour: first in a Renaissance villa in the hills above Florence; then in one he himself had built on the coast of Tuscany. Always he seemed to be in the company of other celebrities. I met him and his wife, Lucy, on only a few occasions but we had mutual friends and I listened to their stories of his life with envy. It was only later that I learned of the struggles, disappointments and emotional turmoil that lay behind this splendid facade. His story came to haunt me, for it assumed an epic quality.

Moorehead's was a biography that needed to be written. Happily for his biographer, he had kept large collections of correspondence, some of his diaries and his wife had saved the letters he had written to her from the time of their courtship for nearly three decades.

In writing this book I am, above all, grateful to his children –

Caroline, John and Richard Moorehead – for their permission to undertake it and for making their parents' papers available to me, and to Caroline's husband, Jeremy Swift, and John's wife, Sarah, for their perceptive comments. In Australia, other members of the family were as helpful: the late Mrs. Phyllis Whitehead (née Moorehead), his sister, and her daughter, Mrs. Gillian Lodge and Mrs. Marjorie Rogers. In the past I had often talked about Moorehead and his war-reporting days with friends who had shared them; particularly David Woodward, Desmond Tighe and Brigadier Nigel Dugdale. I had met his closest friend, Alexander Clifford, when we were both on the staff of the *Daily Mail* and I am grateful to his brother and sister, Mr. H. Dalton Clifford and Mrs. Elizabeth Davies, for allowing me to read his journal and correspondence. I never met Moorehead's other great friend amongst the correspondents, Christopher Buckley, but his widow, Mrs. Cecilia Russell-Smith, has kindly talked to me about him.

I am also grateful to many of his friends for their help, notably Lord and Lady Bangor (the former Edward Ward and Marjorie Banks), Lord Bernstein, Mr. Doon Campbell, Sir Hugh Casson, Mr. Michael Charlton, Mr. Brian Connell, Mr. Don Cook, Sir Geoffrey and Lady Cox, Mr. Roald Dahl, Contessa de Roubilant, Miss Valerie Eaton Griffith, Mr. John Ehrman, Mr. Charles Foley, Mr. and Mrs. Anthony Fry, Miss Martha Gellhorn, Mr. Walter Goetz, the late Mr. Hamish Hamilton and Mrs. Yvonne Hamilton, Mr. Martin Helm, Mr. John Herbert, Miss Clare Hollingworth, Mr. Richard Hough, Group Captain George Houghton, Mr. Derrick Knight, Mrs. Essie Lee, Mr. Drew Middleton, Mr. Richard McMillan, Mr. Gerard Mansell, Mr. Max Martyn, Mr. and Mrs. George Millar, Mr. and Mrs. Leonard Mosley, Sir Edward Pickering, Mr. Cyril Ray, Mr. John Rayner, Mr. John Redfern, Mr. Norman Smart, Mr. Dick Waller, Miss Kaye Webb, Sir Edgar Williams, Mrs. Edith Wilmot, Miss Olive Wood and Mrs. Elizabeth Woodward.

In Australia, I was greatly helped by Dr. and Mrs. Roderick Andrew, Mr. Douglas Brass, Mr. Creighton Burns, Mr. and Mrs. Anthony Casson, Professor Manning Clark, Lady Drysdale, the late Mr. Ian Fitchett, Mr. Allan Fleming, the late Mr. Erl Gray, Mrs. Molly Hetherington, Mr. Bill Holmes, Mr. and Mrs. Colin Laverty, Mrs. Margaret Lodge, Mrs. Joan McClelland, Mrs. Eleanor Rymill, Mr. Frank Sullivan and Mrs. Beth McInnes (née Thwaites).

In London, I am indebted to the Librarians and staff of the British Library and Newspaper Library, the London Library, the reference

library of the *Daily Express*, the Chief Press Officer of the Ministry
of Defence, and the Archivist of the Savoy Hotel; in Australia to
Mr. W.M. Horton, the Director-General of the National Library of
Australia, Mr. Graeme T. Powell, the Manuscript Librarian, and
their staff in Canberra, and to the Editors of the *Melbourne Herald*
and *The Age*.

I must thank Alan Moorehead's publishers, Hamish Hamilton,
for permission to quote from his books.

Caroline and John Moorehead kindly read and commented upon
the typescript of the book and Mr. Jack Carlisle Taylor read – and
commended – Moorehead's reporting from India.

Jill Black and Corinne Hall gave wise editorial advice. My wife,
Penny, helped with research in Australia and nobly accepted the task
of compiling the index.

A final word of gratitude must go to a small group of war
correspondents – among them Alan Moorehead's friend, Paul Holt
– whom I met in June, 1944, on board ship in the English Channel
and whose company inspired my hope of taking up their profession
and so eventually led to the writing of this book.

Tom Pocock,
Chelsea,
November, 1989

Prologue

Despite the activity, it was a peaceful morning. The last four had been quiet, too, but although the guns had been silent and dawn patrols of fighter-bombers no longer rushed overhead in search of targets, it had been the wary stillness of the battlefield. Now this morning, 9th May, 1945, everybody realised that the war in Europe was over. First in Italy and then on Luneburg Heath, at Rheims and in Berlin, the German armies had surrendered to the Allies.

For the journalists accompanying the victorious armies, there remained much to report. A German government, under Hitler's successor Admiral Doenitz, was still in being at Flensburg on the Baltic; several of the Nazi leaders – notably Heinrich Himmler – were still at large; there were reports that concentration camps, even more ghastly than those recently uncovered at Dachau, Buchenwald and Belsen, had been discovered in Poland; and, for the British and the Americans, the triumphal entry into Berlin, which had finally been captured by the Russians a week before, was still to come.

So the journalists were moving on from their billets around the town of Luneburg. Among them three men, dressed in the khaki battledress and green-and-gold insignia of war correspondents, were loading their car for a long journey with kit bags, bedrolls, camp beds, rations and petrol. They were friends, who had been together through many campaigns for more than four years, and had become as famous individually through their reports to their newspapers as they had become throughout the Allied armies as an inseparable trio.

Two of the men were obviously English; both tall, both educated and both combining an air of resolution with gentleness. The elder, aged nearly forty, wore a moustache and round, wire-rimmed spectacles that gave him the look of a schoolmaster, which was what he had been before the war. He was Christopher Buckley, the correspondent of the *Daily Telegraph*. The other was aged thirty-five, handsome but studious in manner; indeed he was said to be fluent in six languages and able to communicate in half a dozen more so that it had been a surprise to the friends of his youth when he had decided to become a journalist rather than a diplomat. He was Alexander Clifford of the *Daily Mail*.

The third and dominant member of the trio was an Australian, aged thirty-four. Short but well-built and muscular, he was remarkable for his large, watchful eyes, which were blue, clear and bright. A fellow-journalist described him at this time as "a trim, slight figure, dark and jaunty, with steady eyes, a scornful, passionate lip and a certain ruthless charm".[1] This was the most celebrated of the three: the correspondent of the *Daily Express*, Alan Moorehead.

When they had loaded their car, the three climbed aboard and, with Moorehead at the wheel, drove away. But they did not head east towards Berlin, north to Flensburg and newly-liberated Denmark and Norway, or south towards Vienna and the Balkans as might have been expected. Instead they took the road south-west to Hanover, then across the Rhine, through Belgium, then to Paris and finally to cross the Channel to London. They were going home.

The three of them had taken a joint decision to return once the fighting had stopped, however important subsequent events might be. They were tired to the point of indifference, Moorehead would say; the fresh and perceptive eyes they had brought to the reporting of the war had become jaded. This had been demonstrated to him a few days before when he had met a British soldier, just liberated from a prison camp, who was staring at their jeep, by then the most familiar form of transport in the Allied armies but which he had never seen before. "What a drum-roll of victories have filled those three years since the first jeep appeared," mused Moorehead in his final despatch from Germany. "Alamein and Tunis. Sicily and Rome. Normandy and the Rhine. And now, at the end, all this ash-heap with the burned-out evil spirit of Hitler at the bottom."[2]

They were driving west through the ash-heaps of bombed cities and bombarded towns, past fresh cemeteries and barbed-wire cages crowded with German prisoners; back across the battlefields of

recent months, like a film of their own memories in reverse. Jolting
through streets half-blocked and ruptured by explosives, they passed
the grey-faced, hungry, shabby Germans with whom the victors
were forbidden to speak except as impersonal conquerors. Each
town reeked of sewage, the smoke of brown coal, decaying bodies
under the rubble and the sour, soapy smell that had accompanied
the defeated *Wehrmacht*. The three men longed for fresh air and
rest.

They felt that they had earned this return to their homes and
womenfolk after so much war. Alan Moorehead had married just
before it had begun and now had a small son and an infant daughter.
Alexander Clifford had married a vivacious girl in London during his
last leave earlier in the year. Christopher Buckley had remained the
bachelor that he looked, but was in love with a girl he knew to be
unhappily married and so he now had his hopes.

They crossed the Rhine, drove through the Ardennes, where
the Germans had counter-attacked at Christmas, and took the road
to Paris but did not linger there, for London was their destination.
There the laurels of their triumph awaited. All three were aware of
their celebrity from their editors' cables of congratulation, the prominence given to their reports on the front pages of their newspapers
and the praise that had been lavished upon them when on leave in
London. For Moorehead and Clifford this had begun at the end of
1940, when they had reported the first campaign in the Egyptian and
Libyan deserts, and for Buckley when he had reported the fighting
in Greece. Together they had discussed their fame and speculated
whether, like the leading war correspondents of the First World War,
they might be rewarded with knighthoods.

In any case, all doors would be open to them and they longed
for the fulfilment of hopes that could now be transformed from
ambitions to realities. Buckley hankered after an academic future,
perhaps at Oxford, his own university; possibly as Professor of the
History of War and a Fellow of All Souls. Clifford talked of a return
to the Mediterranean, living with his wife in some beautiful place
and touring Europe and the Middle East as a political commentator,
unhindered by the need to report daily news. Moorehead was less
specific: he might live in England, or he talked of moving his family
to Paris, and of buying a vineyard on the Basque coast of France. But,
wherever he decided to live, the thrust of his ambition was clear and
had been clear for a decade: he wanted to become a writer rather than
a reporter; not just a well-regarded writer of books – he had already

had three about his war experiences published and was at work on a fourth – but a writer of international renown.

As the three of them returned to London and acclaim, all things seemed possible.

Chapter One

"This is what I had come for"

On the first page of his diary for the year 1926, the fifteen-year-old boy wrote, "One crowded hour of glorious life is worth an age without a name." Sir Walter Scott's words expressed the hope for excitement that then seemed unlikely to be fulfilled in the genteel suburbs of the Australian city of Melbourne, where he lived. A second quotation, taken from the poet Robert Browning and written on the second page, was added because it was dramatic and suggested another reason for his growing sense of frustration. "Sunset ran, one glorious blood-red, reeking into Cadiz Bay."

The imagery of that line was affecting because such skies at dawn and sunset often reddened above the great wilderness that lay beyond the lawns, trimmed hedges and tennis courts of the boy's surroundings. But Cadiz Bay and the tremendous historical events and characters that its name conjured up – Drake and the Armada, Nelson and Trafalgar – were part of his own inherited mythology that was ten thousand miles away, as remote in distance as in time. Indeed nearly all the high drama of history, which had shaped the British Empire of which he was a citizen and which crowded his imagination, had happened a long way from Australia.

At the age of fifteen, Alan McCrae Moorehead seemed a happy boy to his parents, brother and sister with whom he lived. At school, he was not academic but he did try to succeed and was always busy on the cricket and football fields and at the swimming baths. In the holidays his enthusiasm was directed towards expeditions to the edge

5

of the outback, the seemingly eternal scenery of desert, forest and mountain that threw the suburban security of their lives into such cosy relief, and to summer camps arranged by his school. The diary reflected uncomplicated contentment: "We had a great footy match . . . We had the rowing boat up there. There were also fights, swims, extra tucker and many other things. The jolliest happiest camp I've ever been to."

There were the stirrings of a budding libido and wonderings about religion combining with the daily happenings of adolescent life. After the school's swimming sports, he noted, "There is something behind it all – something that controls our destiny. A day of joy and sharp sorrow. I have dropped my fountain pen in the baths – and I have met Bill Bailey's sister." Disappointment followed and was shrugged aside with an entry in the diary two days later: "Delia Bailey is a pretty, naughty, empty little thing."

For his sixteenth birthday on 22nd July, he was bought his first pair of long trousers and on that night he accompanied his sister Phyllis, a tall, handsome girl aged twenty-one, to a dance. "A wonderful night," he wrote. "Crowds and crowds of people. Orchestra, supper – oh, wonderful . . . What do you know? I can do the Charleston!"

Yet beneath this breezy boyishness were frustrations at several levels. One of them had been recognised by some of his friends and, shortly before his birthday, he had confided it to his diary: "Here I am nearly 16 and scarcely five ft. high – it hurts. Never mind, there's plenty of other small people worse off than me." Dancing with his sister on the night of his birthday had sharpened his consciousness of his small size; it seemed all the healthy, athletic Australian girls he was beginning to desire were tall, and certainly his rivals were. This seemed particularly unfair since he also recognised that they could be attracted by his handsome looks and attentive manner.

This recurrent worry merged with that of money, for the Moorehead family faced a continuing struggle to maintain middle-class appearances on the modest earnings of Alan's father, a journalist. An amiable man with a light touch in his writing and in some demand as an after-dinner speaker in Melbourne, Richard Moorehead was not, and was unlikely to become, a success. Although he had written for the two principal Melbourne newspapers, *The Age* and the *Herald*, he had not become more than an amusing feature-writer. Yet he prided himself as "a man of letters", just as his wife Louise was "artistic" and therefore a social cut above their prosperous relations who had made their money in trade.

The Mooreheads had originally been of Scottish stock and, after settling in Ireland, had migrated to Australia in the middle of the nineteenth century. The first Australian Moorehead – also named Richard – had first settled in Sydney in 1849 before moving to Melbourne, where he worked as a carter. His son married into the McCrae family, which had arrived in Australia from Scotland at about the same time as the Mooreheads, after a dreadful voyage in which their ship had been becalmed for six weeks near the Equator and one of their children had died. One of the sons of this marriage was Richard Moorehead, who married Louise Edgerton, the daughter of a prosperous publisher and printer in Melbourne, and fathered three children, Phyllis, Bernard and finally Alan.

Life in the suburbs was not expensive but the Mooreheads could afford no luxuries and certainly not a motor car or travel except into the countryside around the city. To compensate for this they were constantly moving house and, whichever suburb they chose, they usually managed to find a new home with a tennis court in the garden. Even this failed to satisfy Louise Moorehead's restlessness and she would compulsively change the uses of the rooms of her home and rearrange the furniture within each. Once she even took out her paint-box to change all the roses printed on the wallpaper from a yellow she disliked to pink. Her husband, arriving home late from some dinner in the city and making his way to bed in the dark to avoid disturbing his family, would sometimes trip over furniture his wife had moved during the day; one of his more successful newspaper articles was a humorous account of moving house.

Nevertheless, it was a happy family, and Richard Moorehead managed – occasionally with the help of well-to-do relations – to give his three children good educations. Phyllis, the eldest, was a striking, athletic girl so would certainly marry well; Bernard, the elder son, was something of a problem for he was withdrawn, gauche and seemingly without ambition; then, four years his junior, was little Alan, who was so full of energy and enthusiasm that, despite regular setbacks in school examinations, he would probably make his own way. In 1926, Alan was attending one of the best schools in Melbourne, Scotch College, which offered an English education, slightly modified for the Antipodes, in its range of mock-Tudor buildings surrounded by lawns set with large ornamental trees.

It was this education, combined with the books that the children read, the traditions upon which their family life was based and the whole ethos of the British Empire, of which they were citizens, that gave rise to a deeper and less definable sense of restlessness and discontent. The Mooreheads, like nearly all the six million Australians, were proud to be of British stock, to have inherited the British language and laws and to be subjects of the King-Emperor. Apart from the minority who lived by farming and prospecting at the edge of the Outback, their social structure was a reflection of that in the British Isles; indeed it included an occasional custom derived directly from the manners and modes of an earlier British society, as when Louise Moorehead spoke of a ladies' tea-party as a "chevoo", a derivation of *"chez vous"*, a fragment of social parlance from the eighteenth century.

Most of young Alan's reading-matter was British. The magazines of his childhood – *Chums*, *Magnet* and the *Boys' Own Paper* – arrived several months late because they had been shipped from England, and the photographs and political cartoons in the *Illustrated London News* and *Punch*, to which his interest was beginning to turn, were also out of date. The novels of Dornford Yates, P.G. Wodehouse and P.C. Wren, which he had begun to enjoy, were all set in a society somewhat like his own but, it seemed, on a different level of creation and infinitely remote.

For the British – particularly the English – were different from the Europeans. The people of the Continent were all labelled with Alan's preconceptions: as he was to describe these, he saw the French as "lascivious and sharp", the Italians as "unreliable and physically rather dirty", the Scandinavians "clean but uninteresting", the Dutch "clean but gross" and the Germans "quite simply, monsters". But the English were something of a mystery, particularly when seen through the eyes of his favourite novelists. They were noble or comic, subtle or stupid, arrogant or charming but all of them were sprung from that pageant of melodramatic history which Australia lacked.

His first encounter with the reality of this came when he was one of a picked troop of Boy Scouts chosen to escort the newly-arrived Governor of Victoria, Lord Somers, on a brief expedition into the outback. A product of Charterhouse, New College, Oxford, and the Life Guards, and decorated for gallantry in the recent Great War, Lord Somers proved a genial, paternal, middle-aged man with a military moustache and the "nice speaking voice" that Alan's mother said the English had. He also seemed to have a semi-religious status as representative of the King-Emperor, that distant demi-god, and his presence underlined the ambivalence of the Australian condition.

At Scotch College, Alan was taught the history of Australia and the British Empire by masters who were often themselves English but, he was to feel, rejects from the schools of their own country; their failure showing in their "harassed and defeated faces". The Australian history he was taught was less than a century and a half in span and, although it included the early navigators and explorers, their exploits had to be seen beside the miseries of the penal settlements and the rough-and-tumble of the gold rush that had brought prosperity to Melbourne. The real achievements of the pioneer farmers and graziers seemed dull beside the two thousand years of British history.

Australians themselves had first become involved with that when Alan had been aged five. Two uncles were particular favourites; one of them because he would invite the child to force open his clenched fist within which would be a silver coin that would be for him. Then both uncles appeared, one after the other, with their legs no longer covered by well-creased slacks but with khaki breeches and, below the knee, wound with spiral strips of cloth called puttees. Then both went away; one never returned; the other came back but the coin now had to be forced from his left fist, because his right was no longer there and he had only one leg in his pair of trousers. They had been to Gallipoli.

The summoning of the Australians and New Zealanders to Europe and the events of 1915 brought about a sudden and brutal coming-of-age for both countries. Australians had been proud that their young men – magnificent physical specimens, reared in the open air and sunshine – had been called by their King-Emperor to his service, like some cherished Praetorian Guard held in reserve for just such a moment as seemed to have come. Their task – the forcing of the Dardanelles and the capture of Constantinople – seemed as heroic to them as it had to Rupert Brooke; a crusade worthy of their sacrifice. Indeed, of more than three hundred thousand Australian men sent to fight in Europe, more than two-thirds were killed or wounded, a far higher casualty rate than that suffered by any other country in the British Empire, including Great Britain herself: 68.5 per cent as against 52.5 per cent lost by the British. This blood sacrifice had earned Australia the right to be heard, to criticise and to carry more weight in the affairs of the world. So when the opinion of Australia carried no more or less weight after the Great War than before it, the result was an increase in assertiveness and a defensive self-regard.

Life in Australia did not satisfy Alan Moorehead, even though the city where he lived was growing fast and the population was expected to reach one million within the coming decade. Once the family lived in Sydney for a spell but otherwise their knowledge of the world beyond their suburb was limited to the country towns between Melbourne and the outback and the edges of the great wilderness itself. This could have been exciting enough for many boys. It was not only that another uncle had been a gold-prospector and told thrilling stories of his adventures: how he had almost died of thirst in the bush and nearly been murdered by an Aboriginal tribesman; how fortunes had been made and lost in the goldfields and how he himself had missed finding the biggest and most famous gold nugget of them all by a couple of feet. Within Alan's own experience were the terrifying bush fires, which raged around Melbourne in 1926 when the sky above the Dandenong hills, twenty miles east of the city, was dark with smoke. The wild creatures of the outback – the kangaroos, koala bears, the duckbill platypus and the richly eccentric bird-life – was not only accessible to any visitor to the surrounding country, but unique to Australia. Once in an attempt to catch a koala, Alan and some friends chased the animal into the tree-tops until a branch gave way beneath its weight and it fell to its death, leaving him with a guilt he never forgot.

Yet this strangeness was familiar to him and, since it related to family holidays and school expeditions, was not particularly exciting; the history lessons in school and the books he read all suggested that important events took place somewhere else, particularly in Europe.

Following his sixteenth birthday, there were discussions about his future. His brother Bernard, four years older, was preparing to be an architect and showing promise as a painter but was so shy and uncommunicative that he did not inspire his younger brother. Phyllis had tried to follow her father as a journalist and had spent two years at the University of Melbourne taking a diploma course; but women journalists were only supposed to write about fashion, household matters and social gossip, so she had taken another course in dress-making. It was being said that Alan should enter one of the principal professions and become a lawyer or a doctor to ensure a well-paid career and respectable position in society. Then advice was offered by the very man who had introduced the boy to the far-distant, tantalising world where everything seemed to happen, through the medium of English literature. This was the senior English master, W.A. Waller, cruelly nicknamed "Hoppy" by the boys because of his limping gait. On 7th October, Alan wrote in his diary: "Hoppy Waller asked me what I was going in for. He strongly recommended journalism on the strength of my essays. Well, what's to be done?"

Other than eliciting this insight into his latent talents, the boy had not made much mark at his school. His headmaster's report for that year shows him to have been regarded as pleasant but not out-standing: "He is a good lad, who has shown himself diligent and attentive to his studies, amiable in disposition and ever-ready to give help where it is called for." He had reached an academic standard that would qualify him for Melbourne University and he hankered after the prolonged adolescence combined with a carefree social life, reminiscent of the P.G. Wodehouse stories, that undergraduates seemed to lead in and around the mock-English buildings that housed them in the north of the city. Yet, even if he knew which subject he wanted to read, there was no possibility that his father could afford the modest fees. He himself was already decided on another ambition which had developed from "Hoppy" Waller's advice. Journalism had done little enough for his father but it might, perhaps, lead to some-thing that could make him rich and famous. Sometimes the "great writers", whose books were shipped out to Australia, seemed akin to the better journalists, except that, instead of writing a thousand words, they would produce a hundred thousand which would be published in hard covers. Surely, if he could win praise from a schoolmaster for his essays – and any praise from that quarter was a cause for some surprise and celebration – he could write a book and become famous?

At the end of 1926 when he left Scotch College, he planned to combine both the dreams: a lively life at university for a few years, then journalism leading to the writing of books and international acclaim. Yet all such hopes were dashed when it was explained that there was no possibility of raising enough money for the university fees and that journalism would be a possibility only when he was some years older. So he became an office boy, running errands for a small advertising agency and occasionally looking over the shoulders of the copy-writers to envy them their task of writing enticing words.

He was a determined boy and it struck him that many great writers had boasted of their humble beginnings and had had to make their own way towards fame. He knew, too, that in the United States, which was becoming increasingly familiar through Hollywood films, young people worked to pay, or subsidise, their college fees. So, after six months' work as an office boy, during which he began to understand the importance of presentation and the eye-catching phrase in advertising copy-writing, he decided to make a change. His father had once worked for the magazine *Table Talk*, in which his mother's family had had an interest, so he called at its office and asked to see the editor. Would he like to publish a weekly column of social and sporting news from the university? If so, he could write it as he was planning to become an undergraduate shortly. The editor was taken with the idea and agreed to give it a trial, paying £2.10s. a week if it could fill a full column in the magazine. This would provide sufficient subsidy to pay the university's fees.

So, in the spring of 1928, Alan Moorehead enrolled at Melbourne University to read English for a Bachelor of Arts degree. It was not his studies that particularly appealed but the robust social life and the opportunities to write for student magazines. This would also provide shelter from the bleak economic climate, for this was the period between the British general strike of 1926 and the American slump of 1929 and the depression had reached Australia, bringing unemployment and sharpening the genteel poverty of the Moorehead household. Alan could live at home and now eyebrows would not be raised when he returned to bed in the early hours of the morning. This new freedom combined with the pleasure of schooldays: playing hockey and winning a half-blue; skiing in the Victoria mountains and skating in winter; surfing from the wide, empty beaches in summer and riding on sheep stations in the Riverina.

In his contentment Alan hoped that this pleasant, undemanding life could be extended indefinitely, but he also found himself his father's heir because his brother Bernard, who had gone to Hong Kong to work as an architect, died suddenly of pernicious anaemia in 1931, and now the family's future status would be dependent on his own efforts. So, after three years, he took his degree and looked for another subject to read that would offer prospects in a profession and decided that this should be law. The status of lawyer would establish him in the social hierarchy and provide an assured income and such benefits had become clear since his sister Phyllis had just married a promising young lawyer, Jack Whitehead. He also told himself that an understanding of the law would be useful when he began work as a journalist and good training in the grasp of essentials when he became a writer.

This was already beginning to become a reality. The *Table Talk* column had given way to regular reporting of university news for the daily *Herald* and to the lucrative work of reporting examination results at 2½d. a line, which together produced an income more than adequate for his needs. However, the real excitement was in university journalism, for that commanded the attention of his peers. He contributed to the *Melbourne University Magazine* and became its editor for a year, but the focus of attention was upon the students' own magazines; sometimes rather scurrilous, often political, for Australia was reacting to the upheavals in Europe – the Russian revolution and the rise of fascism – and the university was in a ferment of radicalism.

Alan did not hold strongly political views but he did follow his friends in a general admiration of socialist ideals, although he and most of them drew the line at outright communism. Among those who did not was the most charismatic in their circle, Alwyn Lee. A charming, intelligent and quick-witted young man, he combined traditional Australian looks – he was tall, lean and aquiline – with a communist view of the world, softened by a wide knowledge and love of literature and poetry. It was he who weaned Alan from the simple pleasures of the popular English novelists and introduced him to the work of James Joyce, Ezra Pound and T.S. Eliot.

Lee wrote political commentaries for the Marxist magazine *Proletariat*, as did another celebrated student, Sam White. The son of Russian immigrant parents – his father had been one of the few Jewish civil servants in Tsarist Russia and he himself remembered the terrors of the last pogrom and the beginnings of the communist revolution – he became a Marxist and an enthusiastic Australian. His family had changed their name to White and Sam claimed to have forgotten his original surname. Together, Lee and White were regarded as extremists, while others were more interested in the writing than the radical content of their student magazines, amongst them Cyril Pearl who edited *Stream* and Allan Fleming who was editor of the more breezy *Farrago*, which was produced in a corner of the undergraduates' club-room.

A few of the aspiring journalists and writers were apolitical, amongst them a handsome Tasmanian, Noel Monks, who was far more interested in swimming and athletics than in radical ideas. Tall, fair-haired and blue-eyed, Monks was vain yet kindly and gentle, always ready with a sympathetic ear and a generous gesture while glorying in the hero-worship he was accorded, particularly in the public displays of his prowess, such as diving into the Yarra river from the Princes Street bridge before admiring crowds. Another undemanding and apolitical friend was Jim Kilvington, also a law student and the son of a well-to-do surgeon. Diffident and unambitious, he introduced Alan to more sophisticated and less heady pleasures, notably to music, and the two would listen to his recordings of opera while sharing a bottle of wine. Alan did not feel that this was a rival with whom he must compete.

As the correspondent of the *Herald*, through whom the news of the university and the names of his contemporaries could be printed in a newspaper which would find its way across the country and even abroad, Alan enjoyed a standing that could not have been imparted by the lively but amateur activities of student journalists. Occasionally, both would coincide, as in the case of one student prank, which became part of the university's mythology and was reported in the *Herald* by Alan. This was the hunting of Sam White.

While his fellow-Marxist Alwyn Lee tempered the violence of his views with urbanity, White was a militant, seeming to appear at every political meeting or debate at the university in order to deliver a communist harangue, often choosing the British Empire as his target. While the more moderate undergraduates merely tired of his constant interruptions, the more conservative considered him "a commo and a damn nuisance". Amongst these were the conservative stalwarts of the Trinity College rowing club, who finally decided that he had taken his politics too far and must be taught a lesson by being thrown into the lake in the university grounds outside the club-house.

The occasion for this was to be another political debate at which Sam White was scheduled to speak. Something of the sort was expected by Allan Fleming, the editor of *Farrago*, who was in the audience and later recalled, "As Sam began to speak, a number of mighty shoulders arose in the auditorium and advanced towards him. I thought this sort of thing was wrong, so I got up and remonstrated, 'Gentlemen, gentlemen . . . ' But that was not going to stop them, so I grabbed Sam and hustled him out of a side door and he escaped."

His respite was to be brief. Next day, he was in the corner of the club-room where *Farrago* was produced, talking to Fleming when, as the latter recalled, "There was a thundering noise outside, then a thumping on the door and a chanting of 'We want Sam.' It was the shoulders again. But only one pair could get through the door at a time, so when the first of them made a grab at Sam, some of us tried to hang on to him. But it was no good. They hauled him out and threw him in the lake."[1] As he emerged, dripping, to be photographed by his jubilant persecutors, Sam White was philosophical about his fate, realising that martyrdom could only help his cause. "The first thing I did when I got out," he said later, "was to give the exclusive story to Alan for the *Herald*."[2]

Alan enjoyed making the most of describing this mild escapade as much as he would have been bored by having to report the political differences that had precipitated it. At parties which quickly became heated political debates, he was likely to disappear early and usually with some attractive girl. The passionate interest his contemporaries showed in radicalism he devoted to the opposite sex. He had grown into a strong and virile young man, conscious both of his well-built body and its lack of height, for he had now reached his full height of five feet and seven inches. He knew himself to be attractive to women with his large, appealing yet challenging blue eyes and the sensual mouth, which had earned him the nickname "lubra lips", "lubra" being the word for a negroid Aboriginal woman. Yet the lack of height, which had so worried him at the age of fifteen, continued to induce aggressive attitudes in compensation and this was reflected in his attitude to women.

Like so many young men of his time, he saw his female contemporaries in three categories. First there were those to whom he was related by blood, or might one day be related by marriage; who seemed sacred beings, pure in mind and body; who could, or should, prompt no profane desire beyond a romantic longing for those seen as a future wife. Secondly, there were the girls for whom he felt no romantic attachment yet who stimulated lust, which, it was assumed, they could share, or be excited into doing so; these could be regarded as a means of satisfaction and so accorded only the most cursory civilities. Finally, there would be the occasional confidante, seen as a friend to whom loyalty was due. Sometimes the categories would overlap: the goddess would become a nymph for debauching; the sexual quarry could induce chivalry; even the confidante could suddenly and unexpectedly become desirable.

Alan had been accorded the reputation of a "ladies' man" yet it was not until he was aged twenty-one and in his last year at university that he lost his virginity. Until then, what was described as "making love" was confined to urgent kissing and fumbling beneath clothes, such encounters confined to the backs of cars, secluded porches and whatever cover was offered by the countryside or the beach in the hours of darkness. His first conquest was neither a challenge to his powers of persuasion, nor proved as satisfying as the occasion should have been, for it took place on some waste-land behind the girl's house and she infected him with a mild form of venereal disease.

This and other encounters he described to a friend in the third category, Beth Thwaites, also an undergraduate, who was hoping to become a journalist. He had been drawn to her because she was entertaining, forthright and as short in stature as himself. When his sister had introduced them at a dance, Beth, sensing that, if she told him of her ambitions in journalism, he might brag about his own achievements, told him that she wanted to breed pigs. She was small, quite pretty, somewhat in the shadow of a more desirable sister and defended herself with an aggressive repartee. Once it became clear to both that they would not become romantic or carnal lovers, they became, as Beth put it, "good mates – no sex. We were both short-arsed bastards and he was very sensitive about his height. He had big, sparkling eyes, big, sloppy lips and was very sexy – but not with me. Everyone made love to my sister and played cricket with me."[3]

So he would regale Beth with humorous commentaries on his current encounters, such as one on a seaside holiday. He wrote to her:

> Things narrowed down to a pursuit of the blonde. To my amazement I emerged victorious in the teeth of fierce opposition. A positive host of boiled shirts and swarthy faces assailed the lady's room on the last night. But Jack and I (in soft shirts) had the girl and her friend on the beach before the opposition could move . . . I have come to the conclusion that my methods on the beach are my most effective argument against feminine innocence. But in this case the girl is decidedly not innocent. She is in the richest and fullest sense a bad woman and one of parts at that. It was an orgy of moon, sea, beer and woman until three in the morning when we went back to the hotel. I have reason to believe that subsequently she spent the rest of the night with someone else . . . which makes her all the more desirable.[4]

His relationship with Beth Thwaites was flirtatious, if platonic, and he enjoyed writing another teasing letter to her about this affair:

> Dear lass, I'm beginning to realise how futile it is trying to elude you. I sneaked up the stairs last night with a guilty mind. I switched on the light in my room and the first thing I saw was your awful photograph peering at me in the true battle-axe manner. I tried to placate it. It stared at me in cold contempt. "I know," the damn thing said, "you've been out with the blonde." What could I do? I broke down and confessed everything. Picture the scene. My bedroom, midnight. Me on the floor, a pathetic figure . . . you on

the dressing table, glaring with seething hate over a pair of brushes and a bottle of hair oil, muttering thickly to yourself, "Out with it you young pup and God help you if you've done wrong by the girl."

"I was mad," I cried. "Unbridled passion surged within me. I could not live without her." (The family stirred restlessly in the next room at this moment and I lowered my voice to a fierce whisper.) "I sought her in the cool hours of the evening," I continued brokenly. "She spurned me, her cool lips curling in the dusk and the soft lines of her delicate, fragile face hardening at my approach. Even now I hear her silver tones crying, "I'll be damned if you're coming in here." Every word she uttered was a lyric. Madly, I replied, "I'll be damned if I don't." Touched with the pathos of my voice and the neatness of my reply, her demeanour softened and together we passed within. She reclined upon a silken divan whilst I lay at her feet, smiting my brow in an excess of passion. "Darling!" I cried. She waved a bare leg at me. I was utterly disarmed by the charming gesture. For an eternity we lay clasped in each other's arms waiting for the beer to cool on the ice. Presently she spoke, her voice crooning like a young dove, "Dear one, I think we might sock a couple of quick 'uns now." And so the cool hours of the night sped on . . .

I see the girl for the last time on Monday night. No don't laugh at that. It's getting a bit too serious anyway . . . I'm too much of a materialist to lose my wits about the whole business. She says – "If I once start, I'll never want to stop." I think the same. So long as there is any hope of me doing anything worth while in this world I'm not going to succumb to the passion for sleeping with women. I want experience. I may get it before Tuesday morning. I honestly don't think I will. Whatever happens, it's going to stop.[5]

Attempts to discipline himself were more successful when applied to his law studies. The subject did not particularly interest him and his true ambition to become a journalist and a writer rather than a lawyer came into sharper focus as the end of the two-year course drew near. It became increasingly clear that a life in legal chambers would be no substitute for the easy-going years at university and still less for the excitements of reporting and writing of which he had dreamed so long.

But this did not become fully clear to Alan until, in 1933, he sat his final examinations for his degree. He had settled at his table in the examination hall to answer a paper about Modern

Political Institutions and then realised not only that they did not interest him but that he would neither make a good lawyer nor did he want to become one. As he stared at the blank sheets of paper, there suddenly seemed no point in writing on them. He already had a part-time job as a reporter at the *Herald* and felt confident that he could apply for, and be given, full-time work. So, when the interval bell rang to allow candidates to leave their desks for a break, he rose, walked from the hall, took a tram down to the *Herald* office, asked for a staff job and was given it.

Not for an instant did he regret his decision as he settled into the newspaper office. He kept in touch with his closest university friends – notably Alwyn Lee and Beth Thwaites – but that life quickly fell away and his job as the *Herald*'s reporter there was taken over by a forceful young man two years his junior, Chester Wilmot, who was reading law and had become a powerful speaker in undergraduates' debates. Now Alan's talent for reporting – the marshalling of factual information learned during his law studies combining with the light touch inherited from his father's journalism – could be spread far beyond the university but not, of course, beyond Melbourne and the state of Victoria. He reported magistrates' courts and inquests, bush fires and droughts and an early success was his reporting of a plague of locusts that was devastating farmland. His light touch was used to effect when he was sent to cover a race up Mount Buffalo by competitors pushing wheelbarrows laden with sacks of wheat.

He was making new friends among the young reporters and sub-editors on the Melbourne newspapers, amongst them the charming but quick-tempered reporter John Hetherington, the urbane sub-editor Erl Gray, the equally ambitious Frank Sullivan, the robust Ian Fitchett, whose grandfather seemed to have shown the way by writing the best-seller *Brave Deeds that Won the Empire*, and his old friend Noel Monks was already established as a resourceful, flamboyant reporter. Alan, too, took to the life and work with gusto, his pay rising from £4 to £8 a week and occasionally his reports being signed with his own name instead of the usual attribution to Our Special Correspondent. When the young journalists met over coffee before the day's work or over beer after it, their talk was of their calling and their ambitions rather than sport and girls. But now that one ambition had been attained another took its place, for all of them were reading books which reflected the tumult of the outside world and Alan particularly admired the terse, tense novels of Ernest Hemingway, declaring *A Farewell to Arms* to be a masterpiece; a style of writing and an achievement to emulate.

However, his immediate inspiration and trail-blazer was Noel Monks. He was now a shipping reporter on the *Sun* newspaper, had been at sea under sail and round the world in a freighter and was now planning another expedition abroad since it had become apparent to them all that international acclaim would not be accorded to success in remote Australia. He was talking of working his way to England by sea and trying his luck there as a reporter, for, by 1934, tremors were shaking Europe as the violent, alarmingly popular Fascist movement took hold in Italy and was being followed by that of the Nazis in Germany. The idea of roaming the world in search of fame took hold on the young men and Alan, walking out of an old university friend's party which was turning into one of the familiar political debates, with a girl on his arm and heading for the nearby beach, told her, "I'm going to get out of this country."[6]

All eyes were upon Noel Monks and the great adventure he was planning. He was to be accompanied by John Hetherington and finally, in January, 1935, the two of them set out in the liner *Largs Bay*, working their passage as crewmen. After leaving Melbourne, the ship called at Fremantle in Western Australia and from there Monks sent them a farewell letter: "Ah there mates . . . Have been feeling very, very sorry for myself, lads . . . Will feel sorrier tomorrow when we leave old Aussie behind. But Time Marches On . . ." He wished them luck, sending his regards to "Alan the Great Lover".

Those he left behind settled down to reporting the magistrates' courts, bush fires and sport, speculating on the adventures awaiting Noel Monks in the almost mythological country of their origin on the other side of the world. Over the coming months, news of his exploits arrived. In London, he had fallen in with a young South African journalist, O'Dowd Gallagher, who had just been engaged as a reporter for the *Daily Express*, the mass-circulation newspaper owned by the Canadian millionaire Lord Beaverbrook, who tended to favour other sons of the Empire. Moreover, Gallagher was to be sent on the most exciting assignment possible: to Abyssinia. The news dominating 1935 was the threat to invade and annex that strange and backward African country by the Italian dictator Mussolini and the attempts by the League of Nations to stop him. Noel Monks had been to see the editor of the *Express*, the celebrated Arthur Christiansen, and asked if he could go too, the editor's refusal being tempered by his kindly remark that he was glad to see that the spirit of adventure was not dead.

Monks decided to accompany his new friend to Abyssinia at his own expense as a freelance. This he did with some success and he was there when the Italians invaded at the beginning of October, sending despatches to the London *News of the World*, the Melbourne *Herald* and a news agency. Yet he saw no action – although he did hear distant gunfire – and had to leave the country before the Italian victory in the following May. He then returned to Australia and what he hoped would be a hero's welcome.

In this Noel Monks was mistaken. There was an Australian saying about cutting down tall poppies and that egalitarian parable was particularly appropriate to newspapers, where success abroad was resented. So Monks was given what was known as "the treatment"; arriving at the *Herald* office, he was at once sent by his editor to report a conference of the Women's Christian Temperance Union and it was made clear that he would have to work his way into favour by getting back into the routine instead of boasting about any adventures he might have had. So he spent his earnings on another passage to England in the liner *Jervis Bay* and was back in Fleet Street by May 1936, just as news of the formal annexation of Abyssinia by Italy was announced. Ambitious young reporters were casting about for another exciting assignment, perhaps in Spain, which was in the ferment that, two months later, led to a military revolt against the Republican government led by an unknown officer named Franco, and civil war.

The treatment accorded to Noel Monks had a profound effect upon Alan Moorehead and his contemporaries. They would have to make their way to London for opportunities and success. They reckoned that the cost of getting to Britain, seeing something of Europe and launching themselves on a newspaper career in Fleet Street would be £500 and several of them, including Alan, had begun to save. By the time Monks sailed for England the second time, he and several friends, including Erl Gray and Frank Sullivan, had enough for their escape and booked one-way passages to England in the *Ormonde*, a liner in which passengers were not segregated in classes, this appealing both to their Australian egalitarianism and hopes of a sociable voyage. In May, the same month that Noel Monks arrived back in London, they sailed from Melbourne.

It was difficult to realise that the great adventure had begun because life for the *Ormonde*'s passengers was like a maritime version of that in Melbourne: there were so many young Australians on board and the round of parties, accompanied by much banter and the occasional flirtation, continued much as it had ashore. The weather became hotter as they crossed the Indian Ocean and, as the ship entered the Red Sea and approached the Suez Canal, it became apparent to the least imaginative of them that they were about to reach that part of the world where history happened and was still happening. As the *Ormonde* steamed northward through the heat of the Red Sea, the passengers held a fancy dress ball; Frank Sullivan attended dressed as a fairy, became overheated dancing the Charleston and the Black Bottom, then went to sleep on his bunk wearing only pyjama trousers beneath an electric fan, became chilled and soon afterwards was in the ship's sick-bay with pneumonia. Concern for Frank was countered by the mounting excitements of the voyage. The ship stopped at Port Said and the Australians tumbled ashore in the heat, dust and flies and remembered the soldiers' stories that fathers and uncles who had returned from Gallipoli had told about Egypt. They passed south of Crete and the Ancient World familiar from Greek legends learned at Scotch College, then saw the mountains of southern Italy and Sicily and the threatening volcanic mass of Etna. They sighted the Sorrento peninsula, the dramatic cliffs of Capri and the *Ormonde* moored off Naples below the high, dark crater of Vesuvius. Going ashore, the Australians had been assailed by the pungent mixture of architectural grandeur and social squalor and, after a day's sightseeing, Alan wrote to Beth Thwaites in Melbourne:

> Of Naples they promised us excavations and dancing girls, red wine, spaghetti of old brew, fruit and volcanoes; a mixture of immorality, epicureanism and archeology. We got them.
>
> Lovely place. The gendarmes dress in black, knee-high boots, green plus-fours and tunics and they are armed with a great goose-feather stuck in their Alpine hats, enormous revolvers, swords and a sneering smile. Half the population wears uniform. The other half is in the employ of a dive called the Glass House. We missed the Glass House but it will remain for me the brothel of all brothels. Every guide we had, every steward of the ship lavished adjectives upon it . . .

His first sight of Europe had not impressed him with the sense of the past, the sophistication and charm that he had expected and, when he returned on board, he dismissed it lightly, as he told Beth:

I was drunk when we got back. I went with a nice Australian girl on the boat deck and told her that the discovery of a frying-pan and pieces from a chess-board in the ashes of Pompeii had disproved the existence of God. We sailed along under the cliffs of lovely islands piled with palaces and churches and I told her that everything was all wrong with everything. That Naples had the beauty of an over-ripe melon. That its beauty was superstition. That its virility had been aborted even before Vesuvius splurged out ashes over Pompeii. That nothing had been done since. Then I went to bed.

The others are well. Noel left his last letter for us in Port Said and we are to wire him the time of our arrival in London next week so that he can meet us.[7]

The ship's next call was to be Toulon and the Australians expected little from what they were told was the principal base of the French navy and probably more squalid than Naples since the French were notorious for their indifference to hygiene. In the event, their first experience of France was quite different and its impact made a lasting impression upon Alan, as he was afterwards to write. Indeed, he was to conclude, "I date my life from this moment. Everything in my memory either falls into the period before I reached Toulon, or belongs to the years since then, and in fact my life abruptly took a new course that morning."

The *Ormonde* had steamed into the great outer harbour with green, wooded hills to either side and to the north, below a steep, bare mountain, lay the town which slowly came into view:

From the distance it had the effect of a mirage, some turreted town from the East, floating on the edge of the water. We anchored a good way out in the harbour and came ashore in small boats; and once ashore the city swallowed you up. You stepped from your boat straight on to the cobblestones, and, all about you, yelling women were selling oysters and mussels, lobsters and crabs, shrimps and limpets and sea urchins; they were all alive, reeking of the sea and piled on top of one another in sagging wicker baskets. Beyond these stalls was a short open space and then the cafés began, dozens of rickety little tables in the sunshine with coloured sunshades and, sitting there, idly surveying the universe, sipping their vermouth-cassis, were the bottomless cynical French clientele. Wonderfully gay little men, chattering like monkeys. And girls. French girls, doing things or having things done to them, right there in the open in a way that would have caused a riot back in Park Villas, Melbourne. Before my eyes, a man casually reached up his hand to the waitress, pulled down her head and kissed her on the mouth. When, after a long time, she lifted up her head again and caught my eye she smiled pleasantly . . .

The shock no doubt was all the greater because this was precisely the sort of behaviour that I expected from the French – expected but never quite dared to believe was true. It was like having one's secret thoughts dragged out into the open . . . I shifted my eyes away uneasily. Beyond the cafés, the facades of topsy-turvy buildings rose up and they were painted in the brightest possible pale blues and yellows with window-boxes and strings of corn-cobs hanging out from the balconies to dry . . .

I left my friends then and walked on alone . . . Finally I came to an open square . . . It was market morning. The fishermen and peasants had set up their stalls under the plane trees. There it was, the ripeness of the Midi, the colour, the shouting and the confusion . . . I walked slowly up the square between the stalls. This was it. This was what I had come for.[8]

Still bemused by the theatrical bustle of Toulon, he returned to the ship and reality. Frank Sullivan was now gravely ill, in a coma, and there were fears for his life. As the voyage continued, his condition worsened and, as the *Ormonde* steamed across the Bay of Biscay, her captain decided that the only hope of saving him was to call at Plymouth and put him ashore so that he could be treated in hospital. Alan volunteered to accompany him and, when the liner came to a stop in Plymouth Sound and a launch put out from shore and his stretcher was lowered into it, he scrambled down a ladder and jumped aboard. The boat swung away from the ship's side and headed for Plymouth Hoe: up on that grassy rise was where Drake was said to have played bowls while waiting for the Armada to come. Beyond was the great naval harbour where could be seen the grand, grey shapes of the ships of the Royal Navy, whose burnished gun-muzzles were the final arbiters in global dispute. From these shores had come not only his own ancestors but almost all the traditions that had shaped him. If Toulon had confirmed his excited preconceptions of France, how would this half-mythological realm compare with the expectations of his imagination?

Chapter Two

"I am a mixture of happiness, doubt and worry"

Alan Moorehead's arrival in England was not what he had expected. With the pavement still heaving like a deck beneath his feet, he walked past terraces of little houses, prim and self-contained, facing parks and gardens fenced with iron railings. This was not the Plymouth of Drake and Nelson for, as he decided, "those canary birds in the bay windows should have been oath-screeching parrots."

Once Frank Sullivan had been taken to a nursing-home where Alan was also given a bed, he was free to explore the huddled, dowdy but self-confident town. It was not only the mixture of Georgian, Victorian, Edwardian and occasionally modern architecture that he noted but the social stratification which began to become apparent. The less well-to-do citizens spoke with a recognisable country accent whereas those of a social status comparable with the Mooreheads', or more exalted, had what had been called an "Oxford accent". His contemporaries in the professional class would, initially at least, address him by his surname only.

Ashore, Frank Sullivan recovered from his coma but was likely to be bed-ridden for some weeks and so, after a few days, Moorehead took the train to London. For the first time he saw a countryside of extraordinary lushness: cattle knee-deep in grass; green, billowing tree-tops covering gentle hills; all so different from the hot, harsh Australian bush with its snakes and insects and the threat of fires that would sweep through its forests of pale, thin-leaved trees. The suburbs of London seemed interminable – an immense, grubbier version of those tight-packed streets in Plymouth – and the imposing, smoke-blackened buildings at its heart looking haughty and inscrutable, as befitted the capital of an Empire ruling a third of the human race.

Noel Monks found rooms for Moorehead and Gray in the Mecklenburg Square boarding-house where he and Hetherington were staying for 25s. a week and introduced them to Lyons tea-shops and London pubs for food and drink. Bloomsbury was said to be where writers and intellectuals lived but there was nothing about those tall, formal facades of Georgian brick to suggest whether a literary salon or students' lodgings lay behind. All London had this bland, uncommunicative look: not unwelcoming, but unforthcoming; not impregnable, but forcing an entry, let alone conquest, would take time.

Meanwhile the flaunted enticements of the Continent were fresh in Moorehead's memory and beckoned. Thanks to help from Monks and Hetherington, employment in Fleet Street seemed possible but he still had most of the original £500 and it was said that it was possible to live for a year on half that amount, so this was the time for exploration. Although the others were eager to find work, he had fallen in with a young South African journalist, Guy Young, and together they planned an expedition. The talk of Fleet Street was the King's love affair with the American divorcée Mrs Simpson and the possibility that she might become his consort, if not Queen, but the news from Spain was more exciting and that was where they planned to go. Young knew an American correspondent in Burgos who might employ him, and Moorehead had a friend in a London news-agency which he tried to interest in reports he might send. In the agency's office, his eye was caught by a pretty typist and he invited her out to dinner. She refused and he declared, "This may be the last chance. I am going to Spain tomorrow. I may be killed. I may never come back."[1] She replied that she might consider another invitation if he did.

Next day the two young men set out for Paris on the Golden Arrow boat-train. Moorehead's impressions of the journey were mostly of railway stations because of their headlong determination to reach the excitements of Spain. But what he saw made a first and indelible impression: "The porters in blue smocks and cloth caps careering by with agitated families in their wake . . . bulbous French mothers with chalk-faced, black-eyed babies who screamed and screamed and the frantic cries of the little darting fathers"[2] – for it was July and the beginning of the annual holiday exodus.

25

They travelled south that same day, passing the night on the wooden benches of a crowded, third-class railway compartment reeking of tobacco, garlic and sweat. Next morning they were in the strong sunlight of the south which was lighting the deep blue Atlantic and the distant shapes of the Pyrenees. At Hendaye they found the Spanish frontier closed but, accepting this as a challenge, hired a motor-bicycle, rode along the border and, at a remote village, rode over it while the police were questioning farmers waiting to pass with their produce. Wildly exhilarated, they headed towards Burgos, where the American correspondent was thought to be, but got no farther than Pamplona, which they reached that first night. The town was a rallying-point for the Carlist forces supporting the rebel leader Franco and they were almost immediately stopped, interrogated and told to leave Spain at once. This proved no more a deterrent than had the frontier: they found beds in a pension for the night and again took the road south in the morning, though they were constantly stopped at military check-points and they could not buy petrol without a ration-card. Anyway, there was no sign of war so, the pair picked other excitements: they would celebrate Moorehead's twenty-sixth birthday on 22nd July in Paris, then head for Berlin to see the Olympic Games. Back in Paris, they watched Josephine Baker dance dressed only in a girdle of bananas at the Folies Bergères and took in the nocturnal life of Montmartre. Then they took a train to Berlin and found themselves lodgings in the suburbs.

The capital was crowded for the Olympics, which were being exploited by the Nazis to demonstrate their cults of racial purity and physical perfection. Later, Moorehead wrote:

> One day when we were on the Unter den Linden, a gust of nervous excitement suddenly took possession of the crowds. The people ran to the edge of the pavement, thrusting one another aside in an hysterical, almost frantic, kind of way. Hitler was coming. We were talking to a German girl we had picked up and it was astonishing to see the shining-eyed look of ecstasy that overcame her face as the great man came riding by through a forest of outstretched arms. It was the look of a girl meeting her lover.[3]

They lingered in Berlin for a few days, visited the Olympischdorf, where the competing athletes lived, watched some of the events, and Moorehead seduced an Austrian girl met at their lodgings. Now they talked about further travels – perhaps south again to Italy and the

Balkans or even east to Russia – but at last their money was running short and they would have to return to London and start work. They were back in August after an absence of little more than a month and without dramatic stories to tell. In an outburst of youthful braggadocio, Moorehead wrote to Beth Thwaites:

Just back from the wars. For a month I have been breathing the pure rarefied air of excitement and I just can't see any sense in trying to work out a nice safe scheme of happiness. I'm a little monster of blood and thunder. Right now I'm looking out for any sort of binge which will keep me moving. Most of the things I talked sadly about over coffee are coming to life. I know with certainty I'm changing, but I think I'm still a logical extension of my sordid history. Point A – I have even less desire to make money than before. B – I don't want especially to debauch. C – I have much less, much much less desire than formerly to shine in middle-class society. D – I'll resign all chances of being the big shot on Fleet Street, or the author of tremendous novels, if I can get a thrill out of living. And E – most important, I'm a bloody sight harder and more material, according to your standards, than before.

The reasons for this mental upheaval lie in the tawdry background of my existence for the past few weeks and months. I've had a gun shoved into my ribs and seen a certain amount of sudden death in Spain, I've spent a night with 50 naked prostitutes in a Paris dive, I've seen brother Hitler heiling down the Unter den Linden, I've drunk gallons of the nectar they call beer in Germany, I've been in a car smash, I've slept with an Austrian governess in Berlin, etc., etc., etc.

Sounds hot, doesn't it? Was it? No, not very. Exciting to remember . . . You see, I haven't got morality any more. I'm not ashamed of anything I do now . . . Any appetite I gratify is a good thing. Any appetite pushed too far, or over-indulgence, is an evil . . . And I'm having a swell time . . . I'm a big, blustering hero back from the wars.[4]

He ended by asking Beth to buy a bunch of violets for him and send them to his mother on her birthday.

Despite this posturing, he was grateful to Noel Monks for the help he offered in finding work. Directly Monks had returned to London he had been engaged as a reporter by the *Daily Express* because Arthur Christiansen had been impressed by his enterprise in going to Abyssinia as a freelance the year before; now he was to report the war in Spain. There was no work for Moorehead there for the moment, he said; but there was at an Australian news-agency, which employed him in their Fleet Street office while he looked about for something more appealing. Indeed, he would stay late in his office at his typewriter practising the style of writing he hoped would one day bring acclaim. There was another distraction, for the typist with whom he had flirted before leaving for Spain proved amenable, they became lovers and he now had a girl to escort to the little restaurants of Soho and Chelsea and evenings at the theatre and cinema. Meanwhile he moved from Bloomsbury to more comfortable and more expensive lodgings in the Gloucester Road. Soon afterwards she suddenly announced that she was about to marry somebody else, an older man with whom she had been involved for some time. But she slept with her Australian lover on the night before her wedding and a fortnight later returned to him and continued to escape from her husband for brief assignations when the mood took her. Moorehead was excited but rather shocked by her behaviour, unsettled by her sudden arrivals and departures and began to hope for work that would take him abroad again. Finally, early in 1937, Noel Monks told him that at last there was a chance of a job with the *Daily Express* as a reporter working abroad, if not exactly as the foreign correspondent of his imagination.

He had met some of the reporters when visiting the Red Lion, the tiny pub they called "Poppins" in Poppins Court off Fleet Street, where they gathered for beer-drinking. Now he was invited to the black glass citadel, which dominated the view towards Ludgate Circus and St. Paul's Cathedral. It had been opened two years earlier to house the brash but brilliantly presented newspaper, read in all social strata and commanding a circulation of about 3,000,000. The proprietor, the Canadian millionaire Lord Beaverbrook, was an old-fashioned imperialist, favouring free trade within the British Empire and its sons and daughters who hoped to work for him. This was reflected in the grandiose front hall by two metal sculptures illustrating in angular relief on opposite walls the attributes of Great Britain and her possessions.

On one wall a gigantic figure of Britannia presided over the assembled symbolism of British industry, commerce and enterprise: ships and aeroplanes, factory chimneys and locomotives, dockers and builders, engineers and farmers, miners and printers. Facing this was another allegorical figure, possibly representing Fame or Plenty, and around her the Empire busied itself. Turbaned Indians, bare-breasted Polynesians, feathered Red Indians, muscular Africans were surrounded by the crops that made the Empire rich. But in the pride of place, filling the top, right-hand corner was a sheep-shearer in wide-brimmed hat and shorts and around him not only sheep and cattle but koala bears and kangaroos. This suggested to the arriving Australian that, although favoured, he did not belong to the inner family circle.

On the second floor, where the journalists worked, Moorehead was introduced to the editor. Arthur Christiansen was a stocky man of thirty-two with dark hair curling at the nape of his neck, a wide, thin-lipped smile and lively eyes that could reflect laughter or anger. It was he who interpreted and presented the political passions and whims of his proprietor with a slick, breathless pace, using news as entertainment.

Christiansen, knowing Beaverbrook's liking for keen young men from the frontiers of the Empire, greeted Moorehead warmly. There were no staff jobs available, he said, but he could offer temporary work. The big foreign story was, of course, the war in Spain and only senior staff reporters went there. But he needed to keep reporters just off-stage on the French frontier and in Gibraltar, where they happened to be looking for a reporter, and Monks had said that Moorehead was going there. In fact, he had had no such intention but, briefed by his friend, he pretended that he had. Thereupon Christiansen offered him a retaining fee of £5 a week plus some expenses, further payment by results and wished him luck. A week or two later, he was checking into the smart new Rock Hotel overlooking the Bay of Algeciras and the distant hills of Spain: he could call himself a foreign correspondent at last.

On Gibraltar itself nothing seemed to be happening. He met the British officials who governed the colony and the officers of its garrison; he walked endlessly up and down the narrow length of Main Street, noisy each night with the blare of flamenco music from gramophones playing in shops and brass bands in the bars; he scanned the bare hills across the bay through binoculars for signs of war. But only the occasional explosions that rattled the windows when the heavy British guns on the crest of the Rock were fired for target-practice broke the peace. Then on 30th May – a Sunday, when he was looking for a news-item to start the week – a pale-grey warship steamed slowly into the harbour and suddenly there was news.

The German "pocket battleship" *Deutschland* had been lying off Ibiza in the Balearic Islands – as other foreign warships, including many British, waited outside Spanish waters with the declared aim of preventing foreign armaments reaching either of the belligerents – when an aircraft with the Republican markings dived and dropped its bombs with remarkable accuracy, penetrating her armour, killing twenty-three men and wounding another eighty-three. Had the ship been giving covert aid to Franco's Nationalists, or was it a case of mistaken identity? Nobody knew. News of the attack came from Spain and Berlin but no reporter was nearer to the source of the news than the temporary correspondent of the *Daily Express* at Gibraltar. From the dockside he saw the rows of flag-draped coffins on the deck, the ambulances arriving to collect the wounded and the ship's company jumping from deck to dockside against the shouted orders of their officers in a panic to get ashore. Moorehead spent half the night rushing between the moored ship, his typewriter and the cable office.

Next morning the headline "NAZI BATTLESHIP BOMBED" stretched across the top of the front page of the *Daily Express*. Beneath, reports from news-agencies and a dozen foreign correspondents had been blended into the terse, aggressive style of the newspaper by its sub-editors. On page two, a report from Gibraltar by a "*Daily Express* Correspondent" stood by itself and although this, too, was largely couched in the sub-editors' journalese a few descriptive touches suggested that its original author had been an eye-witness. Enough remained to convince Moorehead that the way to success in journalism lay as much in descriptive writing as in the delivery of "hard news".

In London, Christiansen had seen Moorehead's original copy and recognised a reporter with a fresh eye. So when, in reprisal for the bombing of the *Deutschland*, her sister-ship, the *Graf Spee*, bombarded the port of Valencia, which was held by the Republicans, he was ordered to go there and report. In the event, it took him a week to reach it in a small tramp-steamer and another reporter, based in Spain, arrived there first. But his enthusiasm was rewarded with another assignment. Supplies for the Republicans were being shipped into Barcelona and Valencia despite the blockade by Nationalist aircraft and submarines – possibly aided by German and Italian warships – and it was thought that oil was arriving in tankers sent from Russian ports in the Black Sea. Moorehead's task was to identify the blockade-runners and, if possible, sail in one.

After six months at Gibraltar, it was a relief to roam the Mediterranean: first to Algiers and then to Istanbul, where he was able to make contact with a shipping agent who managed to arrange a berth for him in a small oil-tanker bound from Odessa to Valencia. The long, slow voyage that followed, on which the stifling boredom was interrupted only by a storm and by the homosexual captain's vain attempt to seduce his passenger, did not produce the sort of action story the *Express* wanted, for the ship docked at its destination without hindrance. For him, Spain was to remain "a place of forbidden exhilaration", as he put it, and an assignment for senior reporters, while he returned to the periphery of the war at Gibraltar with only an occasional visit to the night life of Tangier across the Straits to break the monotony.

Even in despatches that were never printed, Moorehead had showed that he had an alert eye for the telling detail. He had been receiving small payments – ranging from one to five guineas – for reports that were printed but now he was recalled to London, for Christiansen had other plans for him as a reporter there. But he did not want to work in Fleet Street because he felt more at ease on the Continent where everybody whose native language was English felt equally misplaced. Also the boisterous circle of young Australians who, when together, could disregard the etiquette and social stratification of the English, would not be the same now that Noel Monks had married. Moorehead had long suspected that Beth Thwaites was in love with Noel and had been urging her to come to London in the hope that the relationship would develop. But it was too late – although Beth did come to London – for Monks had fallen in love with a smart and attractive American girl, Mary Welsh, who was also working for the *Daily Express*, and had married her.

The marriage had been in the face of opposition, for Lord Beaverbrook liked his young eagles from the Empire to fly free. Monks had written to Moorehead about the support he had received from his friend, the former Liberal Member of Parliament and aggressive political journalist Frank Owen, who was writing leading articles for the *Daily Express*. He told him:

Frank tells me that the Beaver is sore at me for marrying Mary! The old bastard. Frank had a row with him about it. Told him I was the best man he had. You remember the dirty old bastard made passes at Mary in America, which she slapped back at him. Jesus, how ungreat are the alleged great men! Frank said, "The old shit is going to America soon. When he gets clear, I'll boost you along, Noel. Just lie quietly and we'll lick the old man." Frank sure is a white man.[5]

So Moorehead returned to a London he had not seen for more than a year with a new self-confidence as a foreign correspondent with several major despatches to his credit. His friends thought he had matured and, noticing that his Australian accent was softer, so teasingly accused him of taking elocution lessons. While awaiting Christiansen's offer of a new appointment, he looked about for new companions, particularly female. There was Beth Thwaites with whom to exchange confidences and banter at the Hammersmith Palais de Danse but he was eager to complete his new-found contentment by falling in love.

There were a number of eligible girls at the *Daily Express* office but the prettiest of them seemed to work for the women's and fashion pages and were known to be protected against such attentions as he might have planned by the women's editor, who was said to be a tigress of propriety. Certainly, Lucy Milner appeared aloof but, as she was also attractive and carried her gentle beauty with wit and grace, her male colleagues considered her to be as desirable as she was unattainable. Moreover, she was a journalist of high quality, a brilliant editor of her pages and said to be second to none in making up pages under pressure in the composing room. She not only seemed the quintessence of the remote charm and determination possessed by the heroines of novels such as those written by Dornford Yates and John Buchan, which the young Moorehead had read so avidly, but she was taller than he was and two years older. So she became a challenge, for to be accepted by her would be acceptance in this strange and desirable country. It was not long before she was laughingly asking the girls in her office, "Who is this Australian who keeps saying that he is going to take me out to dinner if it's the last thing he does?"[6]

However, their proximity was about to be ended. Despite his apparent success, Christiansen decided in October that there was no more work for Moorehead at the moment; there were no vacancies on the staff and other young men from the Dominions were to be given a chance to work on the *Daily Express* for a spell. It was then that he was sighted in the big, open-plan office by Charles Foley, a tall young Irishman on the foreign desk, who crossed the room to congratulate him on his reporting from the Mediterranean. "I've just been fired," replied Moorehead. As it happened, Foley had been told to look for a French-speaking reporter to work with the Paris correspondent and he asked whether Moorehead would like to go there and if he could speak the language. His reply to the first question was so enthusiastic that Foley forgot about the second and it was quickly arranged that he would leave for Paris immediately as a member of the staff with a salary of £10 a week and a cost-of-living allowance.

An appointment in Paris was a prize he had not dared to consider, for it seemed the most desirable of all capital cities: beautiful, dramatic, mysterious, erotic and politically important. He would work for the head of the bureau, Geoffrey Cox, a young New Zealander, and there would be three or four others working at the office in the *Paris-Soir* building in the Rue du Louvre. While Cox would handle the major political news, he would concentrate on the general run of events – any disasters, crime, entertainment, sport, social gossip – and keep an eye on the Spanish frontier.

Before leaving London, he succeeded in taking Lucy Milner out to dinner, finding her amusing and not so formidable as she had seemed. They began to confide in each other and it emerged that, until she had gone to Fleet Street, her life had been quietly frustrating. She was now aged twenty-nine and was one of the three children of a country doctor in Dorset. Her father, whose principal interest was sailing, was stern and domineering, refusing to allow his son to study music so that he had to find work as a tobacco salesman. When Lucy had won her scholarship to Lady Margaret Hall at Oxford, he did not allow her to accept it and instead she had to take a secretarial course. She had joined the *Daily Express* as the editor's secretary and had eventually been given charge of the women's pages. Quite tall – standing nearly two inches taller than Moorehead; more in her high-heeled shoes – she wore her clothes with an easy elegance. In her company he did not feel that he had to strike heroic attitudes and soon he was falling in love.

Leaving London at such a moment was less of a wrench than expected because Lucy would regularly visit Paris to report on the fashion collections and indeed would be coming over almost as soon as he himself arrived there. There was particular excitement in this prospect because they would both be free of the inhibiting presence of their friends in Fleet Street and of her neighbours in Donne Place, the little Chelsea street where she lived. They would be able to begin exploring the possibilities of their relationship in a setting that was both neutral and romantic.

Moorehead reported to the Paris office of the *Daily Express*. Geoffrey Cox was a lean, hard-muscled, resolute man of his own age with smooth, dark hair, alert eyes, a predatory, aquiline nose and broad Napoleonic brow. He was known as a shrewd and tireless reporter, but Moorehead sensed that he might be a tense and dour superior which would be in contrast to his own studied nonchalance. There were three others: a French reporter, Bob Chasseuil, the *Evening Standard* correspondent, Jerome Willis, and sometimes a photographer in the office, which was efficiently organised by a White Russian woman of tall, dark and handsome looks, Princess Mara Scherbatoff. Moorehead was told that one of his first assignments was to keep track of the Duke and Duchess of Windsor, the former King and Mrs Simpson, who were planning to settle in Paris.

Then, almost at once, Lucy arrived with the fashion journalists from London. They would meet in the evenings when she was often tired, so their involvement with each other was not so headlong as he had hoped. When she left, he wrote to her, "I think Paris tired you over-much and you are glad to be back in London. There are fine soporifics in London – the pubs, the theatre, men from the most rugged colonies and Law and Order, or whatever it is that makes it impossible to get a drink at midnight. It's your world, my dear, and you have it taped far better than I have . . . I must just keep moving and swooping about until – well until we meet again."

He could not resist tossing into the letter that he was still free of commitments.

After last week's rush of British fashion writers – I got involved with some others after you left – Paris seems quite French today. I skipped my French lesson and went skating at Auteuil. This afternoon I have been to Versailles to see the Windsors safely stowed away . . .

I have moved to a nice little tenth-rate hotel in the Rue Monsigny – the move was chaotic since it took place at 2 am during bouts between Montmartre night-clubs. Result was I was washed up in the backstreets of Paris at 7 am without the faintest idea of where my new home was. And this definitely is the end of debauchery – it just mustn't happen again, not until Friday night anyhow.[7]

Lucy, too, reflected disappointment in her reply, complaining of the dullness of her life in London and the bleak prospects for the future. He answered at length in terms suggesting that the development of love had stalled:

Now see here, my girl, this is all very bad and I don't see clearly what we are going to do about it. I personally run away and run like hell when I get into the state of boredom in which you imagine yourself to be at the moment. I ran away to England in 1936; I ran away to Gibraltar, then back to England. And now I have run away to Paris. Not, mark you, because I think I am following the way of high ambition. In each case I ran away because I was bored, or because I couldn't cope with some difficulty or because I thought someone was going to get at me and hurt me.

When the war comes, you will see me beating up the trail somewhere else. You need a surprising amount of energy to run away but I prefer to be energetic rather than stay and take what is coming to me – like you. Why don't you run away? You could. Better still, why don't you compromise? . . . So why don't you crash out and have a run for your money? . . . Have a shot at taking quick, hard stabs of pleasure and pain. Keep your job. Go and splash all your dough – in buying a set of furs or taking a trip to Switzerland. Do it now, at once. Change your flat and live with a man. Ask the office to send you down to Spain for a series of articles. Write a book. Rent a house in the country. Play golf. Get interested in politics or gardening or lesbianism. Buy a horse. But for God's sake do something . . . If you think all this is fantastic then it only shows how many barriers you have put up against being hurt . . .[8]

Moorehead had told Lucy that he loved her, but both were wary of committing themselves; he sometimes hiding his fear of rejection behind banter and a breezy style that owed something to the prose of Ernest Hemingway. He told her:

Darling, there won't be other girls as there is you. The other girls, if there are other girls, will be only gay and chance departures and not anything to touch, or be thought of in the same way. You are quite the best one; even you saying no with a sour puss are better than all the other girls saying yes with a friendly puss. But you nearly always have a bright and friendly puss so there is no need for other girls at all.[9]

One Sunday that summer, Jerome Willis of the *Evening Standard* and a journalist friend of Moorehead's named Cassidy* decided on a picnic by the Seine and again he described it in the style of Hemingway:

> Cassidy liked Willis and Willis liked Cassidy and we all liked Cassidy's girl. So it went marvellously well. We drove to Villennes, which is so green and remote beyond St. Germain forest and lunched at length, then swam for miles and lay in the hot sun and drank again, and in the evening we went back to the restaurant alongside the river and danced and drank while we ate an enormous dinner under the coloured lights. All the way back to Paris we have been singing in the car, Cassidy, the girl and I and now I am home and there is a letter from you. And abruptly I am glad because I remember that you are much, much better than Cassidy's girl, or all the other girls I saw today not excepting the one with the blue cornflower in her hair . . .[10]

He was feeling himself a man of the world and an experienced correspondent, particularly after taking a chance to air his sophistication to a visitor. One of these was a young Australian, Chester Wilmot, who had been his successor as the Melbourne University correspondent of the *Herald* and was touring Europe with the university's debating society. A tall young man of powerful build, he had the air of an intellectual and it was gratifying to impress him. Indeed, Wilmot noted in his diary:

> Taxi to office of *Daily Express* to see Alan Moorehead. He's been wonderfully successful. He came over here two years ago. Got on to the *Daily Express* eighteen months ago and had made a great name. Sent to Gibraltar last year and then into Spain and now is in Paris – earning a very good salary indeed.
>
> He has been behind both lines in Spain and says there is no doubt about the feeling of the Spanish people. They are almost universally against Franco – except the Church, the feudal landowners and some of the very big businessmen. Franco is holding what he's got only by dint of strong garrisons behind his lines and could never hold out without foreign support. Moorehead thinks it will be a tragedy – disastrous beyond expression –

* Henry Cassidy of the Associated Press.

for the Spanish people if Franco wins – and Moorehead is no radical.[11]

But he was not to feel so self-confident on his next assignment, which was to the northern frontier of Spain, where the last act of the long tragedy was beginning. For journalists watching the border, the two principal vantage-points were Hendaye and St.-Jean-de-Luz and, at the latter, they tended to congregate at the Bar Basque. This was a lively restaurant and bar with tables on the pavement outside in summer, where the food and wine were good and often from the Basque region and where it was pleasant to linger over coffee and the pale, sweet liqueur *Fleurs d'Hendaye*. As in such establishments in such towns were journalists gathered, this was the recognised rendezvous and as soon as Moorehead's train arrived he went there to find them and seek their advice on hotels and communications.

Entering the big room with its murals of Basque peasants dancing the *jota* and playing *pelota*, he asked the barman in his halting French whether any British journalists were there and he nodded towards two men sitting together on one of the red plush banquettes, talking over their lunch. He approached them and introduced himself. They were Karl Robson of the *News Chronicle* and Alexander Clifford of Reuter. The former seemed a gentle, approachable man with a welcoming smile. But the latter appeared forbidding, looking up irritably through round-rimmed spectacles. Clifford was a tall young man with the air of effortless superiority that Moorehead disliked so much in Englishmen who had been educated at public schools and Oxford or Cambridge. He was handsome in a conventional way but his regular features and smooth cheeks were unlined by humour or experience and his mouth was tight. He did not answer Moorehead's question, leaving it to Robson to recommend an hotel. Accustomed to the friendliness of Fleet Street, this cool reception was hurtful and, muttering his thanks, he retreated to the bar to collect his bags and leave. He had decided that Alexander Clifford might be, and probably was, an experienced correspondent and a formidable rival – particularly as his reports to his news-agency might well reach the *Daily Express* before his own despatches each evening – and that he was not the sort of man whose company he would seek.

But he had less need for the company of strangers, or even of new friends, because in October Lucy wrote a letter telling him that she was in love with him, too. "I had never quite believed before that you really had any serious thought about me," he replied. "Now that

37

I see it's true, I am a mixture of happiness, doubt and worry about you." His doubt was that he might not be able to offer her the depth of response that she would expect. He continued:

> In all the little passing things in enjoying life with another person, I'm fine, but as regards anything deeper, I'm just as warped and unresponsive as I was when I ran away from England 18 months ago. Believe me, I'd love to have you here and be with you, but you would give too much and I too little. That wouldn't do at all.[12]

For him, it was still a question of self-confidence.

Chapter Three

"Be prepared to follow me"

In November, 1938, Alan Moorehead told Lucy Milner that he
had taken a flat in Paris. "Believe it you may not, my dear," he
wrote, "but I am setting up house like a staid old family man. It's a
whacking great studio flat at St. Cloud near to the Coxes; very nice,
very new, very fine."[1] It was less than six weeks since the British
and French governments had given way to Hitler's demands at the
Munich conference and allowed him to annex the German-speaking
Sudetenland areas of Czechoslovakia, so acknowledging Germany to
be the dominant power on the Continent. Moorehead, like most
informed journalists, did not expect this to be "peace in our time"
as Neville Chamberlain, the British prime minister, had forecast but
only a postponement of an inevitable war. Yet this awareness of the
Europeans' rush towards the abyss only sharpened his delight in the
pleasures of Paris.

His salary had just been increased to twelve guineas a week,
plus two guineas a week living-allowance and an expense account,
and this – due to the recent devaluation of the franc – allowed him
to live as comfortably as he wished. The flat he chose was on the
seventh floor of a new block – "like a great battleship", he said –
on a wooded hill above the Seine. It consisted of a studio with a
gallery, a double bedroom, a little kitchen and a chromium-plated,
rubber-floored bathroom. By any standards it was luxurious and its
particular attraction was the view from the great window of the studio.
Below, the river swept around the Longchamp race-course and the

Bois de Boulogne and beyond rose the landmarks of the city – the Eiffel Tower and the Invalides, the twin towers of Notre Dame, the Arc de Triomphe and the white turrets of Sacré Coeur on the summit of Montmartre.

The acquisition of the flat (and an Annamite man-servant named Tai as cook and valet) finally freed him from the social complications of being an Australian in England. From his eyrie above St. Cloud he had Paris at his feet and London was over the horizon; near enough to be visited and telephoned but presenting no immediate challenge. There, Lucy was at home, moving with graceful assurance through the labyrinth of etiquette, tradition and prejudice; here, he had the edge over any visitors from across the Channel. It would make his courtship of Lucy easier as he would no longer be under the eye of his colleagues at the office and both of them wanted to keep their meetings as secret as possible; partly to avoid gossip in Fleet Street and also because it was more exciting to meet secretly in Paris.

He kept the extent of his involvement from his family, too. When his mother visited Paris, he took her to the Folies Bergères, told her that one of the girls in the show was a friend of his and when she asked him to point her out on stage he replied that it was too difficult to tell them apart without their clothes. But his mother won his approval by her *sang-froid* in the face of Parisian eccentricity. After taking her up the Eiffel Tower, through the Louvre, around Versailles and to the Comédie Française, they sat at a café table on the pavement in the sunshine. He was sitting with his back to the street when she said gently, "You know, I shall never really accustom myself to the French. Fancy having a lion walking down the street." Her son considered this for a moment, then turned in his chair to see that there was indeed a lion. It turned out to be the pet of a bohemian eccentric, living on the Left Bank. "I am grateful to my mother for her acceptance of that lion," he wrote to a friend. "She had a wonderful gift for taking things and enjoying them as she found them."[2]

He was enjoying Paris more than ever. His man-servant would bring him coffee in bed and a bundle of French newspapers. After glancing at the main news-pages and reading a few editorials, he would dress and go down to the garage under the flats and set out in his new car, an open-topped Ford Matford, for the Racing Club in the Bois de Boulogne. After a swim in the pool there, he would finish reading the newspapers before driving into Paris and arriving at the *Daily Express* office around mid-day. After planning the afternoon's activities, he and the others would go upstairs at one o'clock for a glass of champagne in the roof-top bar before going out to a substantial lunch. They would then return to their office and work through until late evening, sometimes until midnight or after.

There was much jollity in that office and some tensions. Geoffrey Cox was an experienced correspondent, who had reported Hitler's annexation of Austria and the Sudetenland and took his work seriously, without Moorehead's assumed nonchalance. He and his wife Cecily also lived out at St. Cloud and enjoyed physical exercise, yet he and Moorehead were so different in temperament that their relationship, though friendly, was not relaxed.

For his part, Cox found Moorehead an ambitious subordinate, who envied the important assignments that were the province of the senior correspondent. This became more apparent with the arrival of a third member of the reporting staff, who could cover some of the more trivial news that had hitherto been given to Moorehead. This was a burly Scotsman, Donald Robertson, who had learned to speak some French during the Great War and had suddenly been sent to Paris by Christiansen to escape a possible criminal charge in England. When reporting a fight between London gangs, Robertson had pretended to be a detective in order to interview the prime suspect for the *Express*. It had been expected that he would be charged with impersonating a police officer and so he had been sent abroad for a while.

Even more appreciative of the louche life of Paris was Jerome Willis of the *Evening Standard*, whom Moorehead liked and Cox did not. An Irishman and, it was said, none too particular in his habits, he had the manageress of a Parisian laundry as a mistress and frequented brothels to drink an evening aperitif. He was often out of the office when his news editor telephoned but, just when his professional prospects seemed in jeopardy, he would redeem himself by writing a highly-coloured article about Paris, which was just what his readers wanted. He and Moorehead enjoyed each other's company because, as one visiting reporter put it, "they revelled in being there, in the air, the smells, the virility, the beauty, the humour."[3]

Mara Scherbatoff, the chatelaine of the office, disapproved of Willis, particularly after he escorted her to a cocktail party in honour of visiting American journalists at *Le Sphinx*, an elaborate brothel in Montparnasse. Moorehead, on the other hand, was forgiven all indiscretions even when, before his serious courtship of Lucy, he gave her a lift in his car and, as he told Willis, kissed her.

About once a week, Moorehead would be ordered to entertain

41

ALAN MOOREHEAD

some visitors from London. If this was another journalist of the
standing of Tom Driberg, the homosexual gossip-writer, or the
foreign correspondent Sefton Delmer (usually called Tom), the evening would be passed in talking about politics over dinner. But when
the visitor was from the alien worlds of commerce or administration,
the occasion demanded other arrangements: an expensive dinner at
Maxim's or the Tour d'Argent and then drinks at a table near the
stage of the Bal Tabarin. There, wrote Moorehead:

> Naked, six-foot girls come whirling from the roof and debouching
> from the walls. They rise in glittering tableaux on lifts beneath
> our feet and their breasts are not a yard away from the visitor's
> nose. Girls on horses, girls in cages, girls in mountains of flowers,
> girls being flung in the air by fierce Spanish dancers, girls wearing
> nothing but a cache-sexe and a mammoth hat. The band roars
> and a young man in silver tights recites a prose poem through
> a microphone. We talk rubber. We talk shipping tonnages, splits
> in the Nazi party, the Italian shortage of coal and the new Presi-
> dential election in America. We cast an amused and only faintly
> interested eye on all these breasts and thighs and horses because
> we are sophisticated people, because the guest is on a business
> visit to Paris and nothing more . . .[4]

The evening would often end with Moorehead jotting an address
on the back of a cigarette packet for his guest and driving back to
St. Cloud alone.

It was a doomed city. There was now nothing to stop the German
and Italian dictators and some time soon the war would begin and all
this sensuality would come to a shuddering end. But it was available
now and, even if he did not indulge in its almost limitless possibilities,
it gave a gamey savour to life. Increasingly, however, Moorehead
found that it was no longer enough to enjoy this range of pleasure.
He missed Lucy and when both the Coxes, who were aware that he
had been paying attention to the delightful young woman from the
London office, suggested that he invite her to Paris for Christmas
he at once wrote and asked her to come.

Since her last visit, they had been a little wary of each other,
bewildered at the emotions that had overtaken them. His recent
letters had been full of news about his move into the flat but
without the former intensity. When she accepted his invitation, he
wrote back, saying, "Well, that's grand, my dear," ending cautiously,

"You might not want to believe it or care about it, but I am excited at your coming."[5]

Christmas gave a brief, artificial respite from the tensions of the time. Since Germany had occupied the Sudetenland, Hitler's appetite appeared to be gorged, although everybody expected it to return with renewed voracity. It was now Italy that was the hungry predator: Mussolini had just declared Libya to be part of metropolitan Italy and was not only demanding French territory in North Africa but the annexation of specific parts of France itself, his mobs chanting the demand for, "Tunis, Corsica, Nice!" But for a day or two at Christmas the ranting ceased, newspaper offices closed, and, as Lucy arrived in Paris, it began to snow.

For both of them the meeting was happy and fruitful and, as he put it, they "succeeded in pushing the world away for a little time". Their relationship attained an intimacy from which there was no return and when he kissed her goodbye on the boat-train at the Gare du Nord on Boxing Day, their encounter already had an unreality about it. He wrote to her next day from his office:

All the time we were together is now like a film. But, darling, please do not forget it, or change, or be any different and go on thinking of me as I am – remembering you saying, "Oh God, you can't do that" . . . and being with you in the snow and in the train and laughing and it always being you there and you're always saying "Yes".[6]

He had little more time to muse. Although Lord Beaverbrook remained optimistic and the first day of 1939 was greeted with an article by his chief editorial-writer beginning, "There will be no great war in Europe in 1939" – Moorehead agreed with them both – the future was regarded with apprehension. The war in Spain began its final spasm as Nationalist insurgents opened a final offensive against the last strongholds of the government in Catalonia and refugees were struggling over the French border to escape Franco's bombers. This was Moorehead's next assignment and he spent a week in the Pyrenees, watching a war in progress for the first time.

On his return to Perpignan, he wrote to Lucy:

Yesterday I felt like a Roman in the Coliseum as the Government boys came up the valley to France, mining and setting fire to the villages on the way. The thing that makes you most savage is seeing

43

the black bombers come down when the men below are helpless. Each time the explosion is louder and somehow far more drastic than you expect . . .[7]

This was more than an exciting interlude for him because even in the misery of the refugees and the callousness of the bombing, he could find touches that recalled the romantic eye of Hemingway, whose writing he so much admired. There was, in particular, a Spanish colonel among the Republican soldiers who straggled into France:

He was very thin and gaunt . . . He was very tired, much too tired to assert his authority. He stood dejectedly between two peasant women and a soldier, his head bowed down and dirty blood was seeping through a bandage on his arm . . . It was this wounded Spanish officer who especially caught the attention because his humiliation seemed more complete than for the others . . . A Spanish colonel wasn't worth a row of beans this side of the border.

Then a pompous little French officer of the Garde Mobile, who was hustling the refugees towards a reception centre, suddenly, to Moorehead's surprise, also caught sight of the dejected Spanish officer and marched up to him, saluted and said, "Sir. Excuse me, sir. Would you care to lead your men down to the valley?" At first the colonel did not understand, but the Frenchman repeated his question and then, Moorehead wrote:

. . . he saluted and, as he came past me to take his place in front he had his head up and it seemed to me that he had forgotten about his wounded arm, his exhaustion and even, perhaps, his defeat. And when he gave his orders from the head of the column and the Spaniards recognised the familiar voice, they stopped and quickly grabbed up their bundles from the snow as if they had suddenly woken from a trance. They came to attention with a kind of ragged dignity . . . and then stepped forward together. The colonel did not look back to see if they were following. He marched ten paces ahead, swinging his one good arm and it was not possible to watch that pathetic figure . . . or see the pride in the tattered men behind him without breaking into tears.[8]

Moorehead was now ordered back to St.-Jean-de-Luz and in the train he had time to ponder the future of his relationship with Lucy and, with a pen shaken by the lurching of the train, wrote a letter:

> My thoughts on the matter are a little turgid at the moment but the general idea is that I had a fine barrage up against the soft world of suburban homes and respectable wives and there is momentarily a hole in the barrage now. I think you feel that, too. I think that you were doing (and are doing) fine without a love affair and you resent the intrusion. You resent it because you are full of doubt and you don't know whether you have the guts or even sufficient interest to go through with your love affair . . .
>
> Things are beginning to stir in me as well: against the routine, the smugness, the flat, the friends, the conventional *affaire*. I've run away twice from these sort of things – from my home in Australia and from London and now it looks, my darling, as though you are going to be the shock which ejects me from Paris.
>
> Dear me, what a bad-tempered letter . . .[9]

Although O'Dowd Gallagher was in besieged Barcelona and Moorehead's reports from the frontier town were only occasionally published and then signed only by "*Daily Express* Staff Reporter", he was able to up-stage all his rivals with a long and colourful article about it:

> Since the war began not a single shot has ever been fired in St. Jean. When the other border villages were spattered with shrapnel and refugees fled across the frontier from the battle of Irun, leaving their homes blazing behind them, St. Jean sat snug and tight . . . Tourists still came to gamble in the casino, to swim and play golf nearby and occasionally they stopped and listened to the thunder of shell-fire which was smashing up Spain just across the mountains. Yet in all Spain itself there is hardly a town that lives and breathes in the odour of war as St. Jean does . . .[10]

This vigorous exercise in making bricks with little straw was signed with his name in bold type.

At the Golf Hotel by the sea letters from Lucy reached him and there was time to rest and relax. There was also a chance to indulge his moods as worry gave way to playfulness. He wrote in reply:

I have been reading your letter in bed and making my usual morning re-consideration of you. I am extremely objective in these seances. First I consider you as the Fleet Street woman – that's the picture I like least so I always start with that one. Then, in growing order of importance, we consider Lucy at a party, Lucy having a meal in London, Lucy walking on the boulevards and Lucy in bed. Then I turn my face to the wall and ring for the morning chocolate . . . Then there is the after-luncheon session when I am sated with cognac and Basque cooking at a little place we go to in town and I turn slowly over in my mind the ways and means by which we might contrive to live together . . . Finally we have the evening conference, which is altogether practical and is devoted solely to considering you in bed.[11]

His concern about the unsettled future, in which their own merged with the huge uncertainties dominating everybody's lives in Europe, was anticipated by Lucy and, two days later, reflected in a worried letter from her. He replied:

Such a forlorn letter from you this morning, my cabbage. What a mixture you are. You say, "I suppose none of this will last for either of us." Now what in the world does it matter if it lasts 5 minutes or a million years? It exists. And it's just too bad that you are in London and I lounging around the vice hells of the South of France. Ironical that you, the stone-waller, the looker-ahead-over-the-years-to-come, should have all the doubts. I, who merely grab at anything that chances to come my way and have no plans, have no doubts at all . . . There is nothing sad in what is ahead. The only sad thing is that we are not together at this moment.

I'm lecturing again but, dear me, if you knew how I feel about this, if you realised that it is you and not I who will be the first to run away in the end.[12]

Plans to meet in Paris had to be postponed. By February the war in Spain was reaching its climax. Barcelona had fallen, the surrender of Madrid was thought to be imminent, and already Britain and France had recognised the Franco regime as the effective government in Spain. To report on the final moves, Moorehead was ordered to Marseilles, where he hoped to board a British warship and sail in her to the Balearic Islands.

He was also to meet one of the more exotic refugees from Republican Spain. This was Dolores Ibarruri, the communist orator and leader of the women's movement, who had become famous as La Pasionaria. She had escaped to Algeria and was on her way by sea from Oran to Marseilles, where he was to interview her if he could. He joked to Lucy in a letter:

> I am on a highly sinister and dangerous mission. I have to contrive to meet the Passion Flower when she arrives from Oran this afternoon. I have to offer her untold sums of Beaverbrook's gold for her story . . . I shall just sneak up behind her and plant a great big whacking kiss on the nape of her neck crying, "Come little Passion Flower for I am Cactus Bill the Flower of Lust." And we will steal away to the South Seas together. I hear she is a raging Spanish beauty with enormous flashing eyes and constantly walks about with a red rose gripped in her powerful teeth.[13]

But the mockery evaporated when he did meet the sombre Spanish woman, now in her mid-forties. He wrote to Lucy:

> I shook the hand of our old friend La Pasionaria. I know. I know. It makes nothing at all. She's a communist agitator and I am a rubber-necked tourist. They call her "The Red Widow of Spain" in Marseilles. And for me she has more than dignity. Of herself, she knows. You remember, "To thine own self be true." She knows completely, in what she believes and what is right and what she wants to do; or so I think. She has the remarkable courage of anyone who is completely honest. I am not mesmerized by her. I am tremendously impressed.[14]

While he awaited the Admiralty's approval of his intended voyage, he wrote daily to Lucy, his letters reflecting his changes in mood. Sometimes he was the ardent lover, sometimes the detached philosopher and quite often the nonchalant hedonist, presenting a brash, defensive front as the foreign correspondent in dramatic times, snatching his pleasures when he could. Occasionally, when thoughts of Lucy's quiet wisdom, her poise and her Englishness predominated, he became aggressive in these letters, seeming to bolster his own self-confidence by undermining hers. Then he would praise the attractions of other women, although adding that he was currently immune to them. In one letter, complaining about the days of waiting for permission to sail from Marseilles, he wrote with a frankness that must have aroused mixed reactions in her . . .

> I used to have myopic affairs because I loved a woman's legs, or her gaiety, or her breasts, or the way she dressed and laughed. It is quite different with you and I am honest when I say I do not like most of those things with you. You seem very much more of a person than the other affairs just as you are a very much better woman than any woman I met before. I do not think you have gaiety or that people will ever admire you for the way you dress or the way you look. But nearly everyone genuinely likes you and I have never heard anyone say they disliked you. The thing most people usually say is that you are "a companion".

He told her that one of the other reporters at Marseilles, "who knows a little and suspects more, said I 'would be a bastard if I ever treated you badly'. How utterly he is wrong and how utterly I disagree. I could never do other than treat you badly even in the secret ways of our being in love. I shall continue blandly neglecting you and being unfaithful and selfish and superficial and bad-tempered. But I shall, I believe, never deceive you, or be unhelpful when you are hurt . . ."[15]

He read in the *Daily Express* that Lucy was launching a fashion competition under the headline, "What shall I wear with my new yellow hat?" a question she invited readers to answer for three-guinea prizes. "I bought a hat when I was in Paris," she began her article, "a yellow hat with a spotted veil and two cockades of ribbon in front . . . I haven't worn it yet and I can't wear it – because I have nothing to wear with it."[16] Moorehead wrote on the page, "My God, have you no shame?" and sent her the cutting.

His self-knowledge was raising questions about the future of their relationship and increasingly he felt that marriage would establish her as the dominant partner whereas, if they lived together, he could exercise control and predominate:

> More and more I see that I cannot depend on anyone. For so long now I have fought for everything I wanted and taken every pleasure as the price of winning that I cannot bear the idea of waiting for someone else to dish my pleasure out to me. You fight and scheme and cheat for happiness. You never (so I think) get it by patience and sweet, passive reasonableness . . .

Naturally I know that the best thing in the world would be for us to marry. But I do not think it would be so good for you to marry me. I should probably reproach you for giving up so much for so little. Tricky business, however you look at it. Finally, then, the point is this – I do not love you any less, rather more if anything . . . A real downright stinker of a letter. Yet all my love to you.[17]

In the event, he did not go to sea with the Mediterranean Fleet. But he did visit the cruiser *Devonshire* which had arrived from Minorca, where her captain had helped in the negotiation of the island's surrender and gave Moorehead the news that it had been bombed by the Italians even after the capitulation to Franco. This neat piece of news-gathering brought immediate congratulations from Christiansen. He was then ordered back to Paris.

At the end of February, Lucy visited him there for a weekend and worry was calmed by their happiness. When she returned to London, he was grateful to be caught up by a succession of new arrivals in Paris, both *Express* journalists and other foreign correspondents passing through, and talks with them strengthened his resolve to leave Paris. Cox and he were both effective correspondents but were opposites in temperament, Moorehead affecting nonchalance and mocking the other's solemn zeal – when Cox was thrown from his horse while riding in the Bois and slightly injured, Moorehead wrote to Lucy that he was "cracking hardy, with a 'must stand by at the helm attitude' ".[18] For his part, Cox found Moorehead a restless and impatient subordinate, who should be given his head with his own assignments. There was only one major European capital where the *Express* maintained no staff correspondent and that was Moscow and one would surely be needed. The idea occurred to Moorehead that he and Lucy could both, in effect, run away to Russia, so that she would have to abandon the important job, the comfortable life and the English assurance that made her both desirable and daunting.

Then Tom Driberg arrived at the office from London to spend a few days at the Ritz before going to New York for the opening of the World Fair. He confided that he wanted to give up writing the daily "William Hickey" column and go to Rome as the staff correspondent, covering Italy and the central Mediterranean, and he urged Moorehead to apply for the posting to Moscow. He wrote an enthusiastic, light-hearted letter to Lucy about it and ended:

I know that you people in London lead such busy, crowded lives but, should you find yourself free later in the season, do you think you might have time to marry me? It might, I think, be arranged very easily except that I am very much in love with you and can by no means wait patiently until the end of the season. Darling, you are not even listening. You are pretending not to listen . . .[19]

As he imagined it, the shared difficulties of a life together in Moscow would bring them together. He asked in another letter,

Do you remember my saying that we had only been together when things were going well for us and wondering how it would be when things went badly? I can see now that in one way things would be much better between us if they did go badly. We would be forced to take a decision and be together. It is only the world and the devil which really keep us apart – only the fact that you want to go on with your job and I with mine. We already have so much separately that we are not struggling hard enough to be together. There is, as yet, not sufficient dependence on one another. Suppose one of us were ill and completely broke – I think we would find out then very quickly how far we were in love and how necessary to one another.[20]

But, while Moorehead had the pressure of work in covering the tightening tensions of Europe and, as relaxation, the pleasures of Paris to help occupy his mind during their separations, Lucy had only long hours in Fleet Street and the early hours of the morning in which to worry. She was in love but was not convinced that her lover was totally committed or that marriage would be the solution for either of them. If she went to live with him in Moscow, or even in Paris, she would throw away her successful career and create a scandal which would upset her family.

These tensions came to breaking-point in March. Lucy's sister Mary had been giving cautionary advice and Lucy telephoned the *Express* office in Paris and talked to Moorehead just as he had finished dictating a long report to London after a day at the National Assembly. He was irritable and, as he confessed in a letter next morning, "abrupt and unkind". He then set down the state of their love affair and its prospects, as he saw them. He wrote:

What I dread so much is this – that you will insist that anything

1 Setting out. The young Alan Moorehead when the life of Melbourne
  University was giving him his first assignment as a journalist.

2 Lucy Milner, the women's pages editor of the *Daily Express*, in the late 1930s.

3 Alan Moorehead, the subordinate correspondent in the Paris office of the *Daily Express*.

4 The wedding in Rome. Alan and Lucy Moorehead photographed after the civil ceremony in October, 1939, outside the Palazzo Senatorio.

5 Father and son: Alan and the infant John Moorehead in Cairo.

6 Godfather and godson: Alexander Clifford and his friends' baby.

7 A threesome at cards, photographed by the fourth; Alan and Lucy Moorehead at home with Alexander Clifford in their Cairo flat.

8 War correspondents halt for a meal by their truck in the Libyan desert in 1941. Moorehead is second from the left; Clifford, fifth, standing holding a mug.

9 Correspondent and commander: Alan Moorehead interviews General Montgomery during the Sicilian campaign in the summer of 1943.

short of the perfect dream is not enough. My dear, do you think I prefer half-baked affairs and living in and out of brothels, of never having a let-up in the complete knowing of one other person in the world? Do you think that one week I can say I love you and change 5 days afterwards? That I did not mean it when I asked you to marry me? I tell you again that I am not "perfectly" in love – I never will be. And I tell you that more than any other woman in the world, I want you. Can't you see? There will always be a barrier. Cannot you accept that? No, I don't think you can – not easily anyhow. But you must, darling.

It seems that I am giving you everything except the one thing you really want – constant overwhelming proof that I am deeply and perfectly in love. And I am sure that this is the trouble between us, the thing that makes us altogether too heroic and serious. Oh, I know you are hating me for writing like this. I am not doing much better than the telephone conversation. But I am going right to the bitter end this time.

1. I am not *perfectly* in love.
2. I want to marry you.
3. I want in the short time of peace ahead to travel, meet a lot of people, be a success in journalism, to eat and drink well.

There is no adolescent rose-coloured dream about this. I add up the money. I plan to go to Moscow, I want to have a woman. It is all – well, not exactly mathematics, but sometimes damn near it. And always, everywhere there is in the background the great fear that I will be lonely, that there is some gap in my life. You have filled up that gap and stopped the loneliness. And my love for you is therefore precisely this – the happiness I feel at not being lonely any more. That happiness is tremendous to me. It is, at the moment, not sufficient for you. We must work it out together.[21]

The one chance of a happy outcome was, it seemed to him, that they could both go to Moscow. Now that he was away from Paris more often, another reporter had been sent to help Geoffrey Cox. This was George Millar, a young man of twenty-eight, whose fair hair and dazzling good looks had earned him the nickname "Golden Millar", after the famous racehorse Golden Miller, and Moorehead liked him ("He is modest and writes well"[22]). He himself was currently reporting a sensational trial – that of a Eugene Weidmann, who was suspected of murdering six women and whose case he had reported since the beginning – but the verdict was expected shortly and then he would be free to run away with Lucy.

In the event, Charles Sutton, the foreign editor, was not interested in Moorehead's request for a transfer to Moscow. He knew that little exclusive news and virtually none of the lively "human stories" that the *Express* needed were to be had there and it was easier and cheaper to rely on the news-agencies. In any case, far too much was happening elsewhere. Czechoslovakia had, as had been expected, been dismembered by Germany which was now threatening Poland over border claims; the surrender of Madrid to Franco had brought the war in Spain to an end and reprisals had begun; Britain and France were re-arming urgently; then, at the beginning of April, Italy invaded the little Balkan state of Albania. *That* was a good *Daily Express* story: both one of David and Goliath and of Ruritania, since the country was ruled by a King Zog and the beautiful Queen Geraldine. So Christiansen sent his reporters scurrying around the area of crisis. Moorehead told Lucy that he was being sent to Yugoslavia in the hope of getting into Albania.

"We took a car up to the Albanian border," he later wrote to her, "and then, after hours of quarrelling with the soldiers, got into Albania just before the Italians arrived. There was no shooting. It was all very picturesque, dirty and pleasant . . . I'm sorry, darling, but I'm loving it."[23]

From there he returned to Skopje and then Belgrade, where he met Tom Delmer, who was on his way to interview King Zog in exile at Salonika. Lucy cabled her good wishes and Moorehead replied:

Now that was very nice of you to send the wire – small boys went through the streets crying out my name. Actually the message was put into my hand at 1 am this morning in a night-club, where Delmer and I were hungrily eyeing a bunch of immoral Hungarian blondes. I read your wire, blushed scarlet with shame and ran out of the place. If ever the avenging hand of conscience fell on me . . .[24]

What little news and rumour filtered out of Albania was unreliable but he made the most of it with a little help from the sub-editors in Fleet Street, one report beginning:

Mussolini is finding another Abyssinia in Albania. Although tonight

all the main towns . . . are securely in his hands, the wild country in
the interior is holding out bitterly against him. In the mountains in
the north at least 10,000 brown-skinned peasants and mountaineers
have been rallied by their chieftains and are sniping down into the
valleys . . .[25]

Then orders arrived from London to leave for Istanbul in the
hope of reaching the Dodecanese Islands, which were also being
threatened by Italy. From there, he was to make his way to Malta,
the British naval base from which Italy was watched, to Tunis, which
the Italians were demanding from France, and finally to Gibraltar.

After several days' waiting, he boarded a tramp-steamer for Rhodes,
passing the time reading Somerset Maugham, whose work he did not
like, and D.H. Lawrence's book about Australia, *Kangaroo*, which
stirred uneasy memories and gave him:

> . . . the same awful stifled feeling I used to have towards the end
> when I was living in Australia. I am sure I could never go back
> there again happily. How hateful it sounds . . . God, how much
> he makes me hate Australia. And I know what he says is true. And
> I know if I went back it would, octopus-like, close round me again
> bit by bit so that in the end I would say, "Well, it's a damn sight
> better than decayed Europe anyhow." Ugh.[26]

He had flown to Rome but there received orders from London to
abandon his proposed tour. A German naval squadron had entered
the Mediterranean and another correspondent, O'Dowd Gallagher,
had been rushed to Gibraltar. Moorehead was to return to Paris.
When he arrived at the end of April he found a crisis in the office. A
letter awaited him from Charles Sutton saying that he had intended
Cox to go to Albania but that Moorehead had told him that he was
not available and gone there himself. He was thus accused both of
lying and disobedience. Geoffrey Cox readily accepted his plea of
innocence and that there had been a misunderstanding, but suspicion
that Moorehead might have been somewhat disingenuous gave him a
reputation for ruthlessness.

Soon afterwards, Cox went on holiday and Moorehead enjoyed
himself as the senior correspondent in Paris. It was satisfying to be
able to talk in a confident, worldly manner about his experiences, and
the future of Europe as he saw it, when visitors called. One visitor
was daunting. Lord Beaverbrook arrived in Paris unexpectedly and

invited Moorehead and Mara Scherbatoff out to dinner. They sat at the Tour d'Argent until nearly midnight, Moorehead told Lucy, "talking about Daladier, Molotov, Scherbatoff's family, the Russian church in Cannes, the cost of food in London and Weidmann's execution, to which I am invited – especially about Weidmann." Beaverbrook asked Moorehead when he was going to get married, prompting the thought that he might have heard rumours about his affair with Lucy. "I'll tell you why men stop buzzing like a bee from flower to flower and eventually get married," he had said. "Because nature is on the woman's side. The urge is too great. It takes hold of everyone sooner or later."[27]

The idea had taken a strong hold on Moorehead. The *Daily Express* had offered no alternative to remaining in Paris – he still felt under a cloud following the Albania affair – and he was thinking of returning to London. He asked Lucy to look for a flat they could share and live on an income of £15 a week. "That is plenty," he told her. "You'll ride in a bus, you won't have new clothes or lunches at the Savoy Grill but, by God, you will have me in bed with you at night and your life will become just half again as big by having me to look after."[28]

He thought it would be romantic to marry in Paris at the British Consulate. He remembered the last journalist's wedding when Tom and Isobel Delmer had married and they had quarrelled immediately after the ceremony:

Isobel then burst into tears in the street and declared, "It's my wedding and I want some champagne." Delmer told her not to be vulgar. They then drove to the Dôme on the Left Bank and ordered some oysters. Isobel was still unhappy so Delmer called the waiter and said, "Bring a dozen bottles of champagne for *madame*." In the evening they felt better and went to the theatre. Almost immediately after that Delmer left for Spain. It all seems a little too like Hemingway for me.[29]

But, even now, there was an occasional urge to run away. He was ready to go almost anywhere except his homeland: "*Ugh*" was again his response when his parents suggested his return but he did think of asking to report the planned tour of Australia by the Duke and Duchess of Kent if Lucy would first marry him and come too. He could be charmingly flirtatious and flattering and write:

My darling, I have been considering you rather critically while I have been having my bath . . . First we have Lucy the Smiling Wife and Mother. This is very beautiful. It calls for the Gentle Puss, the Infinite Pity and Mercy Puss. A very tender and beautiful spectacle. It seems to call for candlelight at dinner and Rhine wine in crystal glasses and evening dress. Then we have Lucy the Concubine and this is the Hungry and Luxurious Puss. It seems to call for wild music on the lawn outside and the sudden slamming of a window to keep it out and a moment of hot silence in the darkness and I, rather indifferent and determined to have none of it and not to notice a shameless length of naked legs moving underneath a shameless split skirt . . .

And then we have Lucy the Young Woman with a bundle of tradesmen's bills in her hand and the telephone ringing and three of the latest biographies lying on the occasional table. And this is the Set and Intelligent Puss. I make an attempt to reduce it to the Hungry and Luxurious Puss but it is useless . . . I register the Sour Puss.[30]

Or he could be mocking as when, visualising themselves as suburban parents with him working in London, leaving her at home "in a state of cow-like expectation and content", he concluded:

Then after years you would die peacefully and happily, leaving me surrounded with tall sons and daughters and I, in my prime at fifty, still full of roaring lust and health, would marry again, a very young girl and pass the night in gross sport and drinking . . . Ah, my darling, I am going to treat you outrageously.[31]

Their cross-Channel courtship and his pleasure and frustration in Paris was interrupted by a brief but savage scene. The murderer and suspected necrophiliac Weidmann had been condemned to death and both Moorehead and Willis of the *Standard* had been invited to attend the execution. Later that day, he wrote to Lucy:

I feel like death – hangover, no sleep, too many cigarettes. We stayed up all night to see Weidmann get his head chopped off. I am glad I saw it and especially the blood-hungry crowd. Dozens of journalists, of course, all sitting in a café alongside the guillotine, drinking *fin à l'eau* and waiting for the dawn. Willis hoisted me up on his shoulder so I could get a better view. It was all over in twenty seconds. The door opens, Weidmann is shoved out. He was wearing a blue silk shirt torn open at the neck. They pushed him down on to the block, someone pulled the lever, then bang. There was a sort of sigh from the crowd. Only two disgusting things – the blood in the gutter and on the knife and on the solicitor collecting the French journalists around and in a sanctimonious voice describing Weidmann's behaviour in the cell just before the execution. Nice to come home from all this and find your letter.[32]

His next assignment was to visit the fortifications of the Maginot Line and he returned to find Paris "ridiculously pleasant" in summer with so many wives and children away at the seaside and the men "whooping up the town". But, as he put it, the attitude was that of "peasants who insist on setting their vines on the side of a volcano, which they know, sooner or later, is going to erupt over them again. They dread the eruption and watch anxiously for it – but, like us, they will stay on the volcano instead of running away to a good safe place."[33]

The new crisis was concentrated on Danzig and German claims on Poland – although Moorehead expected Hitler to strike at Hungary next – but all agreed that the prospects of peace were now remote. He wrote:

Darling, we might as well make up our minds about it, the war is going to come, but I still think not until next year . . . Please, please, for my sake, don't plague yourself with too many worries and doubts in advance. The war at the worst can be no more than painful death and you don't go around worrying all day about when you are going to die. Let's just admit the thing is coming and forget it as far as possible in the meantime. The French are doing that damn well.[34]

When Geoffrey Cox returned from holiday, the office settled down to its former routine, Cox concentrating on politics and the current crisis, while Moorehead coped with the varied demands for news from Fleet Street, sometimes twenty or more in a single day. On returning to his flat one night he wrote to Lucy that he had just written "stories about opium, a murder and the gold standard".[35] But it was not a happy office, although the misunderstanding over the assignment to Albania had seemed to have been settled with Cox. The two men

– so much alike in some ways, opposites in others – were proving incompatible:

> I cannot remember having this deep personal resentment before. I like him and admire him and I like his family and he is my enemy. There seems to be no logic in it at all. And I feel that no matter how much in the future we may smile and be friends I will try to injure him. He feels the same way about me. It's all very contemptible on both our parts and is probably the answer to the question of why men should want to fight wars. They get the same way in the mass.[36]

Geoffrey Cox, well aware of the antagonism, had decided that the only solution was for Moorehead to work elsewhere and after he had put this to Sutton, he was ordered to return to London. At once, relations with Cox relaxed and, as Moorehead put it, "for the first time in three months we began to behave like normal people again." Cox even suggested that Moorehead might care to rent his flat in London for a modest £2.10s. a week; meanwhile he made arrangements to move some of his furniture to London and sell the car.

Events were moving too quickly and powerfully for any such planning. A British mission had left for Moscow in August and Winston Churchill had urged a military alliance with the Soviet Union; that might have taken Moorehead to Moscow had not the news been overtaken by the mounting German threat to Poland and the determination of the British and French governments to support the Poles. Realising that war might break out within a few weeks, Christiansen was disposing his correspondents because there might be difficulty in moving them once it began. Moorehead had proved himself an energetic and resourceful reporter, who could now be trusted to work on his own in a major capital city; the *Daily Express* had no correspondent in Rome so that was where he would go.

On 22nd August, 1939, Moorehead was travelling past Genoa, along the lovely Portofino coast towards Rome, and he wrote to Lucy, "This dropped out of a blue sky." He told of his friendly parting with Cox: "There is a curious sort of attachment between us. It is very dry and unemotional." Cox had said, "I just want to say how sorry I am we ever had this trouble. It doesn't look as though we will be working together again. You have a wonderful chance now to start up a bureau of your own at Rome."

He had had "a restless, lousy half-sleep in the train last night", brooding about his prospects:

I don't feel greatly worried about getting the news. I do feel a bit worried about being able to write it up sufficiently well . . . The hardest thing, I fancy, is to write the stuff in such a way that it will be printed without infuriating the Fascists. It's damn hard to produce the right amount of sensationalism for the *Express* without being ejected from a country like this.

He brooded about their own future together. He speculated both that "all this might die down in a day or two and I might be on my way home pretty soon" and also that "sooner or later you must free yourself from your job and be prepared to follow me". He was still convinced that war was not imminent and they had a little more freedom left. "I foresee a peace ahead all through this winter and perhaps a neutral Italy afterwards," he told her, "I really do believe that – peace this year."

That afternoon he arrived at Rome and moved into a room at the Albergo Palazzo Ambasciatori, where a telegram of welcome from Lucy awaited him and he added a postscript to the letter he had written in the train: "Darling, how sweet and kind of you to send the telegram. They are playing *Madame Butterfly* on the radio downstairs. It almost seems as if you were here."[37]

Chapter Four

"Quiet but slightly ominous"

Alan Moorehead plunged into Rome with gusto, for with his new responsibilities came a surge of self-confidence. He was at last an important foreign correspondent in charge of a bureau for the British national newspaper with the highest circulation in the world and in the European capital that was exceeded in importance only by London, Paris and Berlin.

On his first day, Sydney Morrell, the *Daily Express* correspondent, who covered Central Europe and had been temporarily transferred to Rome until Moorehead arrived, showed him around the city and introduced him to useful informants. Moorehead wrote to Lucy that evening:

> What a collection. The shrewd little German doctor in the news agency, who said he had it for certain that there would be war in the morning; the 15 dozen Italians, who assured me there wouldn't be war at all; the Americans, who just didn't know and were twice as efficient as anybody else. Nobody seems to really care about it – the weather is too hot. Everyone who can goes down to the beach at Ostia and swaps rumours.

As he wrote, the post arrived. "My goodness, a letter from you, just a minute," he added; then, "Yes, you're a dear. And, darling, would you do that – come to Rome to marry me next month? We will get the Pope to do the job."[1]

59

Next day, Morrell introduced Moorehead "to about fifty people from Carpathian monks to out-of-work grandees" and then flew off to Budapest. He was already being made to feel at home, welcomed at the British Embassy and made a temporary member of the British expatriates' Union Club, where "they all play dice and talk belligerent and it's all very like *Punch* . . . I never saw such a peaceful place."[2]

On the afternoon of his first full day in Rome he cabled a long despatch which appeared under his first by-line as a senior correspondent. Following his own instinct and the policy of his newspaper that there would be no immediate war, he wrote optimistically of "hopes of a peace settlement"[3] because the Italian newspapers were urging negotiations over Poland and there were few signs of warlike preparations in the capital. Next day, he reported that the Pope had called for peace and that President Roosevelt had asked the same of King Victor Emmanuel, the nominal King of Italy. But on the day after that he reported that Italian mobilisation was under way and, with a personal touch that *Express* readers enjoyed, told how the waiter who had brought breakfast to his room had told him that "six of the boys in the hotel were called up this morning and one of the cooks has been sent off, too."[4] But, even at the end of August, he was reporting that Mussolini was using his influence on Hitler to avert war.

Then, quite suddenly, fear of war became apparent "like a monstrous disease slowly creeping over Rome". Moorehead was constantly asked "When?" – "as though I should know" – and the British began making plans to leave via France or Switzerland. Worry was enhanced by the heat, which broke with a succession of spectacular thunderstorms "to complete the Dante-esque scene",[5] as he put it. He revelled in the visual drama of the place, particularly a late-night tour of the city after the "black-out" had extinguished all lights: "the dark Colosseum and St. Peter's and the blue light across the Seven Hills". It was an apocalyptic scene made more exciting by the arrival of a heavily-sealed packet of American dollars from his London office as a "war emergency fund" and when he telephoned the staff on the foreign desk in London, they would end the conversation with "Goodbye, old man", which he said "makes me feel as if I am just about to mount the scaffold".[6]

On Friday, 1st September, 1939, Germany annexed Danzig and invaded Poland. War now seemed not only inevitable but imminent. Moorehead faced the lurid uncertainties of the future, and the possibility of being caught in Rome if Italy suddenly became involved, with a calm professionalism. The past eleven days had changed him. He had matured and the defensive banter and bombast had been replaced by a vigorous and good-humoured determination to survive. In his letters to Lucy, his declarations of love were no longer mixed with teasing about the temptations he was only just managing to avoid. She had now agreed to marry him and both were sure that together they could face whatever was to come.

On Sunday, 3rd September, the vain hope of peace evaporated when no reply was received to the British and French ultimatum that Germany withdraw from Poland. That morning both countries declared war. On that day he wrote to Lucy:

> You must come to Rome and we will be married here . . . You must start making plans *at once* to leave for Italy. Throw up the job, tell them anything but start about it right away . . . Immediately you get a telegram from me, be ready to set off. I don't want you to come until I am absolutely certain this country is to be neutral and until I get definite orders to remain here as a correspondent . . .[7]

Two days later he was convinced that Italy would remain neutral for some time and he asked Lucy to leave for Rome. He suggested that rather than resign from the *Daily Express* she ask for special leave; it might be best to travel by train via Switzerland, but possibly she might fly with Imperial Airways. However, as the Germans engulfed Poland and the British Expeditionary Force was shipped to France, communications with London were disrupted: mail slowed almost to a stop and telephoning became difficult. He wrote daily in the hope that the letters would eventually arrive and urged her to do so, too.

Meanwhile his future was in the balance. He had thought of volunteering for the British Army, then considered the offer of a job at the British Embassy in Rome, which might lead to an appointment as press attaché. Friends like Geoffrey Cox and George Millar in Paris were planning to enlist, but he was now aged twenty-nine and, for any journalist over the age of thirty, an accepted alternative was service as a war correspondent. Delmer, who had just escaped from Warsaw, was, he heard, hoping for that and Moorehead decided on 10th September that it would be his aim, too.

As news of the German advance on Warsaw and sinkings by U-boats in the Atlantic reached Rome, Moorehead seemed to be living in a threatening limbo. No letter from Lucy reached him for more than three weeks and, he wrote to her, he found his surroundings "strange – so quiet, so unnaturally normal and all this sinister undercurrent of diplomatic wrangling".[8] He moved from his grand hotel to a cheaper one, the Luxor opposite Trajan's Forum, because the foreign editor was cutting his expense allowance and he would have little more than his pay, which was now fourteen guineas a week, to keep him. But he began looking for a flat, which he might eventually share with his wife, and learning Italian, reading about Italian history and again dreaming of becoming a writer rather than a journalist. A letter from a literary agent in London, through whom he had hoped to publish a novel, arrived, telling him that there would be no market for it now, but, Moorehead noted with interest, adding that if he was "doing 'war correspondence' " would he think of collecting it as a book?

More than a month after he had asked Lucy to join him, she had not arrived. It was not clear from her letters whether she had talked to Christiansen about their plans, or asked for leave; whether she had enough money for the journey, or had even applied for French, Swiss and Italian visas. By the end of September he had found a flat, which had been abandoned by a British woman who had left Italy:

> It's in an ancient building next to Keats' house in the Piazza di Spagna . . . up four flights of stone steps and no lift and it's pretty much a period piece. There is a hall, 2 bedrooms, dining room, big central living room with a terrace overlooking the Piazza . . . a kitchen maid's room and bathroom . . . there's an ancient female maid, alleged to be excellent, who goes with the place and there's central heating and telephone all found . . . I like it. It's so high and quiet and the air is good.[9]

The cost – including the maid, heating and lighting – was the equivalent of £2.10s a week.

Despite his imaginings of obstacles and delays to Lucy's departure, she had been able to obtain leave, tickets and visas and, at the beginning of October, she left London. In Paris, she stayed with George Millar and his wife, whom she had met before the outbreak of war when visiting Paris but who did not know the extent of her involvement with Moorehead. So they were surprised when, on arrival, she told them that she had to catch a train to Rome next day and even more surprised when they asked why she was going there and she replied, "I'm going to marry Alan Moorehead."[10] Two days later, she was in Rome and, as Moorehead had not yet taken the flat, they stayed in separate rooms at the Hotel de la Ville, overlooking the Spanish Steps. On 6th October, Moorehead wrote to Lucy's mother in Torquay, telling her that her daughter had arrived safely and thanking her and her husband for their good wishes.

"Lucy and I have wanted for a long time to get married," he told her, "and it seems rather ironical that our chance should have come only on the outbreak of war. But already Lucy is enjoying Rome and I think we shall have at least a little time here in peace together." He explained that the legal formalities for the marriage would take about three weeks to complete, that they expected the ceremony to take place at the end of the month and then hoped to spend a short honeymoon at Sorrento, or on Capri. "We have made no definite plans since we must wait to see how the war develops," he concluded. "However I do want you to remember that, whatever happens, I shall be taking care of her and that I am happier now than I can say, now that we are to be together."[11]

The diplomatic community in Rome took Lucy to their hearts. While most British residents and visitors had fled, it cheered them that this charming and intelligent young woman should be arriving to marry the attractive Australian journalist and live amongst them. At a succession of welcoming parties, Lucy quickly made friends, amongst them a number of Anglophile Italians. Moorehead was immensely proud, telling her, "You looked so tall and gracious standing among them."[12] One, Contessa Yvonne Pallavicino, whose father was a close associate of Marshal Graziani, the conqueror and viceroy of Abyssinia, became an early confidante, Lucy showing her the black chiffon nightdress she had brought for her honeymoon.

They were married, as planned, at the end of October in the Palazzo Senatorio in Michelangelo's Piazza del Campidoglio on the Capitoline Hill. They had two months together before her leave ended and she was to return to London, while Moorehead hoped that he would be able to follow soon afterwards, when Italy either settled into permanent neutrality – as was expected – or entered the war. A few days after Christmas, she left Rome just as it began to snow. At the railway station, they discovered that there had been confusion over her sleeping-berth reservation and that the train was crowded. She had to leave, and her husband bullied the managers of Thomas Cook and American Express to make sure that she would be allocated a berth when she reached Milan. On returning to their empty apartment, he wrote to her:

Thank God for the snow. It made a sharp break between now and the past 3 months and even when it clears away Rome will never be the same ever again. Everyone here loved you and wanted you to stay just as they will want you in London – except that they do not need you there as I do here. I walked back from the station through the snow and I am still not feeling anything particularly, just the cold. I don't even know that I am alone yet. I remember how fine you were here and I just feel terribly that I never did enough for you . . . I shall think of you on New Year's Eve and all the time.[13]

On the first day of 1940, Europe was gripped by apprehension. Germany had destroyed Poland in a few weeks and partitioned it with the Soviet Union, with which Hitler had agreed a treaty of non-aggression while the Russians attacked Finland. Rome was full of rumours – most of them false – about imminent disasters: one of a Russian invasion of the Middle East followed by another forecasting a revolution in Moscow while Moorehead had to seek confirmation or denial from various embassies and report the current state of Mussolini's bellicosity. He was miserable without Lucy and it was tantalising to hear that, soon after returning to London, she had been sent to Paris with a fashion artist to report on the spring collections just as she had before the outbreak of war.

Since he did not expect Italy to make any belligerent moves until the spring, he asked Sutton if he could visit Malta and then tour the Mediterranean. The foreign editor agreed and, knowing more about future events in the Middle East than did his Rome correspondent, told him to make his way to Cairo after visiting Malta. "This may take me further away from you," he wrote to Lucy, "but somehow I feel that so long as events are moving and I am travelling I can more easily get back to you. I cannot live for long without seeing you."[14]

On 17th January he flew to Malta. After an uncomfortable flight, stopping at Naples, Palermo and Catania, he arrived first to be surprised by the beauty of the island – "all browns and grey" – and to be appalled by the overlay of British dreariness. "The greasy roast beef, the beer, the clean streets, the self-consciousness, the nameless cheese, the English language, the painful politeness and control in everyone's face and voice, the awful hotel, the shop windows full of English things – and oh, the damned smug control. I hate it,"[15] he wrote to Lucy from the old-fashioned Osborne Hotel within the walls of Valletta.

Everybody was friendly and the Governor was welcoming and informative but the mood persisted. Next day he wrote to her:

> It's fine getting masses of English papers, having bacon and eggs for breakfast and the Governor was charming, but I still cannot get over the feeling that I am in the Borstal institute and with one false move I shall be sent to Coventry. I am afraid that this experience will prevent me from ever getting into the British Army – it will have to be the Australians or nothing.[16]

It was the reserve of the British that he found so irritating.

> Strange myopic people here. They will win the war on self-control, pink gin, private unhappiness and public worthiness. And this eternal under-statement – you know the sort of thing – you say you only have one dog when you have two. Ostensibly modesty. Actually a form of fear. I hate most people who are not boastful egoists.[17]

After a week of such company, permission arrived from the Admiralty in London for him to sail with a squadron of the Mediterranean Fleet on patrol. He joined the cruiser *Galatea*, a notably efficient and happy ship which was the flagship of the destroyer flotillas and was greeted by Vice-Admiral Jack Tovey, who flew his flag in her. Like Moorehead he was a short, dynamic man with wide-ranging interests and, after the ship sailed, the two of them spent hours on the bridge discussing "Italian opera, politics and books". In the wardroom, he was greeted by the officers with friendliness and respect as one who had recently been in a hostile capital and there was much late-night conversation "about the war and the sea and religion and what have you".[18] On the lower deck he was as welcome and treated to more than a share of the rum ration. He was invited to address the ship's company, standing on a gun turret while they were assembled on deck, and tell them about his experiences as a foreign correspondent.

The patrol off the coast of Italy and the mouth of the Adriatic was to catch German blockade-runners and, if possible, arrest suspected enemy agents on board ship. They stopped and searched suspicious Greek, Turkish and Yugoslav merchantmen and sent a few into Malta for further investigation. They did not catch any enemy agents but the alarms and chases and the sending away of boarding parties were exciting and a gale blew and gave a sense of seafaring.

As the squadron turned for Malta, he confessed to Lucy:

I shall be desperately sorry to leave the ship. The storm has died down and we have had a whole series of excitements . . . boarding ships all over the place and a great pother of searchlights, armed guards and signals. I have been on the bridge most of the time. It is more beautiful at night in the bright moon than I can tell you about. I stand watching it sometimes, the spray over the grey decks, the bright snow on the mountains ashore and the moonlight on the ship ahead as we go chasing her at thirty miles an hour. Then the lowering of the boat into the waves and the quiet orders on the bridge. It is bright and cold and I love it. If I could, I would spend all my time away from you at sea. It would be a wild thrill if I could see this machine really go into action.[19]

He knew that he had been liked and admired by men he liked and admired – grave and often intelligent professionals who wore their skills lightly – and when he landed at Valletta they presented him with a caricature of himself and invited him to play hockey for the *Galatea* in a match ashore. His new friends invited him to join them in "a run ashore" and, as he told Lucy, he had "a terrific night with the officers of my ship . . . bowling here and there around the half-blackout between their clubs and the dives of Valletta . . . They have all been so decent."

Nor was this all. The Commander-in-Chief, Admiral Sir Andrew Cunningham, had heard of this lively-minded and amusing Australian and invited him to lunch. He sat down with "a glittering array of aides and captains" and the admiral gazed at him with alert and remarkably blue eyes that matched Moorehead's own and asked him about Balkan politics and the possible interpretations of Mussolini's recent speeches. At the end of lunch, Cunningham suggested that Moorehead should ask his editor to appoint him naval correspondent so that he could spend the war at sea and he, delighted at the prospect, began to dream accordingly. "Give me the sea," he wrote to Lucy, "not these stinking streets. The Navy are really behaving wonderfully for me: the longer I am on land, the more I like them and want to get back to sea."[20]

But his previous idea of a tour through Egypt and the Levant had been approved by the foreign editor and he regretfully left his new friends. Flying to Alexandria, he took the train to Cairo, travelling with "two delightful horsey Englishmen who sat in my compartment roaring and sweating and swearing and talking about horses. The British Raj in action." It was very different from the suffocating gentility of Malta. The entire scene had changed: the light, the sounds and the smells, the people and the places. He arrived at the Continental-Savoy Hotel and immediately wrote to Lucy, "My letters from Malta were bad-tempered and a bit confused. It's better here in Egypt. This hotel is full of fezes and sad chamber music and would-be chic. The country itself is all hard, bright sunshine, blue sky, camels, palms, khaki, guns and sand. It's a queer place."[21]

He wrote an excited despatch to the *Daily Express*, setting the scene for whatever news might emerge in this exotic setting:

I flew down to Egypt over nearly 1,000 miles of the Mediterranean. It is troops all the way – dark-skinned gunners at Malta; Italian riflemen strung along the 25th degree of longitude, where Mussolini has erected a barbed-wire fence to mark the border between Egypt and Libya; Egyptian troops just across the frontier in a dry watercourse at Sollum; then more British again at Mersa Matruh, the place where Cleopatra used to bathe, and so on through the desert to Alexandria and Cairo . . . There, over the tops of the sand dunes stands the world's best air raid shelter – the tomb of Cheops, lying in the centre of the Great Pyramid. British Tommies were swarming up it when I went out there today. Others were loping around the Sphinx astride camels. They are almost the only tourists Egypt sees these days.[22]

All that had seemed to be happening in Cairo was a visit by General Weygand, the French officer who had been appointed to command the Allied armies in the Middle East. But something else was afoot and on 9th February he wrote to Lucy, "A really good story is breaking and I must remain in Egypt until next week. I seem to have arrived at the exact moment. God knows what's going to happen here but something's afloat."[23] What it was did not become apparent for another three days, when the British correspondents in Cairo were invited to visit Suez.

On the 13th the *Express* published his report:

The first of the Anzacs are here . . . in the biggest troop convoy ever to put to sea, they have voyaged 10,000 miles from New

Zealand and Australia and today landed, singing and shouting their war cries, in Egypt. Mr Anthony Eden, the Dominions Secretary, after a secret flight from England, took a launch out to the troopships lying anchored off Suez, carrying in his pocket a message from the King . . .

Even rumour-ridden Egypt was taken by surprise as troop-train after troop-train passed by on the way to desert camps.[24]

But next day he was again ordered to move. "Terrific day yesterday with Australians and New Zealanders," he wrote to Lucy. "And now a cable telling me to go back to Rome to cover the peace moves. What peace moves?"[25]

Moorehead had enjoyed his foray across the Mediterranean to the Middle East and the feeling of being at the edge of great events and mixing with men of power and activity. He had hoped to return via Palestine and Turkey but had to take the most direct route, flying across Libya. Cairo, he could see, was an important centre for news and he would have been happy to stay a little longer only that, as he put it, "the *Daily Express* are constitutionally incapable of allowing anyone to stay long enough on a job to do it properly."[26] His return flight to Rome was delayed by storms over the Mediterranean – first at Benghazi and then at Tripoli – and he was able to take a first, intrigued look at the great deserts of North Africa. He wrote to Lucy from his hotel in Tripoli:

Queer business, the desert. Silent like the sea and the same fascinating monotony. It gives me quite unexpected pleasure sometimes – especially in the early morning when everything turns gold and bronze and vivid red. Then, whack – it's dead night and the sky's as bright as the Champs Elysées on a Sunday night.[27]

He arrived back in Rome to find six letters from Lucy awaiting him. She was staying with Mary Welsh, whose husband Noel Monks was in France, reporting on the British Expeditionary Force, and sharing the marital bed with her in their Chelsea flat, a thought that Moorehead found disagreeable. She had had influenza, was unhappy at the *Express* office and was pining for him. So it was with a shock of joy that he heard from Sutton that he could return to London at the end of February for a month's leave. The days passed slowly with little or no news to speed the time; nothing to report but the daily fluctuations of real or supposed tension and that the British ambassador had invited some Fascist leaders to watch the first British propaganda film made since the outbreak of war, *The Lion Has Wings*, from which mockery of Hitler had been cut for the occasion.

On the first day of March, he travelled by train through Switzerland, then across France, arriving in London to the welcome he had been imagining for the past two months. He wrote a lively, encapsulated account of his 17,000 miles of travel in the past six months for the *Daily Express*, before he and Lucy were at last allowed to leave Fleet Street and be alone together for a little while. Then, on 9th April, came news that Germany had invaded Norway and Denmark and that Britain was to send the Home Fleet and a new expeditionary force to help the Norwegians, for it was already too late to do anything for the Danes. The *Express* correspondents who had been covering Scandinavia and reporting the war in Finland would now go to Norway, while Moorehead must return to Rome in case Italy should enter the war. Sadly he left Lucy in London after making vague plans for a reunion later in the year; but he left her happily, too, for she was pregnant.

Back in Rome there seemed no greater sense of urgency and he began writing to Lucy suggesting that she should travel there in the spring and that they would spend the summer in Italy together. He reported the fluctuations in tension and political speculation, which the *Daily Express* would print so long as each despatch began with a dramatic sentence – or one added by the sub-editor – such as "Late tonight Rome had a quiet but slightly ominous atmosphere . . ." or "As Allied warships are steaming to their stations in the Mediterranean tonight . . ." But he was coming to dislike his exile in "easy, sunny Rome, where people seem to think more about their *cabanas* at Ostia for the summer than anything else". He wanted Lucy to leave London, not only to be with him, but to be away from some of her circle, notably Mary Welsh. A friend in Rome had repeated to him some malicious gossip. This, as he told Lucy, was that Mary had said he had "slept in every brothel in France" and had only married her because she was the only girl who had refused to sleep with him. So he was glad to hear that Lucy and Mary were no longer sharing the Monks's flat and that she was now lodging in Addison Crescent with Osbert Lancaster, the witty caricaturist who was drawing "pocket cartoons" for the front page of the *Daily Express*, and his wife Karen.

Only the thought that Lucy might be able to join him in Rome kept him at his post when Morrell telephoned from Belgrade to say that he was sick of the Balkans and would like to exchange assignments. He stayed where he was "working like a tiger" but with little news of significance to report. As the British were being driven from Norway, the news in Italy was less important there than it seemed in Rome. When he attended the horse show in the Borghese Gardens, he sat near Mussolini and reported his every move: "He stood on a tribune throughout the sunny afternoon, tensely hunching up his shoulders as the horses went over the jumps and snapping into the Fascist salute as each rider passed before him."[28] If Lucy and he could not be together in Rome, which he found "so pleasant and warm and friendly", there might be a chance of a move to Cairo, which, he wrote, would be "less nervous" and much more exotic. Indeed, the more he thought of Egypt – far from the tensions of Europe and the telephoning from the *Daily Express* office – the more the idea appealed. On 6th June, he wrote to her from the pension, to which he had moved, suggesting that she take her holiday in June, come to Rome and then they discuss future moves. Four days later, Germany struck in the west with a sudden, massive assault on France, Holland and Belgium to turn the flank of the Maginot Line and advance on Paris. Neville Chamberlain resigned and was replaced by Winston Churchill as Prime Minister leading a new coalition government.

Lucy now seemed more at risk than he was and he wrote next morning:

> Darling, I am feeling tremendously that I should be with you through this tough period. Should you not give up the job at once? Take a cottage in the country . . . I think sometimes I ought to send you to Australia at once to have the baby in peace and quiet. I'll get you into the sun and warmth of the Mediterranean soon and we will fix it so everything will be fine.[29]

The foreign editor had tentatively agreed that if Italy came into the war and Moorehead had to leave, he might first go to Athens and then, perhaps, to Cairo and it was there that he dreamed of setting up house with Lucy.

On 16th May Moorehead attended "the biggest, roaring success" of a party that the British expatriates decided to call "the Waterloo Ball"[30] because news had arrived that the Dutch army had surrendered and that the Germans had turned the flank of the defences along the Albert Canal in Belgium and broken through the French positions at

Sedan. The armoured columns raced westward, captured Arras and Amiens on the 21st and headed for Paris.

If Italy was to collect a share of plunder from a defeated France now was the time to support Germany with more than propaganda. As well as the familiar demonstrations demanding the annexation of Tunis, Corsica and Nice, the mobs now shouted anti-British slogans and there were cases of British residents in Rome being abused and even assaulted by Fascist youths in the streets. Although both the British Embassy and Italian officials had tried to reassure British correspondents that, in the event of war, they would be evacuated with the diplomats, there was no guarantee of this and the possibility of internment remained. The *Daily Express* did not want to risk losing its Rome correspondent so, at the end of the third week of May, Moorehead was ordered to fly to Athens.

It had been stimulating to work in Italy. Rome, he found "so electric it keeps one buoyed up and the background fear one has of being caught here makes the usual, normal routine of living seem strange" and the demonstrations heightened the sense of drama which found expression in vocal and occasionally physical violence. "I will, I think, in the end be glad to get out of this unfriendly city," he wrote to Lucy. "The crowd were demonstrating again tonight and, although it means nothing, there is a psychological effect created by this hysterical shouting which wears one down a bit."[31] Looking ahead the thought of Egypt appealed and, he told her:

If we get to Cairo together we can go on out to Australia for a few months' holiday – when the war ends. I might even send you sooner if Europe were absolutely cracking up. Bring the baby up on the farm – good milk.

Goodness I am keen on the baby. I turn him over in my mind from time to time and go thinking round the subject and making plans. She will be beautiful and brilliant if she's a girl and with a good strong placid temperament . . . Perhaps a good bit like you. The boy would be a tiger, full of great appetites. Not one of those damn public school pansies with a squeaking voice.[32]

With such thoughts in his head he flew away from Rome on 22nd May, arriving in Athens that evening. At the grandest hotel, the Grande Bretagne, where he was to stay, he found a cable of welcome from Lucy, who had been told of his move by Sutton, and several familiar faces. "Athens is going to be nothing but a holiday in the heat," he wrote to her next day. "There must be half a dozen correspondents swarming round this pub, all old friends of mine and calmly and blandly sitting about without filing a word to London. It seems the censorship is insurmountable." But there were compensations:

> What heaven getting the English papers, English cigarettes, English language and all damn cheap . . . Rome was getting a bit of a trial with hostile demonstrations and whatnot. It's a tremendous let-up to be in a friendly country though it does seem a bit of a small town. The heat is fierce and the terrific light smacks you fair in the puss so that you don't want to do much except just wait and drink around and talk . . . After a week of this I think perhaps I should move off down to Cairo, where at least I will be able to send messages.[33]

Sydney Morrell had been in Athens for a fortnight because his return to Belgrade had been delayed by some mild infection which confined him to his room at the Grande Bretagne. It was when visiting him that Moorehead entered the lift at the hotel to come face to face with someone who had once seemed an embodiment of all that he disliked, distrusted and, indeed, feared in the English. This was Alexander Clifford, the Reuter correspondent whom he had met in the Bar Basque at St. Jean-de-Luz and by whom he had felt slightly snubbed. He had immediately recognised the handsome, rather Prussian head of this tall, broad-shouldered young man and, particularly, "the air of superiority and pernickety indifference".[34] So he was irritated when it became obvious that Clifford was also bound for Morrell's room. There they ignored each other, addressing their remarks to Morrell. Then the doctor arrived and asked them both to leave. So together but in silence they walked along the corridor to wait for the lift and, while waiting, Moorehead felt that one of them should break the tension and so suggested they had a drink. To his surprise, Clifford agreed and they walked out into the hot streets, sat at a table outside a taverna and Clifford ordered two glasses of ouzo in Greek. Then they began to talk.

Clifford said that he thought he did remember their first meeting and, since then, he had been in Berlin for Reuter but had recently joined the staff of the *Daily Mail* – the direct rival to the *Daily Express* – and was on a general assignment in the Balkans. Moorehead told him about his own adventures and then the conversation broadened.

They talked and argued for three hours and more while the bright sky faded over Athens and the street lamps were lighted. Clifford, he found, was a formidable opponent in debate, with a sound knowledge of European politics and languages and otherwise he began to revise his first impression. Instead of arrogance he sensed shyness and found himself stimulated rather than irritated by their different approaches to the issues of the day. When they parted, Moorehead found himself looking forward to their next meeting. He wrote admiringly to Lucy about "Clifford, who speaks six languages including Greek"[35] and after their next meeting, when they went swimming and talking, wrote again, "I like Clifford of the *Mail* very much. He has survived his old school and donnish manner and he swims and thinks very well. I hope he comes on to Egypt. I have not talked so well with anyone for so long."[36]

In these conversations, something of Clifford's background emerged. Of Scottish descent, his ancestors had been ship-builders and engineers. He had been educated at Charterhouse and Oriel College, Oxford, where he had read philosophy, politics and economics, also showing a remarkable aptitude for languages – he could speak French, German, Italian, Spanish, Greek and Swedish and could manage some conversation in half a dozen other languages – as well as for history and mathematics. His was a wide-ranging mind but if one interest had to predominate it would have been music. After coming down from university he had toured much of Europe by bicycle, or travelling cheaply by train, and had acquired a feeling for, and knowledge of, its countries. Although a career in the Foreign Office had been forecast for him, he joined Reuter's news-agency as a night sub-editor before being promoted to work abroad; first in Spain and then in Germany. Gradually, Moorehead came to sum him up as "a walking dictionary, the precise, diffident, unpolitical and unambitious man".[37]

He seemed a lonely figure, now aged thirty-one and without any attachment to a woman, although he clearly enjoyed female company. Thus, somewhat to their surprise, the two were drawn together: Moorehead to this tall, good-looking, intellectual English-man who was proving such good company; Clifford to this short, jaunty, inquisitive Australian who saw the European scene through his clear, candid blue eyes in sharp focus and made every experience they shared seem exciting or fun.

The two of them discussed the pointlessness of staying in Athens, where there was no news and where little could get past the official censorship. "The very pleasantness of the place is a bit galling, seeing what is happening everywhere else in the world,"[38] he told Lucy in a letter. They went on an excursion to Marathon, where they came across "with great astonishment, the Bishop of Gloucester and the Archbishop of Gibraltar sitting high on a crag there, talking about Queen Mary and heresy". They swam a great deal and, at the hotel and diplomats' flats, talked with "the Greeks and French and Levantines who drift in and out like the South Wind".[39] But Clifford did not accompany him when he went with an American reporter, Ed Kennedy of the Associated Press, to the Mimosa night-club, which provided an echo of the Paris which was now threatened by German tanks. Kennedy, he told Lucy:

> [had] a great passion for the young woman in the Mimosa, who stands with great aplomb in the altogether while they project moving pictures and coloured slides on her midriff. Most interesting, but, like a fool, I got engrossed in the film. She seemed a nice girl and spoke in a very friendly way to Kennedy when he bought her French champagne. I went home and read the *Reader's Digest*. What has happened to me? I was bored to tears.[40]

There were frustrations in Athens, but, he told her, "I am bronzed and fit and think tonight I shall buy myself a classy linen suit since linen is supposed to be good and cheap here and all the others are setting themselves up like a team of ice-cream vendors."[41] Moorehead and Alexander Clifford hoped to go to Cairo and there be accredited to the British Army as war correspondents, for, once Italy came into the war, there would be a certainty of action in Africa. Their plan hinged upon a simple act of collusion. Each would cable his foreign editor to say that the other was going to Cairo. As the two newspapers were rivals, it would appear to each that the other's correspondent was going to Egypt for a specific and important purpose and probably news that should not be missed. He would then instruct his own man to follow.

So it came to pass and each was ordered to follow the other. On 29th May – the day after Belgium surrendered and the day that the British Expeditionary Force began its evacuation from the beaches of Dunkirk – Moorehead wrote to Lucy and told her the news.

So, at the end of May, Moorehead and Clifford boarded an Imperial Airways flying-boat and set out. There was the elation of freedom and adventure about that flight away from the heat and smells of Athens and south over the islands of Greece to Crete and then Alexandria, where they would board the train for Cairo. The flying-boat touched down in Suda Bay and when the steward opened the oval door, the blinding Cretan light dazzled them as it sparkled on the clear water. A few men were the only other passengers, so they stripped and dived from the door into its translucent depths, swam for a while among the shoals of little fish that darted among the shafts of sunlight, then heaved themselves aboard, dripping and invigorated.

At Alexandria, they took the train that rattled across the edge of the desert and the bright greenery of the Nile delta and took them into the heat, dust and tumult of Cairo. Moorehead, who had made a study of hotel prices on his first visit, decided that both the Continental-Savoy, where he had stayed before, and Shepheard's, where he liked to dine, were too expensive and they took rooms at the cheaper Carlton. Instead of private bathrooms they now had only shower-cubicles and the nights were noisy not only with the traffic and street-cries, the wail of Arab music and the snapping of dominoes from the cafés below but amplified dialogue, music and gunfire from the soundtracks of films shown in the open-air cinema across the street. Yet, for the moment, it was enough to be in Cairo, the centre of whatever was happening in the Middle East, which enjoyed efficient communications with London.

The two of them visited the British Embassy and the General Headquarters of the Allied armies. There they were told that France seemed to be lost but that the bulk of the British troops had escaped by sea from Dunkirk. Italy was still neutral and so the British, Australian, New Zealand and Indian troops out in the Egyptian desert, the Royal Air Force squadrons on the airfields outside Cairo and the Mediterranean Fleet based on Alexandria remained in a state of alert. Otherwise all was quiet in the Mediterranean and their friends left in Rome and Athens were presumably following the same daily routines as before.

Moorehead and Clifford arranged meetings with officials and officers who could explain the political and military contingencies. The former included the position of Turkey and whether the Turks could be persuaded to join the Allied cause if Italy entered the war. The military position sounded desperate. On the border between Egypt and Libya, the British would be outnumbered by at least four to one and by nearly twenty to one in the Sudan and East Africa. They were also outnumbered in the air and although the

Royal Navy might be able to take the offensive in the Mediterranean, that sea would be so dangerous that it would certainly be closed to commercial shipping.

Already war correspondents were being accredited and both had been nominated to the War Office in London by their foreign editors. So at a newly-formed department in General Headquarters called Public Relations, each was given a licence in hard blue covers as a "war correspondent accompanying a field force", then told to collect their equipment at Kasr-el-Nil barracks and buy their uniforms at the officers' shop. They were issued with steel helmets, gas masks, water bottles and a revolver which, it was stressed, was for use only against an unruly native population, as war correspondents were forbidden by the Geneva Convention to bear arms. They bought khaki drill uniforms, bush jackets and shorts, woollen stockings and suede desert boots that reached the ankle to keep out sand and, as it was believed that sunstroke was caused by exposing the eyes and the back of the neck, a sun helmet. They bought camp beds, sleeping bags, mosquito-nets and canvas buckets for washing. Finally, they were given the insignia of their status, which was equivalent to that of captain, to fit on to their shoulder-straps: small badges of green cloth on which were woven in gold the words "British War Correspondent".

As yet, there was no war and there was time to enjoy themselves. They visited the Sphinx and the Pyramids, the largest of which the long-legged Clifford climbed while his short companion pleaded vertigo. They bought silk in bazaars and watched belly-dancers perform in the night-clubs, where Clifford showed much less interest in the undulating torsoes than did Moorehead, and attended a concert of Beethoven and Wagner, played by a German-Jewish orchestra from Palestine, which Clifford enjoyed more than Moorehead. They joined the Turf Club and began playing billiards, at which Clifford usually won, for half an hour each evening and they joined the Gezira Sporting Club, where they could play tennis, and the outcome was usually the same – swim, eat, drink and talk.

Although they listened to the BBC news from London every evening, Cairo seemed infinitely remote from Europe, as indeed it was. As their memories of it receded, they began swapping those that still remained vivid: the food and decor at the Bar Basque at St.-Jean-de-Luz, the Champs Elysées in the evening, the golf links at Rye and a particular flat in Knightsbridge with furniture and pictures still recalled in sharp focus. As they felt daily more isolated from their pasts, they drew together for support and, as mutual understanding increased, so did the awareness of each other's failings. Moorehead noted that Clifford could be irritable and, forgetting his shyness and courtesy, would suddenly bark at minor officials who frustrated him; he could be mean, too, although he was earning more than Moorehead's fourteen guineas a week and two guineas a day for expenses. Clifford seemed careful not to pay more than his share of any meal and reluctant to buy a round of drinks, pointing out that, as he did not smoke himself, he did not see why he should provide cigarettes for those they jointly entertained.

Even so, the friendship broadened and deepened. Moorehead, keeping his emotional security in his love for Lucy as a private support, realised that Clifford had few ties beyond a brother and sister in England, and no woman to write him loving letters. Moreover, Clifford was deeply pessimistic about the future and seemed to consider the war already lost. To provoke him into further despairing prophecies, Moorehead would say that it would be quite possible for them to cut themselves free from their pasts and start entirely new lives. Even if Europe and the Mediterranean shores fell to Hitler, they could wander east or south like nomads and survive until the world had returned to normal, or they had started new lives elsewhere. When he had reduced Clifford to a new depth of dread, Moorehead would suggest that they go to a party or a night-club and change the subject to one that suited his own mood.

Their lives in Cairo had begun to settle into a pleasant routine of social activity. This was interrupted on 10th June by news that changed everything. Italy had declared war on France and Britain. The political partnership that had been called "the Rome-Berlin Axis" had become a possibly invincible military alliance stretching from the North Sea to the Mediterranean and from North Africa to the Indian Ocean. Cairo would be as much a vortex as London.

Chapter Five

"This was danger, I thought"

On 11th June, 1940, Alan Moorehead and Alexander Clifford, dressed in their khaki drill uniforms, attended the first briefing of correspondents at General Headquarters in the new theatre of war. Already, they were told, Royal Air Force bombers had attacked Italian airfields and the army had been sending out patrols. Afterwards there was a rush to typewriters, and Moorehead was noticed in what was to become a characteristic attitude, sitting at an angle to his portable typewriter, a cigarette dangling from the corner of his mouth and carrying on with a conversation while typing.

Then the copy had to be censored; not by one censor but by four – one for each of the armed services and by the Egyptians – whose offices were so far apart from each other that the journalists joked that they should race in horse-drawn gharries from one to the next and finally to the Cable and Wireless office whence their reports would be transmitted to London.

As war correspondents, they did not want simply to report from General Headquarters, repeating official communiqués and hand-outs from the Public Relations Department and interviewing the official spokesmen. But, even assuming that they would be allowed into the forward operational areas, it was difficult to know where to begin. Would Marshal Graziani advance from the Libyan desert towards Cairo, or the Duke of Aosta attack the Sudan or Kenya from Abyssinia or Eritrea, or both? Could Malta survive and would there be naval battles in the Mediterranean? Most immediately, if France fell, as now seemed inevitable, would the French territories in North Africa and the Levant – Algeria, Morocco, Tunisia and Syria – surrender or fight on?

Four days after Italy declared war, Paris fell. Two days later, Marshal Pétain became prime minister and concluded an armistice with Germany. On the 24th it was announced that the terms of the French armistice with Italy included the neutrality of the French colonies. Moorehead had already reported on the implications of this to British strategy in the Middle East and flew to Jerusalem to see if there was any sign that the powerful French forces in Syria might refuse to obey Pétain: there was not.

Now the British Empire stood alone in the Middle East and Africa as Britain was already standing alone against a Europe dominated by the two dictators. The most crucial scene of action in the Middle East was expected to be the border between Egypt and Libya, where fighting was already reported. The war correspondents knew, but were not allowed to report, that the British commander, General Sir Archibald Wavell, could field only 36,000 men in Egypt against the Italians' 157,000 in Libya. Raids and counter-raids had begun in what became known as the Western Desert and, at the end of June, a small party of correspondents – including Moorehead and Clifford – were accorded the necessary permission, given conducting officers and trucks loaded with camping equipment, rations, water and petrol, and set out for the front.

The road from Cairo to Alexandria and then west to Mersa Matruh, where Force Headquarters had been established, was met-alled and relatively easy going for most of its three hundred miles. After Alexandria, it ran beside a single-line railway track with the sea to the north and the limitless desert stretching away southward into the Sahara. The desert was not as Europeans imagined it, with golden sand-dunes rolling away to the horizon. It was more as Moorehead had known it in Australia, except that it was mostly hard grey earth and yellow rocks and sometimes a crust of hardened sand over soft. He welcomed the hard, cleansing life of the desert once their little expedition had left behind the supply dumps and tented hospitals and had taken to the open. But on this first morning, heading for Mersa Matruh, the *khamseen* blew and he described it as "the most hellish wind on earth . . . it picks up the surface dust as fine as baking powder and blows it thickly into the air across hundreds of square miles of desert". It blew through every chink of staff car and truck, it choked mouth, nose and throat and made the eyes smart. "Just for a moment the billows of brown sand would open, allowing you to see a little farther into the hot solid fog ahead and then it would close in again."

The sand-storm eased as they reached the deserted township of Mersa Matruh and found Force Headquarters: "Dug-outs nosed up to the surface amid sandbags and rocks. A few low tents flapped pathetically in the wind. Camels plodded about moodily through trucks and armoured vehicles that were dispersed over a couple of miles of desert."[1] But the stories they were told in this desolate place were thrilling.

During the three weeks since the outbreak of war with Italy, General O'Connor, who commanded the Western Desert Army, had taken the offensive although outnumbered by almost three to one. He and Wavell had realised that they must use the desert rather than try to overcome it as the Italians had with fortresses, comfortable camps and the barbed-wire fence twenty feet wide along the frontier. The British had faded into the desert, dispersed, then concentrated and attacked and vanished again. They had seized the huge castellated forts of Capuzzo and Maddalena but were not there when the Italians counter-attacked. They had captured nearly a thousand prisoners and spread alarm among their enemies.

Moorehead sent a despatch back to Cairo for the *Daily Express* at the beginning of July after the first week in the desert and a first look towards enemy territory from the heights of Sollum, where cliffs rose from the coast to the vast table-land of the Libyan desert. "That was the position when I first climbed the cliffs at Sollum last week and looked across in the starlight to the enemy lines," he concluded his summary. "From Bardia, an Italian searchlight was playing across the still desert trying to pick up the roving British patrols."

In this strange vacuum, images and contrasts tumbled over each other in his mind. There was something romantic about warfare away from civilisation, cities and civilians. "It is the Lawrence of Arabia kind of warfare – mechanised," he wrote in this despatch. "At times the men fight in an eerie, yellowish light, like the pea-soup fog of a late winter's afternoon in London. Sand fills the ears and nostrils, clogs the back of the throat and bites into the eyes." And he was the first of many reporters to note the similarity between this kind of fighting and war at sea: "Desert warfare is much like naval fighting. Each force I visited was operating as a semi-independent unit, sometimes hundreds of miles from a base. As at sea, communication is by radio . . . In half an hour, I saw a general take his whole force of tanks and disappear over the horizon . . . like an admiral in his flagship."[2]

The correspondents went into the forward area where, after the metalled road ended at Sidi Barrani, the cars plunged across soft sand that billowed around them like smoke, enveloping each in its own little sand-storm. They saw some shells burst and ran for slit-trenches when Italian aircraft cruised overhead. Finally they were told they could visit the captured Fort Capuzzo if it was still in British hands. It was not and they watched from a distance – munching biscuits spread with raspberry jam, which gave Moorehead the odd thought that he was having tea in a London theatre during the interval – while British tanks lurched forward through shell-bursts and clouds of smoke and sand in an unsuccessful attempt to take it again.

He was excited by what little action he saw, but the principal gain of this first visit was to learn the lie of the land. Just inside the Egyptian frontier was the little town of Sollum on the shore beneath the cliffs six hundred feet high beyond which lay the Libyan desert. Westwards into Libya itself ran a modern coastal road and another, winding up the face of the escarpment and known as Halfaya Pass – Hellfire Pass to the soldiers – and beyond this lay the barbed-wire fence, Fort Capuzzo and, along the hundreds of miles of coast, the towns with names that were already beginning to become familiar: Bardia, Tobruk, Derna, Benghazi and finally Tripoli in the far west.

By day there was always a sense of danger from distant artillery, roaming aircraft or even the self-induced disaster of driving over a mine. Except when a *khamseen* blew, a burning sun was usually hanging in the wide blue sky and produced effects which surprised the others more than Moorehead, who had seen mirages in the Australian desert. As he later wrote:

Often, towards mid-day, the horizon quivered in a watery haze and mirages grew up into the air, turreted medieval cities floating on a lake, mysterious forests trailing grey and purple mists and groups of bedouin in their robes advancing upon us upside down. Then, in the evening, when the terrible, blasting, stultifying heat of the sun began to subside at last, we returned to our camp on the coast and ran naked across white sand beaches into the transparent sea. Lying on one's back, feeling the clotted dust washing away from one's ears, eyes and throat, one saw the cliffs turn scarlet in the sunset light and presently we were once again under the protective cover of night.[3]

No lights could be shown, so there was no reading and nothing to do but to go to bed at dusk, lie under the stars and talk. Moorehead and Clifford would set up their camp beds side by side, lie on their backs staring at the brilliant canopy of stars and as the latter recalled:

> From astronomy we went on to poetry with a ludicrous argument about Wordsworth. Boldly we advanced to deep emotional matters which, face to face, we should never have thought of mentioning. We pared things down to such a transcendental refinement of subtlety that we finally argued furiously about the principles of argument.[4]

They became detached from everything around them in the darkness and, as Moorehead put it:

> . . . our two camp beds sailed out into space and time and we were exactly poised and at peace . . . We were free and there seemed at last in this murmured exchange of ideas to be an explanation for the mystery of simply being alive . . . We were, in fact, perched on a kind of mental frontier; our old lives had come to an abrupt stop with the war and with our arrival here in the desert and no one could say what was going to happen to us after the war was over. When at last we went to sleep it was because we had nothing more to say that night.

At dawn, they would wake to find the hollows in the groundsheets they had spread over their blankets filled with dew. Then came "an hour of grace when the sky was filled with a cool, apple-green light, but then the sun lifted its mad, glaring eye over the horizon and the sense of dread returned . . . We were now uncovered to the sight of the enemy and we had so long to wait for the next holiday of the night."[5]

The excursion over, it was time to take the long road back to Cairo and find out what else was happening in the Middle East and in Europe. It was strange to be back in the sleazy theatricality of the city and hear the appalling news from the outside world. The British were now beleaguered in their islands and under attack by German bombers. In France, Marshal Pétain had set up an administration to co-operate with the victors at Vichy and seemed to have been successful in persuading almost all of the French Empire to follow his lead. Early in July, the British had asked the French naval

10 A friend and fellow-campaigner, David Woodward of the *Manchester Guardian*, on his return from a battlefield in Normandy.

11 Christopher Buckley at a correspondents' briefing in Normandy, 1944.

12 Before the Rhine crossing in March, 1945, General Dempsey, commander of the British 2nd Army (left) is interviewed by British and American correspondents, including Moorehead and Clifford (centre).

13 Jenny Nicholson – in WAAF uniform – joins The Trio in Brussels soon after its liberation in September, 1944.

14 At their wedding reception in the Savoy Hotel, London, Alexander and Jenny Clifford pose, she holding the SS officer's dagger with which they cut the cake.

15 "The prince of war correspondents": Alan Moorehead about to set out in
   his jeep during the campaign in north-west Europe.

16 Literary triumph: Alan Moorehead being presented with the Duff Cooper Memorial Prize for *Gallipoli* by Sir Winston Churchill in 1956 at the Savoy Hotel.

17 Social success: Alan Moorehead with Sidney (now Lord) Bernstein at his home in Sussex with the actor Charles Laughton in 1959.

commanders in Algeria to join them in fighting the Germans or sail their ships to neutral ports and, when this ultimatum was rejected, shelled those ships into wreckage. The French warships at Alexandria had been immobilised and interned and, on 9th July, Moorehead reported with good reason, "Syria has suddenly become an ominous question-mark . . ."6

His own expectations were suddenly transformed by news that Lucy was at last coming out to join him. With air battles swirling over London and south-east England nobody was interested in the latest fashions and she had taken to reporting women's part in war work after giving her resignation to Christiansen and while awaiting a passage to Africa. In mid-July, he heard that she would be travelling by sea to South Africa and expected to land at Durban after calling at Capetown. So he was delighted when the foreign editor asked him to go to Khartoum and cover any Italian moves against the Sudan, British Somaliland and Kenya from their bases in Abyssinia. At least he would be moving south and towards Lucy's destination. It might be relatively easy to fly from Khartoum to meet her at Durban, or, failing that, at Nairobi.

So, while Clifford remained in Cairo, Moorehead and several other correspondents began the five-day journey up the Nile, first by train then by ancient stern-wheel steamer. They passed the hot days drinking beer from an ice-box, sweating and trying to sleep, while Moorehead was reading Winston Churchill's account of his campaigning there at the turn of the century, *The River War*. When they eventually arrived and moved into the dignified halls of the Grand Hotel, that long-past campaign seemed more real than the present war and Moorehead wrote in a long despatch from Khartoum, "I followed the route Winston Churchill took with another British Army over 40 years ago . . . and now this morning I can see across the White Nile the mud roofs of Omdurman where Churchill, as a young cavalry lieutenant, swept through the Dervish line in the famous charge of the 21st Lancers." And, in this report on the current strategic position in East Africa, he echoed a phrase that recalled many a colonial administrator's report and book of memoirs, "There is a restlessness among the native tribes . . ."7

British forces in the Sudan and British Somaliland were weak but, he was told, a squadron of Blenheim bombers was being detached from the Desert Air Force in Egypt to attack Italian warships in the Red Sea and their positions at Kassala, the Sudanese town near the border of Eritrea, which they had already occupied. Elsewhere in the

Middle East, correspondents' requests to fly on air operations had been refused so Moorehead and two others were surprised, excited and apprehensive when they heard that they could do so now.

From Khartoum, they were flown for five hours to an airfield in the desert north of Kassala and told that they would fly next morning on a bombing raid. "I went to bed that night with a little constriction in my throat, a faster, uncomfortable beating inside my chest. This was danger, I thought, asked for and accepted and one might be dead tomorrow."[8] When they were woken in their tents at half-past five next morning and taken in trucks to collect their flying suits and parachutes, there was plenty to occupy the mind. They were briefed by the wing commander who explained that they were to bomb a compound built to house railway workers where it was thought that Italian troops were now billeted. Moorehead squeezed into the observer's seat in one of three aircraft and they took off into the bumpy air for the flight of an hour and a half to the target.

It was a routine operation. The Blenheims made two runs over the target and dropped their bombs on the buildings their crews glimpsed below. Moorehead found himself "suddenly lifted with a wave of heady excitement, more sensuous than release from pain, faster than the sating of appetite, much fuller than intoxication"[9] as the bomber dived, climbed and turned and the brown hills reeled about them. When they returned to their airfields, he climbed out on to the wing and caught his foot on a splinter torn from the side by anti-aircraft fire. In the long and vivid report he cabled to London, he began, "I have just returned from a three and a half hour bombing raid over Italian East Africa . . ." and he went on to describe it, concentrating on the crew "with set, intent faces. Clearly they had forgotten everything else in the world except this whirling little arena of battle." There was nothing the *Daily Express* liked to promote more than the adventures of its own correspondents and his despatch led the principal foreign news page beneath the headlines, "DAILY EXPRESS MAN GOES OUT TO BOMB ITALIAN FORTRESS. WAVES OF RAF PLANES SWOOP."[10]

But, back at Khartoum on 10th August, he found the wider scene transformed. From Libya, Marshal Graziani had advanced into Egypt with a hundred thousand men – two-thirds of his total strength – brushing aside O'Connor's little force. The Italians were sweeping through British Somaliland and threatening Kenya, Aden and the Sudan, for the British could muster only some 19,000 troops in East Africa to face the enemy's 370,000. At once he knew that his

plan to take leave and fly to meet Lucy at Durban was impossible.
She would have to look after herself until she could make her own
way to Cairo by air or sea or both. He knew she had left England
but not when she would arrive in South Africa, if, indeed, she did,
because sinkings by U-boat in the Atlantic had increased sharply. So
he wrote a letter to be forwarded by the Thomas Cook travel agency
in Durban.

I have just come back from an RAF camp in the desert to find
everything in an uproar: threats from Libya, war in Somaliland
and Sutton wanting to know what I propose to do about it. He
has set his face firmly against my going to Nairobi and I don't
blame him . . . so, at the moment, I am under orders to fly to
Aden and am just waiting in Khartoum to see if I can be flown
there. If not, they will certainly order me back to Cairo. Oh God,
the indecision of all this . . .

I quite see that I can't run out on the war just as it's starting
in a big way but I have just got to get to you or go crazy . . .
Darling, are you all right? . . .

Do not be angry about this bloody mess. My dear, I do need
you terribly. I have kept myself for you all through these long
months because I am in love with you beyond all caring about
anything else. This job has gone well and everything I have done
is for you. I have been so frightened for you sometimes; not
frightened for myself any more, even once or twice when it has
been a bit tricky . . . I don't outwardly feel pathetic about this;
rather tough, except when I talk to you and can say everything
and admit that I worry.[11]

When he learned that it would be impossible to reach Aden and, from
there, British Somaliland, he cabled Sutton and asked if he could fly
down to Durban to meet his wife. The request was dismissed and he
was ordered back to Cairo as quickly as possible. He wrote to her
again, explaining this and reassuring her that he could reach her by
air from Cairo in four days and that all would be well in the end. But
he did not even know where her ship was, except that it was thought
to be about a week behind schedule so he poured his frustration into
another letter:

All this dumb waiting and wanting is not much good to you at
this moment, but it means that I am not one person any more

– or you either – and neither of us is ever alone if you are in love as I am now. My dear, you can take me into your arms now. I have you thousands of times. I remember you and know everything about you more clearly than anyone I see here. There is nothing that anyone says to me which I understand as clearly as the littlest things you said in London months ago . . .

The memories had calmed his anguish and he told her that it would be best if she waited in Durban, tried to enjoy herself there and, if she thought it best to stay there for the baby to be born, choose a doctor and a hospital and he would make his way there somehow. After covering fifteen pages, he ended:

It has made me feel a little better writing; it's as though we had been very close to one another this last hour . . . I have had no news of you now for three weeks. It's been a long time. But I know you are all right. I would not live now if you were not. How easily we go from hell to heaven. How much more it will be than anything that has gone before when we meet.[12]

He had been offered a lift to Cairo in a bomber by an American pilot in the RAF that same day and next morning left at dawn and flew up the Nile all day, arriving back at the Carlton Hotel in the evening to a welcome from the other journalists he had not seen for a month. Clifford, it turned out, had been having even more exciting times than himself. He had flown on a long-range reconnaissance flight in an RAF Sunderland flying-boat, which had been attacked by Italian fighters near Sicily. When a gunner had been hit, Clifford had taken his place and was thought to have shot down one of their attackers before the Sunderland managed to land at Malta, riddled with shot-holes and sinking.* This exploit would have to be kept quiet or Clifford could be executed if captured for having broken the non-combatant rules of the Geneva Convention that applied to war correspondents.

"We talked half the night," Moorehead wrote to Lucy on his own return. "Alex Clifford has to go off with the Navy today and

---

* As the fighters attacked, Clifford had just begun writing a letter to his mother: "Dear Mama, I am writing this high above the Mediterranean, where I am out on patrol with the RAF." When the battle was over, he continued: "I had just got as far as that when alarming things began to happen . . . I cannot tell you more about them now but will reserve the full story until we meet."[13]

I shall miss him very much as he is my best friend here and knows just what a spot I am in."[14] Then, just as Moorehead hoped that, as all seemed quiet on the desert front, he could fly down to Durban, he, too, was also ordered to report the naval war. Probably the *Daily Express* had heard from the Admiralty that the *Daily Mail* was sending Clifford to sea, but, this time, it did not suit Moorehead to follow him. Just as he was about to leave for Alexandria, a cable arrived from Lucy saying that she had arrived in Durban. He had to cable that he could not get to her and, when he arrived at Alexandria, another telegram from her followed him from Cairo, saying that she was planning to travel by sea to Mombasa on her way to Egypt. He wrote back desperately trying to dissuade her and urged her to wait until she could get a seat in the flying-boat which would make the same journey in four days. Meanwhile, he told her, "I am going away for a little bit."[15]

At the beginning of September, he joined his ship, the battle-ship *Warspite*, flagship of the Mediterranean Fleet, flying the flag of Admiral Cunningham with whom he had lunched at Malta at the beginning of the year. As soon as he had unpacked in his cabin, the Commander-in-Chief summoned him to his sea-cabin high in the bridge structure and greeted him warmly. "Action and responsibility had made small but very definite changes in him," Moorehead recorded. "He was obviously enjoying life. He had colour in the flat cheeks criss-crossed with tiny red veins. His cornflower-blue eyes were brisk and alight."[16] Cunningham said that there was to be an important sweep across the eastern basin of the Mediterranean but divulged no more. He suggested that Moorehead's action station should be somewhere commanding a good view and advised the searchlight platform just abaft the admiral's bridge.

At sunrise next day, the ships sailed beneath a flaring pink sky. The *Warspite* led another battleship, the *Malaya*, the old aircraft carrier *Eagle*, a cruiser squadron and flotillas of destroyers out of the harbour, steaming north-west. On the third day reports arrived of an Italian fleet of approximately similar strength approaching at fifteen knots. A night action seemed certain and Cunningham had trained the Mediterranean Fleet for that. But the Italians sheered away and no action was seen until the brown cliffs of Malta were sighted. Then the main purpose of the cruise became clear: the admiral was meeting reinforcements which had forced their way through the narrows south of Sicily, the first British convoy to reach the island since Italy had declared war. They were the huge new aircraft carrier *Illustrious*, the modernised battleship *Valiant*, two anti-aircraft cruisers, destroyers and supply ships. With such a combined force Cunningham could confidently accept battle with any fleet the Italians could put to sea.

Action began on the return passage when Cunningham planned an attack on the Dodecanese Islands, the bombardment of shore targets and the bombing of airfields on Rhodes by carrier-borne aircraft. All the way there and all the way back to Alexandria, the Italians attacked with bombers, submarines and torpedo-boats and the raid itself was described at length by Moorehead, who sat with his portable typewriter on the searchlight platform until the blast and vibration of the guns drove him to shelter. He told readers of the *Daily Express* in a long despatch which covered much of the front page:

> An hour before sunrise, the fleet was in position, lapped by a long, easy swell. One after another, over 50 miles of ocean, silhouettes of the battleships and cruisers, destroyers and aircraft carriers detached themselves from the sea mist. By a sickly yellow dawn light I could just see our bombers sweeping off the deck of the nearest aircraft carrier, each one heavily-loaded with ochre-coloured bombs.[17]

It was not just the visual excitement of colour and atmosphere that he injected into his report but a touch of tragedy, which was not easy when censors excised most of the horrors of war. Most of the Dodecanese action was out of his sight but the bombing by the Italians was all too vivid and, although no ship was hit, raised towering columns of sea-water alongside. Then, as the last attack died away, another Italian bomber was hit and it plunged in flames, three parachutes appeared and Moorehead wrote, "Thousands of British sailors watched fascinated as these white dots hovered delicately for a few minutes, then gently lowered their burdens into the sea to drown. No ship would stop for them in that submarine-ridden sea."[18]

Cunningham had demonstrated that, for a while at least, heavy ships and aircraft carriers could operate in a landlocked sea within range of airfields ashore. Moorehead himself had seen action with the army, the RAF and now the navy and could consider himself an experienced war correspondent by the standards of that time. He returned to Cairo and resumed his companionship with Alexander Clifford, playing billiards at the Turf Club for half an hour each evening after filing reports of the day's news and listening to the news broadcast by the BBC and discussing it at length. Their friendship had become so close that both were aware that it would be disrupted by the arrival of Lucy, however welcome to Moorehead that would be. Getting a seat on the flying-boat to Cairo had proved difficult for a woman without military priority and it was not until October that a telegram arrived announcing her arrival in four days' time. Clifford, realising that, as she would be staying with her husband at the Carlton Hotel, his own presence might seem intrusive, arranged a brief assignment out of the city. Moorehead had told him that he was sure he would like Lucy but privately suspected that his new and rewarding friendship could not survive the arrival of his wife.

For months he had been dreaming of their reunion, remembering their happy times together in Paris, Rome and London. But both had changed. Moorehead had assumed the heaviest responsibilities a correspondent could expect and been exposed to danger and this was reflected in his looks: thin, sun-burned, his mobile face tightened by experience. As he waited by the choppy brown water of the Nile, blown by a desert wind that threatened a *khamseen*, he imagined that Lucy, although seven months pregnant, would essentially be the same lively, poised young woman he remembered. Then the flying-boat came swooping from the overcast sky at the end of its long flight through the rain-clouds and electric storms and turbulence of a violently wet season in Egypt and a launch brought the passengers ashore. Then he saw her "wearing a shapeless blue and white maternity dress. I had last seen her as a slim, active woman in London and now this blue and white bundle . . ."[19]

Lucy had had an exhausting journey, but the happy meeting with her husband was only a short respite. It was suffocatingly hot and humid and he took her back to his room at the Carlton Hotel, which was hotter still. Clifford had reminded him to buy her flowers but the room buzzed with flies and through the window came the noise of street cries, the cafés below and the open-air cinema. So he took her to dinner in the open courtyard of a restaurant and they exchanged news; he telling her about his friend Clifford, whom she would meet soon. In fact, they met next day and exchanged polite greetings but neither seemed to take an instant liking to the other and Moorehead suspected that his friendship would now wither. A few days later, he had to leave Cairo for a short assignment in the Western Desert to report on the Italian failure to advance eastward beyond Sidi Barrani although there was little serious opposition. On his return to Cairo, he would have to concentrate on making Lucy content and confident and Clifford could not, quite obviously, have any part in that. For a start, Lucy and he would have to leave the discomforts of the hotel for a flat when they could find one in a city which was rapidly filling with an expanding headquarters and base staff.

He returned to be met by Lucy and Clifford and an extraordinary surprise. As he wrote afterwards:

> Both of them seemed brisker and more relaxed than they had been before. I bathed, we went to a restaurant together and they began to tell me the news of Cairo. They had some private joke about the Levantine porter at the hotel, they had been shopping together in the bazaar and had gone to a party the night before. Lucy now said decisively that we could not continue to live in the hotel; we would have to find a flat which would be cooler and more comfortable . . . I was astonished to hear her say that she and Alex had already been looking for flats together and had, in fact, found a possible place on the bottom floor of an apartment block on Gezira Island. It seemed to be accepted that one of the bedrooms should be reserved for Alex.[20]

What had happened during those few days in Cairo was that just as Moorehead had been attracted to Clifford as an opposite in almost every way, so Lucy had been attracted by similarities. Both she and he were serious-minded and pessimistic; their instincts were intellectual and their tastes English; both were gentle, tall and good-looking and anybody seeing them together would describe them as a well-matched pair. Just as Moorehead needed Clifford to balance his own ebullience and ambition, so Lucy found his calming presence complementary to the volatile husband she loved. It was a strange, three-cornered relationship and, when they all moved into the flat a few days later, eyebrows were raised at what might appear as a *ménage à trois*.

The three seemed happy in each other's company and, once installed in the flat, seldom went to restaurants or dinner parties. Lucy and Clifford organised the domestic arrangements, buying the furniture, engaging the cook and the house-servant and paying the tradesmen's bills. A few were admitted to their circle, amongst them Edward Ward, the charming, urbane BBC correspondent who was pioneering war-reporting by radio, and David Woodward, the large, gentle and amusing correspondent of the *News Chronicle*, who had been in Berlin and just managed to escape from the Netherlands.

Social activity was further limited by Lucy's advanced pregnancy but happily the demands of news-reporting did not take Moorehead or Clifford away, although Italy finally invaded Greece; so much of the Balkans and Middle East were on the brink, that, while the invasion of Egypt remained an imminent threat, all was to be reported from Cairo. From the news-agencies and the daily briefings and interviews they assembled their reports and Moorehead had perfected the technique of dressing them with an eye-catching opening paragraph. When Anthony Eden, now War Minister, who was touring the Middle East, returned from a visit to the troops in the desert, he began the report: "Looking a little dusty and travel-worn and still wearing his brown slouch hat, brown suit and red tie, Mr Eden is back from the desert . . ."[21] Through such small, personal details, he felt, his readers could relate to events otherwise beyond their imaginings.

Then, on 2nd December a baby boy was born to Lucy. They named him John – although his father had originally favoured Gerald – and Alexander Clifford was appointed godfather. The four of them lived together in the flat on Gezira Island and it was noticed that it was usually the godfather, rather than the father, who pushed the pram. Some would gossip that Lucy was in love with Clifford; others that she would have married him were she free to do so; while those closest to them saw the trio as bound together by an exceptionally devoted friendship that could be described as love and which left the unity of husband and wife not only unimpaired but strengthened. In fact, Clifford lacked his friend's strong libido and, while enjoying friendship with women, had had no recent attachment and, at the time, seemed somewhat uncertain as to whether that was his inclination.

The domestic peace was not to last. On 9th December, General Wavell summoned all the correspondents to his General Headquarters in a block of flats in a European suburb. In his own office, "leaning cross-legged against his desk with his hands in his pockets", as Moorehead noted, he said quietly, "Gentlemen, I have asked you to come here this morning to let you know that we have attacked in the Western Desert . . ."

As unassuming as usual, the Commander-in-Chief described an "important raid" rather than an offensive, but the first of the Italian camps had been captured and the British advance was continuing. "I wanted to tell you this so that you can make your own arrangements,"[22] he said and within the hour the correspondents were loading their trucks for the two-day journey to the battle. On arrival at Mersa

Matruh, they were told what was happening. It had been discovered that a new range of huge fortified camps constructed by the Italians inside Egypt had been sited too far apart to support each other with artillery fire. So, on the night of 7th December, O'Connor had sent his armour, followed by infantry, between them and attacked from the rear. The Italians were routed, thousands were captured and the survivors had fled west to seek refuge in Bardia.

At first, Moorehead saw only the aftermath of the extraordinary victory. His first despatch was spread across the front page of the *Daily Express* under the headline, "OVER 34,000 PRISONERS" and, as he moved forward to join the fighting troops, he reported the scenes of victory and defeat, using touches of colour to bring them to life for his readers at their breakfast tables. He wrote:

I saw an entire captured Italian division on the march back to Sidi Barrani. A great column of dust, turned pink by the sunset light behind them, rose from their feet as they plodded four abreast in the sand on either side of the metalled road. They came on, first in hundreds, then in thousands, until the stupendous crocodile of marching figures stretched to the horizon.[23]

He described the loot in the enemy camps:

Uniforms heavy with gold lace and decked with the medals and colours of the parade ground hung upon hangers in company with polished jack boots richly spurred and pale blue sashes and belts finished with great tassels and feathered and embroidered hats and caps . . . Dressing-tables in the officers' tents were strewn with scents and silver-mounted brushes and small arms made delicately in the northern arsenals of Italy.[24]

A few days later he was himself camping before the fortress of Bardia, where 45,000 Italians were besieged and his millions of readers in Britain read next morning, "For three days and nights now the guns around Bardia have been in my ears. Lying on open ground in this bitter wind I wake at night to see flashes against the brilliant moon and wake again at dawn to feel the desert floor trembling with the impact of high explosives . . ."[25]

The British victory far exceeded any hope, let alone expectation. Half the Italian army in Libya had been destroyed and their invasion of Egypt turned into headlong retreat, and all for the loss of less than a hundred British soldiers killed and less than one thousand wounded. There would now be a short lull while O'Connor regrouped and prepared to assault Bardia. Meanwhile the British troops and the war correspondents were exhausted. Alexander Clifford had contracted sand-fly fever and jaundice – one day they left him huddled in blankets in dunes by the sea to spare him an exhausting, jolting expedition across the desert and had difficulty finding him again after dark – and he was in no condition to continue. So they decided that there was time for a short rest and that they could briefly return to Cairo for Christmas.

It was the happiest time that Moorehead had known. He was together with Lucy and their infant son, and his best friend was to hand for discussions of the war, politics and the future. On Christmas Day, they sang carols at the Anglican cathedral and afterwards talked in the sun outside in a crowd that included the quiet, thick-set figure of Wavell, the Commander-in-Chief, whose one good eye – the other had been blinded in the First World War – "gleamed brightly from a face that was usually as expressionless as a statue",[26] as Moorehead described him that day.

There was news from home. A sheaf of congratulatory cables awaited him from the *Daily Express*, praising his "brilliant despatches" on its front page, echoing the sentiments expressed to Christiansen by Lord Beaverbrook. There was news of old friends in England. Both Geoffrey Cox and George Millar had joined the army as private soldiers on the same day on the principle that they should fight in the war that they considered a moral crusade. Both Moorehead and Clifford felt that they could have achieved more – both for the war effort and, incidentally, for themselves – by working as war correspondents. Both were now past the age of thirty, after which war-reporting was an allowed option for fit men, and both expected to face risks as often as those under arms.

For Moorehead himself the war was the ultimate challenge as a reporter and one of startling changes, contrast and excitement. He was aware that, so far, he had been spared the worst horrors and fear, but that those would have to be faced in due course.

Chapter Six

"We smelt powder too"

The beginning of 1941 and of the second phase of Wavell's offensive in the Western Desert was marked by the summoning of the Australians. They were called from their camps in Egypt, where they had been training since Moorehead had watched them disembark a year before and where they had become restless for war. They came to the battle like the Imperial Guard of the British Empire and nothing, least of all the humiliated Italian army, could stop them.

They moved up through the Indian Division and the New Zealanders, who had already seen action, for the attacks on the defences of Bardia and then Tobruk. Moorehead watched them with curiosity and wrote, "These men from the dockside of Sydney and the sheep-stations of the Riverina presented such a picture of downright toughness with their gaunt dirty faces, huge boots, revolvers stuffed in their pockets, gripping their rifles with huge shapeless hands, shouting and grinning – always grinning – that the mere sight of them must have disheartened the enemy troops. For some days the Rome radio had been broadcasting that the "Australian barbarians" had been turned loose by the British in the desert."[1]

On 3rd January, the attack on Bardia began and the garrison of 45,000 men, armed with 462 guns and 129 tanks, surrendered. Now it was the turn of Tobruk, which fell on the 21st with the capture of 30,000 prisoners, 236 guns and 87 tanks. The Australians, supported by the dwindling number of tanks still serviceable with the 7th Armoured Division, headed for the next objective, Derna, a hundred miles to the west. Here the country had changed from desert to fertile country which had been colonised by the Italians and where mud replaced dust and sand. The welcome was as unexpected as the scenery and Moorehead reported to his newspaper:

All day I have been driving through territory conquered by General Wavell's army. A great region of rolling uplands that looks like the Yorkshire moors and is a third of the size of England, has just received the Imperial Army with white flags and gifts of food and wine . . . By the time I arrived in Giovanni Berta, the Australians had received its submission from a priest standing on the town hall steps and had swept on . . .[2]

After Derna, there would be no major fortified positions before reaching Benghazi, the capital of the province of Cyrenaica. Moorehead was trying to keep up with the vanguard, sending reports of each surrendered city and garrison back by despatch rider in the hope that they would reach Cairo and London. He and Clifford had abandoned the transport arrangements provided by Public Relations, which involved several correspondents travelling with a conducting officer and a driver in a fifteen-hundredweight truck, and sometimes having to take their turn with the other correspondents, for they could not all be allowed to roam the same stretch of battlefields at the same time. Instead they would follow other trails. Sometimes they would attach themselves to Squadron-Leader George Houghton, who commanded the RAF Public Relations unit in the desert, and would use his transport, ostensibly to report on the siting of forward airstrips for fighters.

On other occasions, they would follow a dashing young captain, Geoffrey Keating, who commanded the small Army Film and Photographic Unit and had offered them space in his little eight-hundredweight Ford utility truck, built like an estate car. With a driver at the wheel, the three of them were able to move more freely in keeping up with the advance and be less conspicuous to the Italian artillerymen, who were shooting with skill.

Captain Keating had caught Moorehead's attention as he had attracted everybody else's. A handsome young man of twenty-five with lively blue eyes, he was Irish, the son of a Member of Parliament, and put the characteristics of his nationality and his father's calling to good use. He had worked in London as a photographer for the *Daily Sketch* before the war when he had joined a Territorial Army

95

regiment, the Queen's Westminsters, from which he had been able
to transfer to the King's Royal Rifle Corps – the fashionable 60th
Rifles – and become an officer-photographer. He had been in France
with the British Expeditionary Force and had now made his mark as
a photographer in the desert and as a social aspirant in Cairo. There
he had charmed and cultivated not only leading military figures but
also wealthy Egyptian families, particularly the Coptic Christians who
felt an affinity with the British. He had sometimes initiated friendships
with the latter and subsequently often won large sums from them
playing bridge at the Gezira Club. He was known to seat himself
near one such party, ostentatiously reading an Egyptian newspaper,
of which he could not understand a word. When one of the Egyptians
remarked how pleasant and surprising it was to see a British officer
reading Arabic, he would reply that he was by no means a linguist
and then strike up a conversation. Keating, it was said, could arrange
anything from an introduction to the prettiest or richest girl in Cairo
to an extra supply of petrol in the desert. Moorehead, recognising in
him another outsider in the British environment, took to him and,
just as he was learning something of the disciplines of the intellect
from Clifford, he picked up some of the tricks of the opportunist from
Keating, who was good at his job. Once at the Italian fort of Rudero,
they had watched Australian infantry charge through the barbed-wire
defences with bayonets fixed. There seemed to be no opposition and
Keating was so struck with the drama of the scene that he shouted to
them to come back and repeat their charge for his camera. Twice he
persuaded them to re-enact their assault and when he finally allowed
them to take possession of the fort they found that it was crowded with
Italian soldiers, albeit ready to surrender. Thereupon both Moorehead
and Clifford were able to make themselves useful to the Australians
with their knowledge of Italian in the interrogation of prisoners.

Rudero was some distance inland. Throughout most of the
campaign there would be two lines of advance: one along the
coast; the other to the south, which could offer short cuts and
opportunities to deliver outflanking attacks, so while on this latter
route with the Australians, they heard the BBC announce that
Derna had fallen. Heading back to the coast they discovered that
this was not only true but that the other correspondents, who
had remained with the organised parties, had been there some
hours and already written and despatched their reports. Both the
Express and *Mail* had missed the most important news since the
fall of Tobruk.

In Derna, the disappointed pair joined Squadron-Leader Hough-ton's party and he installed them – together with Patrick Crosse of Reuter and Richard Capel of the *Daily Telegraph* – in Marshal Graziani's villa by the sea. It had the ultimate luxury of a bathroom where they could wash away the caked dust and bathe the desert sores on their legs, and a cellar stocked with good wine. They enter-tained lavishly and the British United Press correspondent, Richard McMillan, who was billeted in a lesser villa nearby, was invited to demonstrate his skill in cooking and use the captured wine in one of his specialities, *coq au vin* (another being *spaghetti McMillanese*). It was noticed by the other correspondents that although Moorehead and Clifford were direct rivals they were inseparable and were so highly regarded by those in authority that they seemed to be accorded special favours, such as being given the best house in Derna.

The next major objective would be Benghazi, the capital of the province of Cyrenaica, and the Italians were falling back upon it and abandoning the coastline that ran west from Derna and then south for three hundred and fifty miles. Moorehead and Clifford were eager to push on and redeem their failure at Derna by being first into Benghazi. So again they set out with Keating and his driver in the little truck to catch up with the vanguard of the Australians, who were chasing westward along the road that ran towards Barce and Benghazi through the hills between the massif of the Jebel Akhdar and the sea. Somewhere near Barce they caught up with the forward platoon just before dusk and were told that in advance of them was a fighting patrol of armoured cars. So, leaving the infantry behind, they headed along the road past groups of Italians who had thrown away their weapons and were trying to surrender. Half a mile ahead they sighted the three sand-coloured armoured cars halted on the road and the Hussar major in command studying a map with an Australian officer. To Moorehead's surprise the latter turned out to be a friend from both Scotch College and Melbourne University, Allan Fleming, once editor of *Farrago*, now a lieutenant and the intelligence officer with the battalion leading the advance. There was no time to exchange news and the major explained that he must push on to prevent Italian engineers from mining or blowing up the road ahead and he invited Keating and the correspondents to join them, driving their truck between the first and second armoured cars.

Under other circumstances, Fleming would have been pleased to see Moorehead but now he was annoyed, seeing him and the others as unnecessary intruders, whose journalistic enterprise would delay the advance. As he put it later, "I could read in Alan's eyes the opening of his despatch, 'I was first into Benghazi . . .' "[3] Then Fleming returned to his battalion and the three armoured cars with the correspondents' truck moved forward along the road. The road curved away to the west between scrub-grown banks and as the column turned the corner they saw ahead in the fading light figures of Italian sappers laying mines. At the sight of the armoured cars, they scrambled into the bushes, while the British column halted and the crews clambered out to dig up mines already planted in the road. Just then the Italians reappeared farther along the road, gazing back at the British but not surrendering. The Hussar major called to his gunner, "Give 'em a burst!" At that instant they were ambushed.

"Tracer bullets came down the road towards us in continuous streams of bright yellow light," wrote Moorehead later. He had dived for the ditch just as enemy heavy machine-guns and anti-tank guns hit the armoured cars and their truck and set them ablaze. In the light of the flames he saw a British soldier dragging a wounded man to cover and Keating running along the road to find a first-aid dressing. Then the soldier was felled and as Keating, dressing in hand, threw himself beside Moorehead he was hit twice. Their driver was lying there, too, his arm torn open by an explosive bullet and Moorehead ripped the dressing off the desert sores on his own knee to bind it. Clifford, lying prone, was cut in the buttock by a bullet and another tore the sleeve of Moorehead's greatcoat. He lay there, pressing himself to the ground, thinking, as he wrote later:

This is too cruel, they cannot realise what they are doing to us . . . There could be no hatred or anger in the world which would want to hurt us so much . . . I did not pray or think of my past life or my family; I simply wanted to get away . . . With all my senses I longed for the darkness so that I could crawl away and hide.[4]

Still the shot hammered around them but they began to crawl away from the road, dragging the wounded. They came to a deeper ditch and took cover there, Moorehead breaking a phial of iodine into the wound in the driver's arm. All the armoured cars and their own truck had been wrecked, several of their crews killed or wounded and the Italian infantry might now come after them, so they scrambled into the scrub away from the flames and gunfire, Moorehead supporting Keating and Clifford the driver. Eventually they heard English words shouted in the darkness ahead and called out. Australian soldiers appeared and soon the wounded were being lifted on to a tracked Bren-gun carrier; Moorehead and Clifford were helped to a medical post and there lay on unoccupied stretchers and slept.

Next day they heard that the Australians had captured the ambush position but when they themselves returned to the scene of the action, they found all their equipment, clothing and rations that had been in the truck smashed or burnt. Afterwards, Moorehead wrote:

> I do not think that I ever recovered from this incident. Often afterwards we were obliged to put ourselves briefly in the way of danger but I never again did it with any confidence or even with any feeling of dedication. Whenever I went into danger I did it as a duty, or because I thought that others were watching me.[5]

Both he and Clifford were mentioned in despatches for their rescue of the wounded driver and this was reported in a London newspaper under the headline, "VERY GALLANT CORRESPONDENTS". He felt purged of any need to prove himself in battle.

But there was another view of the incident. After the ambush, Lieutenant Fleming had watched the Australian infantry attack the Italian position. One soldier was killed and a number injured. Probably the ambush would have been as successful as it was whether or not the correspondents had been with the armoured cars, but Fleming could not help thinking, "For Alan to get himself into this 'I was first' situation, one of our men was killed. I had a rather sour outlook on him after that."[6]

Repeatedly, such unreasoned but understandable judgements were passed on war correspondents by fighting soldiers. The correspondents would appear at a moment of tension and danger to watch and ask questions. They were unarmed and might have arrived from comfortable billets for a brief experience of what was continuous for soldiers, who had no occasion to consider that the risks taken by correspondents might be less intense but that many of them would go on taking them year after year.

On 7th February, Benghazi fell. Moorehead entered the city with the vanguard. There was no opposition as the column of armoured cars and trucks laden with tired, muddy soldiers arrived that cold, wet, windy morning. It was odd to be in a city with hotels, shops, restaurants, banks and cafés again. The Albergo d'Italia, where Moorehead had stayed overnight on his return from his brief visit to

Egypt a year before, had been used as Graziani's headquarters and now the correspondents stayed in comfort at the hotel, enjoying hot meals and beds with clean sheets. Exhaustion and reaction to the ambush overwhelmed them but, just as they were relaxing in the unexpected comforts, news arrived of a great battle. While they had been entering Benghazi in triumph, the Italian army that was retreating into the westerly province of Tripolitania had been intercepted and destroyed by General O'Connor twenty miles to the south. At once the correspondents boarded their trucks and set out for the battlefield.

When they arrived it was over. The coastal road was strewn with burnt-out tanks and trucks and the final wreckage of the Italian army that was to have captured Cairo. As it retreated westward, falling back upon Tripoli, 750 miles away, O'Connor's flying column of tanks had cut across the open, roadless desert and caught up with them on the road at Beda Fomm and their destruction had been almost total. Three thousand British troops had taken 20,000 prisoners, 216 guns and 120 tanks. It was the crowning victory of the brilliant campaign that had routed the Italian invaders of Egypt. But while it was being fought all of the war correspondents had been enjoying hot baths, soft beds and rich food in Benghazi, except one.

On the battlefield of Beda Fomm, Moorehead met another old friend from Australia. Chester Wilmot had arrived in the desert as a low-paid correspondent of the Australian Broadcasting Commission. Unable to afford to live with the others in Cairo and preferring to roam alone in the desert, he had been the only correspondent with O'Connor's column when it had trapped the Italians. So there he was, this big Australian with the small, shrewd eyes and the calm, collected manner of an experienced staff officer, who was able to write the news that they had all missed. But to Moorehead's amazement, Wilmot unfolded his map and told them exactly what had happened and what he had seen. Like the others, Moorehead took down Wilmot's words verbatim and wrote his own despatch. "What struck me about Chester," he said afterwards, "was his complete freshness, when we were all feeling pretty tired, his generosity and his very clear brain."[7]

At first it seemed that there was no reason why the British should not push on to Tripoli and complete the conquest of Libya. But Wavell's forces were at the end of their tether, not from fighting but from the wear and tear of the terrain and climate and the length of their communications with their depots in Egypt. Also, there was the prospect that they would be needed elsewhere. The Greeks had held the Italian invasion of their country in the mountains but there were persistent reports that the Germans were to support their ally. In Syria, General Weygand, who had tried to rally the broken armies in France the year before, had assembled powerful forces but these still seemed determined to support the regime in Vichy rather than join the Allies. In East Africa, the British, outnumbered six to one, were struggling with the Duke of Aosta's armies in Abyssinia and Eritrea.

So, as the remnants of Graziani's army straggled back towards Tripoli, and Cyrenaica was given a British general as Governor, the campaign in the Western Desert was declared at an end. Moorehead was given a seat in an aircraft flying seven captured Italian generals to captivity in Egypt. He arrived, tired but exhilarated, to be greeted by his wife and child and also by a cable from the *Daily Express* instructing him to cover the expected fall of Addis Ababa. Now that the desert front was quiet, the news would be the success of the British in ousting the Italians from the heights of Keren in Eritrea to open the way to the capital, Asmara, and the port, Massawa, and a small British army had driven from Kenya through Italian Somaliland into Abyssinia and was now threatening the capital. The return of the Emperor Haile Selassie to his palace in Addis Ababa would be a dramatic story for the *Daily Express*.

For Moorehead, the assignment was fraught with frustration and most of the coming weeks were spent waiting for aircraft which never arrived or departed or, if they did, were already full of passengers. He managed to fly to Khartoum and then Nairobi, which he found bustling with military activity but louche:

It is so improbable a place, such a survival from some lost world along the pre-war Riviera, that you pause at first, unwilling to believe . . . They *do* drink champagne, they *do* dance through the night on soft-lit terraces, or go riding under the moon . . . and there is a carnival of intrigue. They say the altitude at Nairobi makes people go slightly crazy but, after the desert, I found it all delightful as though the world were enjoying one long holiday.[8]

But then he was plunged into the lost world of Abyssinia, its titanic scenery and apocalyptic storms. Delays and a journey through unconquered territory kept him wandering in the wilds and he finally reached Addis Ababa to find that it had been captured some days before and that, because the city was still full of surrendered Italians, some of them still armed, it had been decided that the Emperor should not return yet. The fighting continued sporadically in the mountains but, he heard on the BBC news, the real war had erupted again in the Middle East.

At the beginning of April, he learned, a German armoured column under a young general named Rommel had suddenly attacked the British and driven them out of Benghazi. Three days later the Germans invaded Greece and were being resisted by a British expeditionary force of five divisions, all taken from Wavell's little army in the Western Desert. With his forces so dispersed it was difficult to see how Wavell could defend either Cyrenaica or Greece against determined attack once the Germans were involved. In the Libyan desert, the Germans had caught the British off balance and their success was compounded when, by chance, one of their flying columns caught a British staff car and captured its passenger, General O'Connor. Without his direction the British fell back in confusion and by 11th April had been swept out of Cyrenaica.

Moorehead had to return to Cairo but transport was again the problem. Eventually he managed to fly to Aden in a Blenheim bomber and there join a troopship bound for Suez. On arrival in Cairo he was told that many correspondents – among them Clifford, David Woodward, Edward Ward and Richard McMillan – were in Greece but that Athens had fallen to the Germans and that the British were being evacuated to Crete. In the Western Desert, the British had lost almost all the territory they had won at the beginning of the year even more quickly than they had conquered it, although a garrison was still holding out in the fortified port of Tobruk. Moorehead himself took a ship to Cyprus, which might itself be the next German objective but, in any case, offered a vantage-point to cover the next moves in the eastern Mediterranean. After a few days it became clear that the next battle would be for Crete, where more than 27,000 British, Australian and New Zealand soldiers awaited a possible assault by the German airborne division that was known to have arrived in Greece. So he returned to Egypt in the hope of reaching Crete.

While he was waiting to cross – and he had a theory that waiting to go to war was a worse strain than being there – the attack began and, it quickly became apparent, was succeeding. The German airborne troops suffered heavy losses but, as the surviving defenders were evacuated by warships under continual bombing, it became apparent that they had lost almost half their number. Moorehead never reached Greece or Crete and when both disasters were over

– and the correspondents had managed to return to Cairo – he took Lucy and John for a week's holiday to the cooler air and more gentle atmosphere of Jerusalem. On arrival they heard that, that morning, British and Free French forces had invaded Syria.

No news would come through Jerusalem, so they headed for Haifa and installed themselves in an hotel on Mount Carmel from which they could watch nightly air raids and sea battles as the French in Syria fought their former allies. It was proving an ideal campaign for the correspondents: before visiting the forward positions, they could swim and drink hock in the sun and on their return from the front sleep between sheets. It was much less so for the fighting soldiers; Vichy France had a strong army in Syria, including regiments of the Foreign Legion and colonial as well as French troops, and they fought as professionals. For two weeks, ugly fighting achieved little and it was not until reinforcements reached the British that the French defences began to crack. Then, just as Damascus was about to fall, news arrived that relegated all else to the inside pages of the newspapers: on Sunday, 22nd June, Germany invaded Russia.

From that moment the campaign in Syria seemed a side-show. Beirut fell and in mid-July the fighting was formally ended. Moorehead returned to Cairo to assess the situation. Despite the conquest of Italian East Africa and Syria, the British had been driven out of Greece and Crete. It had become clear that the big ships of the Mediterranean Fleet could no longer operate freely within range of shore-based bombers, although they had performed a spectacular final service in March by destroying an Italian cruiser squadron at night off Cape Matapan. Yet the Allied armies in the Middle East now numbered about half a million men and new arms and aircraft were arriving in vast quantities from the factories of the United States as well as Britain.

In July, it was clear that, while war spread through Russia, its first phase in the Middle East was over. This was underlined in a cable to Moorehead from his editor: "Your messages magnificent but with Russian war other news difficultest give you space you deserve consequently down-file unless sensationalest."[9] In fact, a few days after the German invasion, Christiansen had asked the Soviet embassy in London whether Moorehead could be accredited to the Red Army but it had become apparent that foreign journalists were not being allowed anywhere near the fighting. Meanwhile the Middle East would certainly offer more dramatic news and ease of travel and communications.

Inevitably there would be a lull while the opposing armies in the desert regrouped and refitted, and most of the other correspondents returned to Cairo. Lucy was now working as a senior secretary in an Intelligence department at General Headquarters, leaving the baby in the care of his Armenian nursemaid. Moorehead settled down to write a book about the first year of war in the Middle East, typing for ten or twelve hours a day. Amongst their friends who had escaped from Greece and Crete was Geoffrey Cox – now an Intelligence officer with the New Zealand division – who was writing his own account of the campaign. Some of the returning correspondents had escaped from the Germans for the second or third time, like Edward Ward and Richard McMillan, who had escaped from France, David Woodward from Holland and Desmond Tighe, the tall, unruffled Reuter correspondent, from Norway.

Two new arrivals stood out as curiosities. Clare Hollingworth, a forceful, attractive young woman with candid blue eyes, had been the first to report the outbreak of the Second World War by waiting on the Polish frontier with Germany, since when her reports from Bucharest had appeared in the *Daily Express*; now she had escaped from Athens to work in Cairo.

The other was Christopher Buckley, whose scholarly manner, spectacles and moustache suggested the schoolmaster that he had once been. Five years older than Moorehead, he had some private means which had enabled him to indulge a taste for travel in unexpected places and a little journalism. He had reported the civil war in Spain as a freelance for the *Christian Science Monitor* and travelled the length of the North African coast from Morocco to Egypt. When war broke out, he had been in Warsaw and had been editing an English-language digest of news in Athens, where he had been invited to join the *Daily Telegraph*, whose war correspondent he had now become. He had much in common with Clifford for both had been at Oriel College, Oxford, although they had just missed each other, Buckley being four years the senior. Both had an academic turn of mind: Buckley was an historian rather than a linguist but both were as fascinated by the causes of the war and the reasons for strategic decisions as in the battles they reported; the two quickly became friends and any friend of Clifford's became a friend of Moorehead's.

There was now time for short expeditions from Cairo to explore Egypt for their own amusement or watch the newly-arrived reinforcements on exercises. After two such jaunts, Clifford showed a curiously hard and insensitive side to his character in his diary. "Alan and I drove out along the road south-west of the Nile to photograph some Egyptiana," he wrote. "We managed to line up various picturesque girls, goatherds, old women, floundering water buffaloes, date palms, et cetera. But even in the country the revolting Egyptians flocked around yelling for backsheesh, trying to sell us their women and generally behaving in a thoroughly abject way."[10]

Later, when they were visiting an airfield near the Suez Canal, he noted, "We had a wonderful picnic lunch including such delicacies as quails in aspic. Just as we finished, a Wellington side-slipped into a landing, crashed and went up in a terrific burst of flame. All the occupants were blown clean through the fuselage by the explosion. They were dead, of course."[11]

Work on Moorehead's book was interrupted by having to move to another flat when the short lease of the first one ended. They found alternative quarters nearby on Gezira Island, close to the senior officers they were getting to know. One, Colonel Astley of Public Relations, was the controller of transport and communications and also an ornament of the social scene, who had returned to the army at the outbreak of war having earlier resigned his commission in a smart regiment on marrying the film star Madeleine Carroll. Moorehead was now confident enough of his position with the *Express* to write his book whether or not his editor approved and it was not until it was almost finished that he sought permission. Christiansen cabled, "As you've been a good boy will give you permission to publish book."[12]

This cable was shortly followed by another: "Can you fly to Persia at once?"[13] Christiansen clearly knew more than his correspondent in Cairo but the order was not wholly unexpected. While the armies had been fighting elsewhere, both sides had been struggling for ascendency by intrigue and political pressure elsewhere in the Middle East. The British were still hopeful of persuading Turkey to turn against Germany, while the Germans had been making successful efforts to win Iraq and Persia, or, as it was now beginning to be called, Iran. In April, a German puppet, Raschid Ali, had staged a coup in Baghdad and besieged the British airbase at Habbaniyah before being crushed by a punitive expedition. But in Persia, the Germans and Italians seemed to be more firmly established and now Britain and Russia were, in a remarkable combined effort, to put an end to this. At the instigation of Major Randolph Churchill, the Prime Minister's son, who had taken charge of British propaganda in Cairo, a party of journalists, including Moorehead, was flown to Persia the day before British and Indian troops invaded from the south and the Red Army from the north.

It was a military movement rather than an offensive and, at Basra, Moorehead found time to note the details of the English Club, which he rightly saw as a world-wide institution on the brink of extinction:

> It was almost a perfect specimen. A ramshackle, single-storeyed wooden building by the river with a library, a billiard room and a bar. A wide verandah and a big reception room for the dances and social evenings on Saturday night. Barefoot servants in white robes and turbans, a broad table on which lie six-months-old copies of the *Tatler*, the *Bystander*, the *Sketch*, the *Sphere*, the *Illustrated London News*, *The Times*, and the *Daily Telegraph* . . . The wicker chairs are just as they should be and always have been. So is the boy who presents a chit for you to sign for your drinks. So are the silver cups and the shield in the corner. Only the wireless set is out of place. When the day's work is done, launches slide down the river and drop off the white-trousered English residents and they call for drinks as they slump down in the wicker chairs among their friends . . . The English Club is the place where you "get away from the local people for a bit".[14]

Very different was his uncritical view of another set of men he came across a few days later. These were soldiers of the Red Army and he told his readers, "These Russians, a thousand miles from Russia, seem to have . . . almost a Prussian discipline, combined with downright ruthless toughness."[15] Later he became even more admiring of "these young men, athletes all of them, with their iron discipline, their brand new modern weapons, their wonderful shining health. They had that strange thing you see occasionally in young men's faces. It is a mixture of adolescent strength and spiritual resolve and something else – pride maybe. I had never seen troops like this before."[16]

There was no need for the invaders to fight. The Shah, Reza Pahlevi, who had been expecting the Germans and Italians to win, was quickly deposed and his country occupied by the unlikely allies. Before returning to Cairo, Moorehead, Clifford and a few others took the opportunity to explore the spectacular country in the north towards the Caspian Sea, which varied between harsh mountain scenery ("A tumbled mass of fiery peaks . . . the effect of this awful country was to fill the mind with images of huge sprawling dragons and fabulous monsters") and the damp, flowering shores of the inland sea ("A beech forest dripping with fine rain and, along muddy lanes, willows, oaks and elms . . . meadows of a Devon greenness, where cattle were grazing . . . the wet, fresh smell of the forest").[17]

When the correspondents returned to Cairo they found a change of mood. Reinforcements – particularly tanks and fighter aircraft – had been arriving in convoys routed round the Cape of Good Hope, much of them at the expense of the future defence of Singapore and the British Empire in the Far East which seemed to be increasingly threatened by a militant Japan. In London, Lord Beaverbrook, who had proved such a galvaniser of industry as Minister for Aircraft Production, had been appointed Minister of Supply in June and it was now tanks rather than fighter aircraft that he was demanding. "BEAVERBROOK TO DIRECT TANKS DRIVE"[18] the *Daily Express* headline on the front page had announced and a succession of news stories followed, boasting of his success in mass-producing such as "Valentine, Britain's new 16-ton killer tank".[19] War correspondents in the field were expected to heighten the awareness of the need for more tanks and report on the prowess of those that reached the battlefields.

General Wavell, in whom they had had such shining confidence, had been dismissed following an abortive attempt to counter-attack Rommel's surge across Cyrenaica. He had exchanged places with the Commander-in-Chief of the Indian Army, General Sir Claude Auchinleck, a quiet, resolute, fine-looking Scot of fifty-eight. He made many changes as he prepared to take the offensive; his force in the desert was now named the 8th Army and its commander was to be General Sir Alan Cunningham, who had been so successful in East Africa. The most personal change was in his own office at Grey Pillars, the block of modern flats in the European suburb of Cairo where the senior officers of GHQ were housed. He wanted an intelligent, trustworthy and personable private secretary to stand between himself and all those clamouring for attention and he chose Lucy Moorehead.

This was obviously an honour but to her husband it was unwelcome. She would be privy to almost all the secret information that reached the Commander-in-Chief; the very information that her husband was, as a journalist, trying to discover and which, within the bounds of censorship, he wanted to be free to disclose and criticise. On the other hand, she would meet all those in authority and that would be useful to him. Both might find themselves in invidious positions but soon Lucy was installed behind a desk in the converted scullery adjoining the living-room of the flat where General Auchinleck had his private office. Lucy and her husband had convinced the Commander-in-Chief of their integrity but many of the other correspondents were suspicious, envious or both.

Late in October, Moorehead and several others toured the desert positions of the 8th Army, noting the vast increase in armaments, transport and munitions. They drove deep into the desert to visit the most southerly positions as far as the oasis of Siwa and were finally able to assess the relative quantity and qualities of the opposing armies. Cunningham now had about a hundred thousand men, more than 700 tanks and nearly that number of fighting aircraft. Rommel had assembled about 120,000 men – the infantry predominantly Italian – and about 170 effective German and 150 less effective Italian tanks and 320 aircraft. Both commanders were clearly preparing to take the offensive. Moorehead began his report of the tour:

> I drove back into Cairo last night after a thousand-mile tour of the desert front. In all that way – from the Pyramids to Libya and back – the only shots I heard were a few bursts loosed by troops in the early morning to clear the barrels of their machine-guns and get the army out of bed. It is a strange, tense quiet along the front . . .[20]

Cunningham struck first. On 16th November he had summoned the correspondents to his command bunker in the desert and told them that he planned to attack at dawn on the day after the morrow. Moorehead walked out into the night with sombre thoughts of the vast numbers of men now camping peacefully around them who, in thirty-six hours' time, would start killing one another. "The inevitability of catastrophe – the actual knowing of the zero hour – was the hardest thing to take," he concluded. But he kept such thoughts out of his despatch, writing instead:

> It is a dramatic thing seeing this fine army on the verge of battle. There is no outward excitement, no show of nervousness, or hatred, or impatience, or bravado. The men know nothing of the battle plan, have not even been told that there will be an offensive yet. But they know all right. Their voices are pitched a little lower, their talk is a little abstracted . . .[21]

The following day they moved forward in their little column of trucks to position themselves for the opening of the offensive, which had been codenamed "Crusader". Cunningham's basic plan was to assault Rommel's force directly in front of his with one corps, while sending the other in a wide arc around its flank to destroy the enemy armour and relieve the besieged garrison of Tobruk. The battle began according to schedule early on 18th November.

The ensuing three months of fighting that swung to and fro across the desert and for and against each opponent was almost impossible to follow on the battlefield. As Moorehead had written, it was like naval warfare with little more to be seen than smoke on the horizon and, later, charred wreckage. Occasionally the correspondents had an unexpected close-up, as when they came across the British tank commander General Gatehouse: first when he was ordering his new American light Honey tanks – never yet tried in battle – to charge so as to get close enough to the enemy to fire their own little guns before being demolished by the German artillery; again when he was rallying the few survivors from an armchair strapped to the top of his own tank, a plaid rug around his waist.

For days the fighting swirled indecisively, mostly around the key British position at Sidi Rezegh. Then, on 24th November, Rommel gambled on a deep thrust with his mobile striking force into the rear areas of the 8th Army and this produced the final confusion. At the headquarters of the British corps that had been deputed to destroy the enemy's armour, the correspondents awaited news by the big armoured vehicles that housed the operations, Intelligence and signals staff. As reports became more ominous and fugitive tanks and trucks came racing by in full retreat, they themselves began to pack. "What's the flap?" asked a staff officer. "Ops will tell us if we have to get out." "Take a look at Ops," replied Clifford, and they saw the operations staff loading their camp kit and rations into trucks and, as Moorehead put it, "the stampede began."

The British – or, at least, all those visible through the dust clouds – were running away. Moorehead wrote later:

All day for nine hours we ran. It was the contagion of bewilderment and fear and ignorance. Rumour spread at every halt, no man had orders . . . I came to understand something of the meaning of panic in this long nervous drive. It was the unknown we were running away from, the unknown in ourselves and in the enemy.[22]

He could not write this in his report at the time; it would never had been passed by the censors. But he did tell his readers:

There is no front line. British and German tanks have met and wiped each other out. That is all. On both sides there are thousands of prisoners, thousands of casualties . . . Just this is definite – the hard, armoured casing around both armies has been pierced and broken and the soft inner core of the infantry, light gunners and supply columns stand opposed and at places hopelessly intermingled. Occasionally, tanks from both sides are cutting loose in this soft stuff . . . It is like a shark among mackerel.[23]

At last they came to the Italian barbed-wire fence on the frontier with Egypt and found a break in it: "We plunged through it with a feeling of relief – even a fence between us and the unknown pursuer was something."[24] They were the last party to reach the war correspondents' camp that evening. The scatter of tents sunk three feet into the sand were busy with tired and dusty men who had just arrived from the battlefield and now sat on sofas fashioned from sandbags, glasses of whisky or gin in hand, telling each other of narrow escapes while a worried Colonel Astley counted heads. Several were still missing and were thought to have been taken prisoner; amongst them Edward Ward of the BBC and Patrick Crosse of Reuter.

The 8th Army was in chaos and, although it had inflicted heavy loss on the enemy, Cunningham decided that the only solution was to withdraw into Egypt and regroup for another attempt. But now Auchinleck flew down to the desert and not only forbade any such withdrawal but relieved Cunningham of his command and replaced him with his own chief of staff, Major-General Neil Ritchie. It was the rear areas and headquarters of the 8th Army that had been so badly shaken rather than the fighting troops. Moreover, reinforcements – particularly in tanks – were reaching the British but not the Germans and the Italians. So the British fought on.

Early in December, Moorehead cabled a long article, assessing – so far as the censors would allow – the merits and effects of the opposing armies. Answering the question, "Are British and American tanks good enough to beat the Nazis?" he could not express his own opinion but he quoted that of a Scottish sergeant and this was printed prominently. "We have got to get a six-pounder gun like the Germans," said the sergeant. "They start firing at 1,500 yards and we have got to come right in to 800 yards before our two-pounders can make any reply." Moorehead himself summed up, "We have learned at heavy cost some of the great lessons that have governed this desert tank fighting."[25] This was not the sort of report that Lord Beaverbrook, busily promoting the qualities of British tanks, wanted to read from his correspondent.

After a brief lull – during which Moorehead and some others flew to Cairo for baths, clean clothes and a few good meals before returning to the fighting at Sidi Rezegh – a decision was reached by exhaustion rather than tactical or strategic brilliance. Both sides were spent, most of their tanks destroyed, but the British were getting more tanks and a new resilience. It was Rommel who had to withdraw from the battlefield.

The way into Tobruk was clear and Moorehead and Clifford set off across the battlefield which had suddenly fallen silent. Clifford wrote later:

Our route lay through the vast, stretched-out rubbish-heap that had been the battlefield. It was quiet now, the sand was silting in to cover the waste of brutal, stupid, twisted wreckage, but still the odour of death was brooding over everything. The mind jibbed at trying to assess the significance and horror of it all. Alan and I argued about Jane Austen as we bumped past little groups where violent action had been suddenly frozen by death into grim, silent tableaux.[26]

Explicit accounts of the carnage would never pass the censor but in letters and his diary Clifford occasionally touched on the horror to which he had become accustomed. He wrote of this journey:

We found several British tanks – one contained two roasted bodies and an Edgar Wallace – and not a few German. I acquired a German rubber ground-sheet fitting into a neat sachette – most useful. I got it from a truck where a young fair-haired hero was sitting at the wheel with his brains piled on the seat beside him. On the floor of the cab was a postcard from his mother saying that she would bake him another cake when she could but there was nothing to make it with in the house at the moment.[27]

After Tobruk, the coastal towns were recaptured, one by one, all the way to Benghazi. Near there they arrived at the bend in the road where they had nearly died at the beginning of the year to find that somebody else had just been ambushed there and, wrote Clifford later, "Alan and I rather posed as experts on ambushes outside Barce and were prepared to give a few hints."[28]

They spent a cold Christmas in a bombed and desolate Benghazi, passing the time by wondering how to cook two turkeys they had acquired. Clifford, who was usually the cook, considered three methods, "boiling them in a hip-bath, cooking them on spits over a bonfire or coating them in mud and building a fire around them".[29] Finally they managed to light the huge kitchen range in the abandoned hotel, where they occupied rooms, and enjoyed one cheerful day.

On the way they had heard the most important news since the German invasion of Russia. Japan had entered the war. Pearl Harbor had been attacked, Singapore and Hong Kong seemed about to fall and Australia could be threatened. Moorehead and Clifford cabled their editors suggesting that they should go to the Far East but, while this was being considered in London, the tide turned again in Libya.

At the beginning of 1942 a sense of triumph seemed unreal in Cairo. After that long battle, Rommel had been beaten. Enemy casualties had numbered some 33,000 against 18,000 British; but most of the enemy's had been expendable Italians or rear echelon troops, whereas the British had been mostly experienced fighting men. When Moorehead and Lucy lunched with two corps commanders, Gott and Norrie, with whom they were now on friendly terms, thanks as much to her position as his, he noticed that they did not seem confident. The fact was that Ritchie's army was now as over-stretched as Rommel's had been a few weeks before. "The ancient law of the desert was, in fact, coming into play," wrote Moorehead in retrospect. "The trouble was that the farther you got away from your base, the nearer the retreating enemy got to his. Consequently, as you got weaker, the enemy got stronger."[30]

That January, a convoy of six ships laden with German tanks had managed to reach Tripoli and this gave the Afrika Korps a sharp new spearhead with which Rommel struck on the 21st. The 8th Army, thinly spread and much of its forward troops inexperienced reinforcements from Egypt, crumpled and was soon in headlong retreat. It did not stop until it was two-thirds of the way back to the Egyptian frontier where it rallied behind prepared defensive positions in the desert between Derna and Tobruk at Gazala.

More than a year of war in Libya had achieved little beyond keeping one British army at grips with the enemy. It had, however, established the fame of one war correspondent and every week congratulatory cables reached Moorehead from London. Messages from Christiansen or Charles Foley, who had replaced Sutton as foreign editor, would say, "Splendid desert stuff frontpaged today",[31] "You're once more miles ahead your competitors"[32] and "We smelt powder too."[33] Christiansen was punctilious in passing on compliments whether from another newspaper – "Hope you won't need extra large size hats after *Evening Standard* statement tonight quote here is one of really great reporters of war unquote"[34] – or from an editor of *Life* magazine: "London editor *Life* says if you American would win Pulitzer Prize."[35]

But Christiansen liked to keep a tight rein on his correspondents, however much he praised them. When Moorehead had spent two or three days in Cairo in December he sent him a sharp message claiming – wrongly as it emerged – that one of his rivals was still in the desert so "Hope you're returning soonest missing your brilliant dispatches."[36] And he could not resist a touch of rough banter when passing on the praise of the Minister of Information himself: "Brendan Bracken says how much he appreciates your articles stop still waiting find something kick you pantwards."[37]

Much as he liked and admired Christiansen, such tugs at the rein were irksome and Moorehead took much pleasure at the first sign of future independence when an advance copy of his first book reached him at the beginning of 1942. This was his account of Wavell's campaign, *Mediterranean Front*, which had just been published in London by Hamish Hamilton to acclaim, which, even in distant Cairo, rang sweetly in his ears.

Chapter Seven

"The Inside Set"

By the beginning of 1942, Alan Moorehead's life had evolved into two interlocking triangles. The one he formed with his wife and baby son carried his hopes of increasing happiness and ambitions for fame into the indefinite future, adding another spur to that which had brought him from Australia to his present height of success. The other, he comprised with Alexander Clifford and Christopher Buckley and they were already being talked about as "The Trio", who not only seemed inseparable but together represented a major section of the British press and were thus of world-wide influence.

The vital link between the two triangles was Lucy, whose attachment to Alexander Clifford had become as strong as her husband's. She was now working long hours in the Commander-in-Chief's office and, although this was tiring in the heat of Cairo, it was fascinating and rewarding in terms of status. The exchanges of telegrams between Auchinleck and the War Cabinet – including personal messages from Churchill – passed across her desk, and, although she became one of the best-informed people in the Middle East, her discretion was trusted. Other journalists might grumble that she was passing nuggets of news to Moorehead; this was not so but Auchinleck would occasionally suggest to her lines of enquiry for her husband. When such gossip was heard, Squadron-Leader Houghton, the RAF public relations officer, would defend her, saying that she had known, but not told Moorehead, that a brief visit to Palestine, on which he and the others had been invited, was a deception trick aimed at diverting

German attention away from a planned British attack in Libya.

On the social level she was indeed privileged. All visitors to Auchinleck passed through her office and while they waited they talked and were charmed. Motherhood and a happy marriage had added serenity to her beauty, and her intelligence and cool wit were as sharp as ever. As in Fleet Street, men fell in love with her and dashing young colonels and brigadiers from the desert, who had no time to waste, would invite her to dinner; invitations which she declined without offending. But she and her husband did share tables at the Gezira Sporting Club and the grander hotels with the most important military and political figures, who only saw the other correspondents at press conferences; Moorehead made particular friends with General Gott (nicknamed "Strafer" from the German slogan of the First World War *Gott Strafe Engelland*"). When he was writing his first book, as well as articles for American magazines and the script for a documentary film of the desert war, Gott lent him his diaries and maps. Inevitably he came to know Auchinleck himself and soon Clifford was noting in his diary, "Alan lunched with Auchinleck, who apparently was very cordial and informative. He came home very pleased with himself."[1]

As Moorehead's closest friend, Clifford enjoyed some such privileges, too, and in any case, was universally liked and admired. His courage in the damaged flying-boat and in the ambush was well known and regarded all the more highly because he remained as unassuming as ever. Other correspondents, less intelligent than he, enjoyed his company, for he was unfailingly courteous and a good listener. Surprisingly, he seemed to read little beyond detective novels he found in the flat, or his Arabic grammar, as if his intellectual interests had to wait until after the war. He loved children and would often wheel his godson's pram around the gardens of Gezira, writing to his own mother about the infant's progress: "I have been superintending the baby for the weekend and it has come out in spots and lost weight. But I think this was because they did something with its feeding against my advice."[2] The gossip about his exact relationship with Lucy lessened after he was seen about Cairo escorting a smart Greek girl met at one of the parties given by Copts or Levantines, or in the fast and louche civilian circles which Geoffrey Keating liked to frequent.

At thirty-six, and the eldest by five years and the last to join The Trio, Christopher Buckley was on less intimate terms with the Mooreheads than Clifford. He was his own man in his tastes and habits and lived apart from them in another "chummery", as shared flats were known, on Gezira Island. His links with high authority were not through Lucy but his own contacts with Intelligence officers, which had begun long before he had arrived in Cairo; indeed there were some who suspected that his ties with them were even stronger than they seemed. Unlike the others, he tended to wear civilian clothes in Cairo and, as a man of some means, could afford to pay the considerable rent of £50 a month for his share of the flat when he was away for many weeks, or even months.

His daily routine in Cairo was to rise early and read some serious historical book – the works of Clausewitz were prominent on his shelves – until the morning newspapers arrived at nine. At noon he would attend the daily press briefing on the second floor of the Immobilia building in central Cairo, then have a drink with the others at the Churchill Bar and lunch before returning to write at his flat instead of in the press room. Most of the other correspondents were in some awe of him for he was clearly a scholar (he enjoyed little exchanges in Latin or Greek), he could be startlingly abrupt with those less intelligent and his usual manner was correct rather than courteous. His bearing on the battlefield had, like Clifford's, attracted attention, and in his case it was said that it was not so much that he was brave as without fear.

Another occupant of Buckley's "chummery" was Clare Hollingworth, whom he had first met in Athens. They were constantly together and a romantic attachment – rather than a love affair – developed. Their friends speculated that marriage might follow but they were not suited for this, perhaps because Buckley seemed so self-contained a bachelor and Clare was a forceful woman with a career. Once, after lunch at Mena House Hotel at the edge of the desert at Ghiza, they walked to the Great Pyramid of Cheops and she asked him to climb to the top with her. When he refused, she went alone and, on her return, announced that she had left her notebook at the top and asked him to retrieve it. This was too unsettling a companion for so orderly a man of thirty-seven, middle-aged by the standards of the time and place.

Others found Clare Hollingworth's professional demands irksome, for the war correspondents felt that they belonged to a masculine club for which the qualification was reporting from the battlefields. Colonel Astley did not allow women journalists – or the correspondents of magazines and evening papers – to go into the desert, but Clare and a few others had managed it. The influential, like Clare Boothe

Luce, wife of the proprietor of *Time* and *Life*, and Eve Curie of the *New York Herald Tribune*, managed to get into the forward areas by flying there for the day with Randolph Churchill who would be irked by having to drive his guests miles across the flat desert to achieve their privacy from time to time because of the absence of lavatories for women in this masculine reserve. Clare Hollingworth went more often and for longer through the influences of Intelligence officers she had met with Buckley, or the public relations officer of the Free French brigade in the 8th Army, and it was always possible to ask Squadron-Leader Houghton for a flight to a desert airstrip.

On these occasions, she would sometimes camp with The Trio, or "The Inside Set" as some of the correspondents who spent most of their time in the desert – like the news-agency reporters – would call them. At dark, they would climb into their sleeping bags around their parked truck and lie on their backs, gazing up at the brilliance of the stars, and talk. Confidences would be exchanged and ambitions discussed without inhibition. Once they had covered the state of the war and the prospects of the current campaign, they would speculate on what they would like to do after the war. Their ambitions diverged: Moorehead would leave journalism and become a famous writer on the scale of Hemingway; Clifford would stay, probably moving to a more serious newspaper, and become an eminent commentator, rather than correspondent, touring the world; Buckley would leave Fleet Street and become a don at Oxford, perhaps as Professor of the History of War. All such fancies now seemed to be within the bounds of possibility.

The three had realised for some time that they were the most celebrated war correspondents and knew that several of those who had reported the First World War had been knighted for their services. They therefore expected the same and even considered the eventual possibilities of peerages. They jokingly asked Clare if she would like to be a Dame of the British Empire and Moorehead remarked that when knighted he would have to change his Christian name because "Sir Alan" did not sound melodious.

They discussed religion and invariably ended by agreeing at some level of agnostic fatalism. Moorehead professed no religious faith and when Clifford was once asked to enter his on some document, he wrote, "Employer's choice". The three men talked about sex without prurience; Clifford and Buckley, who were inexperienced and a little apprehensive about it, were fascinated that Moorehead should have found it so natural and enjoyable a part of his life for so long; he was surprised that they should fear it could be anything else.

Only when there was the possibility of air attack, or long-range bombardment, would they dig slit-trenches like individual graves and sleep at the bottom, when they might awake to find that they were sharing it with a large lizard. Dawn would be as beautiful as sunset had been and they would brew tea over the flames of petrol-soaked sand in half of one of the flimsy cans in which fuel was carried. Then they would set out on a compass bearing towards the next desert headquarters somewhere over a horizon that was beginning to shimmer with mirages. They were fit in body and alert in mind, stimulated by the outdoor life and the dry air; Moorehead's physique seemed particularly suited to the life, Clare Hollingworth noting him as "small, lean, sweaty (we all were) and down-to-earth, a good raconteur but with no politeness, unlike his two English friends".[3]

At the outset of each expedition to the battle-areas, Moorehead and Clifford both confessed to a feeling of dread but, while the former could feel excitement and appear jaunty on the journey forward, the latter would, his friend said, "sit hunched in the corner of the car as we bumped over the desert, morose, shut in on himself and hopeless"[4] until they arrived, when he would appear transformed and sometimes seemed the more decisive of the two. Yet when they came to a headquarters it was Moorehead who took the lead in asking the pertinent questions. He was the apex of The Trio and had learned much from the other two, his knowledge and perception broadened by Clifford and deepened by Buckley.

Occasionally, they would also be accompanied by another correspondent of quality, David Woodward, whose experience on the Continent matched Clifford's and who was well versed in the more picaresque byways of European history yet seemed without the ambitions that drove the other three. He and a few others were on easy terms with The Trio but there was still resentment amongst many of the correspondents over what they considered the favouritism shown to them. Clifford and Moorehead were nicknamed "Mutt and Jeff" after cartoon characters, with the latter known as "Little Mutt". Buckley was resented by one or two who had met and formed a "battlefield friendship" with him in Greece and now felt that they had been dropped since he had made important new friends. Several of the Australians particularly disparaged Moorehead as having become "more English than the English" and certainly he had taken to speaking of the British as "we" in his reporting and referring to "the Australians" instead of "us". Richard Hughes, a generally genial Australian reporter, known for his tendency to address friends in ecclesiastical terms as "your grace" or "your eminence", was dismissive of Moorehead as "The Little Digger". Even friends were sometimes irritated by the apparent self-satisfaction, if not arrogance, of The Trio, as when they spoke collectively of their joint, considered opinion, beginning, "We think . . ."

They were also accused of spending more time in Cairo than in the desert and that was true. All three were covering the whole of the Middle East and were liable to be sent to East Africa and Asia. When Moorehead was away from the 8th Army, that was covered either by another staff reporter like Alaric Jacob or his old friend O'Dowd Gallagher, or a temporary "stringer", notably a tough Australian, Ronald Monson, who, it was said, would have won the Victoria Cross for rescuing a wounded soldier under fire had he been in the army. When Moorehead arrived at the desert press camp he bandied about the names of generals with whom he was on lunching terms and his talk of smart political dinner parties in Cairo did not get a reverent hearing from those – particularly the news-agency correspondents – whose assignment was to cover the news of the 8th Army and who thought of themselves as "desert rats".

This degree of hostility towards Moorehead and his circle found an echo in Fleet Street. The foreign editors of both the *Express* and the *Mail* expected their war correspondents to produce a succession of exclusive reports and to conduct themselves as the rivals that they were supposed to be. But, as Foley of the *Express* put it, "they had become inseparable, to my chagrin, virtually writing the same story and Alan simply ignored demands for exclusive beats. I tried sending identical congratulatory cables to Alan Moorehead and Alexander Clifford but that, too, was ignored."[5] Once, after a series about the life of the British soldiers in the desert by Moorehead which was matched by Clifford's article on the same subject, Christiansen cabled to him, "Congratulations your series its talk of town stop can you tell me whether Clifford received his instructions for parallel article following Express boost your series last Thursday query."[6] These had been articles in which Moorehead had again reported the relative weakness of the guns mounted in British tanks and many readers would assume that, but for the censors, his criticism would have been more trenchant. Christiansen knew perfectly well that the two friends had written their articles in collusion.

Yet both Foley and Christiansen – and their equivalents on the

Daily Mail – refrained from taking matters further. They knew their correspondents were – together with Buckley of the *Telegraph*, which was not a direct rival – the best and were setting new standards amongst war correspondents, some of whom had been known to invent stories and prefix a report from Cairo with the dateline "Somewhere in the Western Desert". As Foley decided, "Their unchallenged superiority shamed lesser mortals into assuring the accuracy of their material; faking and 'flying carpet' datelines were soon exposed." They also set a new standard of general conduct: although war correspondents held a status equivalent to that of a captain, they need only salute officers of the rank of colonel and above; the risks they took entitled them to live on their expenses and save their pay but not to profiteer. "Their integrity generally won the respect and confidence of the top people,"[7] Foley concluded.

Moorehead himself was generally regarded as pre-eminent. The radio reporters were known to an even wider public but their recordings were too brief to develop much individuality, make use of their descriptive powers or expand upon any one aspect of the news. Television in Britain had been closed down for the duration of the war and the commentaries added to the newsreels were the most simplistic propaganda. But the newspaper correspondents could spread themselves and Moorehead's despatches – even those written in the midst of battle – often ran to one or two thousand words. His style was personal with a buttonholing intimacy and the pace of his narrative headlong. Deftly, he mixed the news of the day and interviews with participants, vivid flashes of description and background dissertation, historical allusion and speculative forecast with, always, his own travels and adventures, modestly but excitingly told. At the end of a Moorehead despatch, the readers might feel a little breathless and almost as if they had been there, too.

His criticism of Allied tanks was causing disquiet in Whitehall as well as annoyance to Beaverbrook. This would be slipped into his assessment of the military position whenever opportunity offered, whether he stressed "the weight and vigour of the German panzer divisions, which, at vital moments, took possession of the battlefields";[8] whether he was maintaining that, in response, "we have got to build a tank round a 25-pounder gun";[9] or whether he praised the dash and flair of Rommel, as a general who could think fast and improvise on the battlefield.

Christiansen regarded Moorehead as something more than a brilliant war correspondent. Moorehead's experience with Cox in Paris, on his own in Rome and now his association with more seasoned and better-educated journalists than himself had given him a breadth of vision and depth of understanding worthy of a foreign correspondent who could be assigned to cover any major news anywhere. With the triumph of the Japanese throughout South-east Asia and the South Pacific and their capture of Singapore in February, it seemed as though the next blow would fall on Australia and that was where Moorehead now wanted to be, particularly when his friend Noel Monks arrived in Cairo on his way there from London. So he cabled Christiansen asking to go and, when provisional agreement was received, booked his passage to Sydney. Then Rangoon fell and the Japanese plunged into the Burmese jungle on the heels of the British defenders and it seemed that India might be the next objective instead. Foley told him enough correspondents had escaped from Singapore to Australia to give him all the coverage he needed there, so, instead, he should go to India to report on this threat and also the mission of Sir Stafford Cripps, the Lord Privy Seal, who was shortly leaving London for New Delhi to present to the restive Indian politicians the British Government's new terms for granting independence. Later, it would be decided whether he should return to Cairo, stay in India or go elsewhere.

Moorehead and his family had just returned from a short holiday in the Lebanon, where he and Lucy had been ski-ing; she for the first time since a pre-war holiday in Grindlewald and he for the first time since he and Geoffrey Cox had slithered on skis through the snowy woods at St. Cloud one night when they had drunk in the Boeuf sur le Toit off the Champs Elysées, where, he remembered, a girl had sung the haunting song "You Go to My Head". All that now seemed to belong to another world and another age.

In March, leaving Lucy and the baby in Cairo, he set out for India and new experiences in company with the Canadian corre-spondent Matthew Halton of the *Toronto Star*. He was confident that Clifford would care for his wife and child with whom he would be sharing the flat. No husband could have been more attentive – taking Lucy to lunch, giving her driving lessons and wheeling the child in his pram – so that those who did not understand the platonic nature of the relationship raised their eyebrows yet higher. This was understandable, as entries in Clifford's diary showed. A typical day was 27th March when:

Lucy had the day off so we spent the morning shopping . . . Met

Lucy at Groppi's for a coffee before going home. After lunch we took the baby out to the desert a little bit along the Fayoum road and let him play about in the sand. He adored it and didn't want to come home. Lucy tried to drive a little but the child laughed at her so heartily that she had to give up. Spent the evening quietly at home.[10]

Meanwhile her husband's eyes were focusing on the strange scenes of India. As the flying-boat alighted on the lake at Gwalior, he noted that everything seemed to be brown: water, earth, rocks, villages and people. Soon he discovered the extraordinary realities of India, a vast, polyglot, chaotic country ruled by a tiny and efficient cadre of British administrators and soldiers headed by the Viceroy, the Marquis of Linlithgow, and the Commander-in-Chief, General Wavell. It was a sign of Moorehead's new standing that in New Delhi an invitation to luncheon with Wavell should be awaiting him and that he should then deliver private letters entrusted to him by General Auchinleck for both the Commander-in-Chief and for his own wife who had not accompanied him to Egypt. This was followed by lunch with the Viceroy and he recorded both the splendour of Sir Edwin Lutyens's purpose-built capital and of the demi-god himself. He wrote later:

The British wanted an Imperial City, a place of spreading avenues and fountains, of massive administrative blocks and ponderous monuments. They got it. Lutyens spared nothing. The central post office went *here*, the commander-in-chief's house went *there*, the imperial arch at this end of the park and the Viceroy's house at the other . . . New Delhi, as a result, looks exactly like it was in the beginning – a set of architect's drawings . . . It is a mistake, however, to imagine that New Delhi has anything to do with India. It still is an enormous English club, the finest in the world.[11]

Lord Linlithgow himself presided over a formal luncheon at which Colonel Peter Fleming, the dashing author of pre-war books of travel and his own adventures, confided with the self-confidence of a seasoned orientalist the way to distinguish between a Japanese and a Chinese soldier: the Japanese were accustomed to wearing shoes with a thong around their big toes, so a man with a jutting big toe would be a Jap. The Viceroy was lordly and uncommunicative during the meal but later accorded Moorehead twenty minutes of gloomy opinions about the future of India, which, noted Moorehead, "with his habit of passing his hand wearily across his face, combined with the effect of what he was saying, left me with an even stronger feeling of pessimism than the one with which I had arrived".[12]

The prospect was indeed dark. Not only were the Japanese "at the gates of India", as it was said, but the Indians themselves longed to throw off British rule. Yet they were not united in means or ends and the British, preoccupied with trying to stave off the invaders, had to deal with the demands of those Moorehead listed as:

> Gandhi, still the greatest personal force in India . . . Jawaharlal Nehru . . . and the others of the All India Congress. Then Jinnah of the Muslims, their bitter enemy. Then the princes and the Untouchables, the Hindu Mahasabha, the Sikhs and the Gurkhas, the Parsees . . . communists and pacifists, pro-Axis groups like the Forward Bloc and many, many others.[13]

The mission led by Sir Stafford Cripps had arrived in New Delhi to offer these bickering and occasionally warring factions a new constitution which would lead to independence. To gain this they only had to agree to fight and defeat the Japanese. He attended Cripps's press conference at which he gave details of the offer, noting, as few did, Sir Stafford's persuasive charm and occasionally sharp tongue. When questions were invited, he dealt with them, wrote Moorehead, "with the air of an auctioneer selling a particularly good lot to an eager market".[14]

As presented by Cripps, it sounded so reasonable. Once the war was won, with the Indians and the British together defeating the Japanese invaders, a new constitution would be formed for India, first as a dominion within the British Empire but with a final option of cutting those ties. Now Moorehead had to discover the Indian view. One of the most important, and certainly the most striking, figures was Mahatma Gandhi, now aged seventy-three and still the charismatic saint of the Indian poor. Moorehead visited him and described how Gandhi

> . . . came into the room, a twist of white cotton around his loins, his black barrel of a chest quite bare, nothing on his sinewy legs or feet, steel spectacles on his nose. He shook hands, smiling, and teed himself up comfortably against his white bolster. From that moment, I could never quite catch up with the argument or bring it under control. It was not so much Gandhi's quickness or his

wits. Not his really overwhelming charm and the amiable wealth and patience of his pinched little face. It was that from first to last he had the tremendous advantage of being absolutely convinced that he was right.[15]

Thus, although Gandhi would not comment directly upon Cripps's proposals, he repeated that under no circumstances would he resort to violence, even in an extreme of self-defence and even against the Japanese. Therefore there could be no hope whatsoever of his agreement to the key clause that India should initially help to win the war. Moorehead began his despatch, "I have just had an interview, or, rather, an argument, with Gandhi . . . In the end he said, 'I would not surrender India. I would let the Japanese land and fight them by non-violence.' "[16]

Moorehead went to see the leading Hindu politician, Nehru, and found him "a socialist of formidable intellect, an aristocrat of great charm, a lawyer with immense persuasion . . . very much like Cripps, in fact".[17] He was willing to fight and rally his supporters against the Japanese but only on one condition: that India be granted a degree of self-government – including an all-Indian legislature, an Indian defence minister and Indian involvement in the higher direction of the war – as a first step. Both he and his interviewer knew that the British would never agree to that.

Finally, he saw Jinnah, the Muslim leader and Nehru's rival. He, too, was willing to advocate the whole-hearted support of Britain against Japan but only on condition that the Muslims were accorded more power at once and a guarantee of their own separate state immediately following victory, rather than being forced into a system of government shared with the Hindus.

From these and other Indian politicians he interviewed, Moorehead realised that nothing could come of the Cripps mission. His proposals had come too soon, or too late. The problems of India were far too complicated for any neat settlement. Sir Stafford departed for London saying, "The offer is simply withdrawn and I do not think we will be able to make another one. The position is just as it was before I arrived."[18] Moorehead summed up his failure as due to "passive resistance – by that mass of weak, helpless, hesitating humanity that lies, layer on layer, like a London fog, so that the deeper he went down into it, the more it gave way in front of him and closed in behind and got darker. He could find no foothold in this slippery space."[19]

He himself left for Ceylon, which had just been attacked by Japanese carrier-borne aircraft. They had been repelled, although the Royal Navy had suffered heavily at sea, and here, at least, the Japanese seemed to have been stopped. However, the theatre of war to which he belonged was in the Middle East, a new British offensive in the desert was forecast and he had to be there. He was ordered back to Cairo to control several other *Express* reporters as the head of the bureau and senior war correspondent.

The interlude in India and Ceylon had not only enhanced his reputation as a foreign correspondent, but given him time to think about the future. He was hankering after a return to Australia with his family so that he could report the war against Japan and the threat to his own country, and he was tired, having, like many in the Middle East, been subject to a succession of ailments from stomach upsets to desert sores. On his return to Cairo in May 1942, he wrote to Christiansen, telling him that, although he expected the desert fighting to begin again, he would like to return to Australia and then be accredited to the forces commanded by General MacArthur, the American commander of the counter-offensive against Japan in the Pacific, even if only for a spell. Above all, he wanted a rest and a change:

I am sure you will want me to cover at least the opening stages of a summer campaign in the Western Desert, but I do not think I can usefully continue here longer than July . . . I have had such a succession of minor illnesses in this climate that it is simply not worth waiting until I become really unfit. I would like to make it clear that it is only a temporary change of scene I am seeking. I am perfectly ready to go to any front outside the Middle East and the tropical area.[20]

That letter was written on 27th May and the night before, unknown to him as yet, Rommel had attacked in the moonlight, so forestalling the British offensive which was to have been launched three weeks later. His aim was not to assault General Ritchie's defences at Gazala but outflank them, cut through to the sea in their rear and take Tobruk. If he could then destroy the 8th Army, the way to Alexandria and Cairo would be open. Moorehead, like the other correspondents, was taken by surprise and it was five days before he arrived on the battlefield.

This time, the British were confident of victory. They outnumbered the Germans and Italians in tanks, guns and aircraft and, unlike their enemies, could call upon substantial reinforcements. Not only had Ritchie new and more powerful anti-tank guns but hundreds of the new, American-built Grant tanks mounting a 75mm gun, which, although it was mounted in the hull and so could only traverse forty-five degrees, was more effective than the guns in the latest German tanks to arrive in Libya. The 8th Army was disposed in a series of "boxes" – large, self-contained positions protected by minefields and barbed wire – sited between Tobruk on the coast to Bir Hacheim held by the Free French brigade far to the south.

While Rommel tried to outflank the whole Gazala front, tank formations fought swirling battles around the British "boxes". The most vital of these had been named "Knightsbridge" and was held by the Guards and, noted Moorehead:

. . . their strange and slightly automaton code of behaviour was particularly suited to this sort of action. It was something they understood. A position was given to you to fortify and then you got the order to hold it to the last round and the last man. It was simply a matter of progressing to that final point, unless, of course, the enemy got tired first . . . So these odd, gawky officers with their prickly moustachios, their little military affectations, their high-pitched voices and their little jokes from the world of Mayfair and Ascot kept bringing their men up to the enemy and the men, because they were the picked soldiers of the regular Army and native Englishmen and Scots, did exactly what they were told.[21]

Such stubborn defence and the unexpected appearance of the new Grant tanks on the battlefield not only held Rommel but for a time threatened him with defeat. Yet instead of using his tanks as boldly as Rommel, Ritchie launched his counter-attacks piecemeal, so that nowhere did he achieve overwhelming impetus while, over a fortnight's fighting, his superiority in numbers was whittled away by battle-damage and breakdowns. By 13th June, Rommel found that he had a superiority in armour and still held the tactical initiative. On that day, he finally took the "Knightsbridge box" and it seemed to Ritchie that the bulk of his fighting formations were about to be cut off from their supplies. He therefore ordered a general retreat. As Moorehead realised, Rommel was winning by employing exactly the same tactics Wavell had used to destroy the Italian army in Cyrenaica more than two years before.

Again the correspondents found themselves swept up in a stampede to safety and Moorehead cabled to the *Express*:

As the light was fading into a gaudy red sunset, we unpacked our bedrolls and cooked our bully stew in the back of our truck. It was precisely when I was half-way through this stew that the enemy began to come over the horizon. You don't see much in these quick thrusts. Mostly it is just a lot of blown sand and lines of vehicles – yours and the enemy's – coming over the most distant rise like a line of surfers riding a breaker to the beach . . . It took just seven minutes to pack and get away.[22]

He tried to be as optimistic as he could during such retreats because they were not always significant and rarely did loss of a swathe of desert make much difference any more than movement across the sea necessarily gave advantage in a naval battle. "In lines of streaming dust, the enemy columns have flowed around the British boxes," he reported. "Gaps and empty spaces in no man's land have been filled in by the enemy."[23] But this time it was more serious and the enemy's advance was more than a temporary tactical manoeuvre. Sometimes, as they drove eastward, Moorehead's party would be cut off from their communications and no despatch riders would come bouncing over the desert to collect their reports for transmission. Nevertheless the *Daily Express* almost always had a first-hand report from the battlefield for its front page because it now had three correspondents covering the fighting; the others being Alaric Jacob and Eric Bigio, who had moved from Turkey to help Moorehead in the desert.

Back across these old battlefields retreated the British, leaving a garrison of 35,000 men again besieged in Tobruk. This time the defenders – the bulk of the fighting troops belonging to a South African division – were infected by defeat and had neither the time nor resolve to put their defences in order. On 20th June, a bombardment by artillery and dive-bombers was followed by an assault on the perimeter. It broke; that afternoon the German vanguard reached the ruins of Tobruk itself and the garrison surrendered. It was the worst disaster to befall the British since the loss of Singapore.

The other coastal towns – Bardia and Sollum – fell without a fight, for the British had now lost almost all their tanks and had nothing to stand against the hundred or so that Rommel could still send forward. Ritchie had planned to make his stand on the prepared defences at Mersa Matruh, which had been Force Headquarters in the time of Wavell. But on 25th June, he was dismissed by Auchinleck, who himself came down to the desert and took command. He saw that this line would not hold any longer than the others and ordered a further retreat to the one and only position that might be held between the enemy and the Nile. This was at El Alamein – only 60 miles from Alexandria and 150 miles from Cairo – which had the advantage of being impossible to outflank. To the north, of course, was the sea; in the desert stood low ridges which offered vantage-points and defensive positions and, 40 miles south, lay the soft sand of the Qattara Depression, which could not support the weight of tanks. Rommel came up to what was called the Alamein Line on 1st July.

If these final defences were broken, Egypt would fall and that, as Moorehead put it:

would precipitate a chain of misfortunes almost too disastrous to contemplate. With Egypt would fall Malta and all British control of the Mediterranean. The Suez Canal would be lost and with it the stores and equipment worth fifty Tobruks. Suez, Port Said, Alexandria, Beirut and Syrian Tripoli might go. Palestine and Syria could not then hope to stand and, once in Jerusalem and Damascus, the Germans would be in sight of the oil wells and Turkey all but surrounded. The Red Sea would become an Axis lake and, once in the Indian Ocean, the Italian fleet could prey upon all the routes to Africa, India and Australia. India would be approached from both sides by the enemy. Finally, Russia's left flank would be hopelessly exposed.[24]

It was all too easy to see that victory for Rommel at Alamein could mean total victory for Germany, Italy and Japan.

The causes of the British defeat, despite what had seemed to be a decisive advantage in numbers and supplies, were set out by Moorehead in a long article which was passed by the censors and given prominence in the *Daily Express*. "These in my judgement are the reasons for our retreat," he wrote. "The Germans still have the better all-purpose gun – 88mm. The better tank – the Mark Four. The better plane – the Messerschmitt 109."

He also blamed the lack of experienced senior officers, since so many had been killed, wounded or captured: "quick-decision men – that's what we lacked most of all."[25] The enemy had been under-estimated and, he continued, too many junior officers seemed to think that courage alone was enough to win desert battles. Next day, a second article was published and returned to the inferiority of British tank design and armament.

This stung his proprietor, Lord Beaverbrook, into defending the tanks that he had instructed his editors to praise. He addressed the House of Lords, claiming that there was nothing wrong with British tanks, except that the latest models had been delayed by production problems and that not enough of the new six-pounder guns had yet reached the desert battlefield. He even praised the puny two-pounder gun, with which so many British tanks were armed, although his correspondent with the 8th Army had repeatedly written of its inadequacy.

Moorehead and most other correspondents were back in Cairo since their communications had been disrupted in the rout. Now that Auchinleck was in direct command and had moved out of General Headquarters, Lucy was working for General Corbett, the senior officer in Cairo and the link between the otherwise-occupied Commander-in-Chief and his masters in London. There was a sense of unreality. The city was crowded with refugees from Alexandria and there was a new exodus from Cairo to Palestine. A thin haze of smoke hung over GHQ and the British Embassy as secret documents were burned. Yet there was no panic; indeed there was an almost unnatural calm as if it was understood that this was just a nightmare from which awakening would bring escape. Moorehead and Buckley drove to Alexandria to find it strangely quiet and almost deserted; the harbour empty of warships and the Hotel Cecil, once the centre of social life, inhabited only by small groups of officers in transit who exchanged the latest rumours in whispers.

But, for the moment, Rommel had been held, or had run out of petrol and ammunition, or his men were too exhausted to continue, or a combination of all those factors. On 6th July, Moorehead cabled:

The first German assault on the Nile Delta has failed. By radio and in a special Order of the Day, the German High Command announced that the first objective was Alexandria, which was to have been entered at noon yesterday. Today, the nearest fighting German soldier is 60 miles from Alexandria . . . The battle is still going on around El Alamein.[26]

Returning to Cairo, they met Lucy and Clifford at GHQ, where she had just been ordered to burn Auchinleck's correspondence with

Churchill and the War Cabinet before being evacuated with the head-quarters to Palestine. With difficulty, Moorehead found seats for her and the baby on the night train and waved them farewell. He now made his final dispositions: he himself would remain in Cairo, while Alaric Jacob stayed with the 8th Army; James Cooper accompanied the Mediterranean Fleet; a third correspondent should go to Jerusalem and a fourth would remain in Turkey. He and Clifford then went out to dinner, which, to his surprise, was cheerful. The surprise was particularly in Clifford's uncharacteristic and unexpected optimism. While others saw nothing to prevent Rommel's triumphant entry into Cairo and all the consequent disasters they had imagined, he was convinced that the tide had turned. This was because, once again, the physics that controlled the functions of war in the desert had again become active. It was now the enemy's turn to be at the end of his communications, supplies and energy. Reinforcements were still arriving by sea for the British in Egypt, while to reach Rommel they had to cross the Mediterranean and a thousand miles of desert under risk of attack.

Throughout July, the opponents attacked and counter-attacked on the narrow front at Alamein, dominated by the low Ruweisat Ridge. When Moorehead returned to the 8th Army, together with Clifford and Buckley, he began by describing the scene of action. The British held this "rocky, yellow-coloured hogback ridge, running parallel with this coast and in sight of the sea. Whoever holds the full length of that ridge holds the Alamein position."[27]

For once, there was a battle to report within easy reach of communications and the press camp and, day after day, The Trio watched it develop. He wrote long, discursive despatches, mixing reports of tactical moves with sketches of battlefield incidents and his own sensations. "It was hot and there was no shade," he wrote on 14th July for his readers' breakfast-time newspaper next morning:

> Sitting there in the sun, smoking and drinking a mug of tea and occasionally looking through binoculars, you felt as though you were sitting in a grandstand waiting for a cup-tie to begin.
>
> It started not on the ground but in the air. A wave of Stukas and Messerschmitts swept over – going fast and low. By one of those freaks of desert air war, a big group of Boston bombers and Spitfires came over at the same time and, despite the cloudless sky, they did not see one another. Childishly one wanted to stand and shout to the Spitfires, "Look: there they are!"[28]

As always, he never forgot to include the personal stories of the men involved. He was particularly heartened to see the Australian division, which had held Tobruk in the first siege and were regarded, as he said, as "among the finest shock troops of the Empire". After visiting them, he assessed the apparent changes in their behaviour since he had seen them come ashore in 1940, and later wrote:

> To Europeans at first they had seemed boastful and quick to take offence, lax in their discipline in the field and quarrelsome on leave. The usual thing you heard was that the Australians had an inferiority complex and adopted a truculent, noisy manner to hide it. As an Australian living abroad, I had had many arguments about them. I had tried (quite unsuccessfully) to explain to Englishmen that the Australians' manner was the sign of their independence and the freedom of their way of life and that some of their physical vigour might not come amiss in England. To the Australians I tried (even more unsuccessfully) to point out that the Englishman's voice and reserve did not indicate animosity or contempt or weakness, and that some of the Englishman's quiet mental tenacity might not come amiss in Australia.[29]

Like these Australian soldiers, Moorehead himself had acquired a relaxed self-confidence through experience and achievement and the calming, thought-provoking presence of Lucy, Clifford and Buckley, but he had also had enough of war and needed a rest. He decided to alternate with Alaric Jacob in the desert and so, at the end of July, returned to Cairo, confident that Auchinleck could hold Rommel and that eventually the British would take the offensive again. He had written to Christiansen before that he was determined to take a rest and, on 6th August, he wrote again. He began with a brief summary of the military position: "We are holding Rommel on a short line and have greater strength in men, guns and tanks than he has . . . Rommel, of course, may try another offensive before the end of August but personally I believe now the thing is going to sway back and forth indefinitely."

Now he came to the point:

> In these circumstances, I would like to go away at once. It is getting on for two and a half years since I left England and came to the Middle East and it has been pretty nearly continuous work in a bad climate. If only for reasons of health, I am afraid I cannot

carry on without a break. I suppose after all this time I might ask for home leave, either in England or Australia. But Australia is so hard to get to now and there does not seem much point in my coming to England unless a second front develops. On the whole the best plan would be an American trip. I can get there direct either by air (about ten days) or by ship (something over a month) . . .

Before leaving Cairo I would like to get myself accredited to the American Army. This would enable me to take advantage of many facilities which have already been offered me by the American command here – an entrée into war factories, interviews with Army commanders and in Washington, trips with the fleet. I propose a series on the American war effort from the point of view of the man who has been watching their weapons in the field. I propose only a limited trip – six months at the longest. I shall be ready then to return to the Middle East, to go to Russia, England, Australia or anywhere you decide.[30]

The editor cabled his reply a week later: "Since you unquestionably entitled respite agree reluctantly forfeiting brilliant services Egypt critical period therefore OK arrange departure America whence commentary welcomest providing not overcritical stop if Western Europe outbreaks shall want you home quickly biggest assignment regards Christiansen."[31] It was not just the permission to go, or the prospect of his first visit to the United States that delighted Moorehead so much as the new standing that the granting of what amounted to paid leave on the other side of the world conferred upon him. It was all the more of a concession and an honour because during that August the tempo of the war again mounted and yet Christiansen did not countermand his agreement. During the week in which it arrived, a huge convoy – codenamed "Pedestal" – was steaming from Gibraltar towards Malta under the heaviest escort of warships that had ever been assembled, under constant attack and suffering heavy losses. At the same time an amphibious attack was launched against Dieppe and was repulsed by unexpectedly strong German opposition with the loss of some 3,500 men, most of them Canadians.

There were tremendous changes in the Middle East, too. Following the last British débâcle in the desert, Winston Churchill had flown to Cairo to make new political and military dispositions. On the same day as the slaughter on the French coast, he had removed Auchinleck from his command and replaced him with General Sir Harold Alexander, an imperturbable Guards officer, and given command of the 8th Army itself to Moorehead's friend, "Strafer" Gott. But, before taking over, General Gott was allowed a few days' leave; as he took off from a desert airstrip in a transport aircraft next day, two German fighters, returning from a sweep, shot it down and Gott was killed. It was then announced that his replacement would be an officer from England who was unknown to the British public and had the reputation in the British Army as something of a martinet, General Sir Bernard Montgomery.

As Moorehead prepared to leave and made final visits to his Cairo haunts – Grey Pillars, the Gezira Sporting Club, Shepheard's Hotel and the Turf Club – he tried to sum up the events that he had described since he and Clifford had first arrived in the summer of 1940. So much had happened yet so little seemed to have been achieved. The British Army was still in the Egyptian desert, only it was farther to the east and nearer to the Nile than it had been two years before. Since then, so many lives and so much effort and material of war had been expended.

What had gone wrong? Partly, Moorehead considered, it had been the superior quality of German weaponry. Their tanks were designed to present a low profile and deflect shot, whereas the British were flat-sided and under-gunned, and the Allies had nothing to match the 88mm dual-purpose, anti-tank and anti-aircraft gun. In the air, only the Spitfire fighter could match the Messerschmitt and there had been hardly any of them in the skies of the Middle East. Yet the British had failed even when they outnumbered the Germans – although that position was reversed when the Italians were involved – so that it must have been a question of morale, strategy and tactics, all of which stemmed from Rommel's brilliant generalship. In the field, the British generals tended to commit their armour piecemeal so that it had itself been outnumbered and destroyed by the more highly-concentrated Germans; the few commanders who had shown flair for desert fighting had been killed, wounded or captured. Now it would put to the test this new commander of the 8th Army, Montgomery. If he, too, failed to defeat Rommel, the war might be lost.

On 19th August, 1942, Moorehead cabled a long article, summing up his views of the past, present and future in the Middle East. He began with an optimistic forecast, "This is the last message I shall write from the Middle East for some time. Looking back over the last two and a half years, I cannot remember a situation which was more full of possibilities than this . . ."

He concluded, "When I am a long way from this country, I fancy the thing I shall remember most is the bare-backed, begoggled and dusty trooper perched on the open turret of his tank, having a last cigarette before he goes into action." It was such small touches that had brought the war home so vividly to millions far from the sound of gunfire and made Alan Moorehead famous and widely recognised, as his own newspaper put it, as "the most brilliant battle reporter the war has produced".[32]

His editor agreed that he had earned a respite from the demands of reporting news but, even though he was sailing for America, his aspirations would ensure that he would remain restless.

Chapter Eight

"I can't deal in trivialities any more"

The voyage to America was not a restful interlude. Japanese and German submarines had been active in the Indian Ocean and the crossing of the Atlantic had to be made in the face of German U-boats, long-range aircraft and surface raiders. Nor were the risks only external. Most of the passengers in the liner *Zola*, which had been converted into a cramped and uncomfortable troopship, were German prisoners from the Afrika Korps. Although, of course, guarded, other such prisoners on the ship's last passage from Egypt had plotted to seize her and force the captain to steer for Madagascar and freedom since the island was controlled by the collaborationist Vichy regime. The plot had been discovered just in time but the constant awareness of such possibilities remained.

Yet the shared degree of danger further strengthened the Mooreheads' marriage. Both of them were tired and had been almost totally preoccupied with their respective work and the war. When they could relax it had nearly always been in the company of friends, particularly Alexander Clifford. Now he was to go on leave to England, while Christopher Buckley remained in the Middle East. For the present, The Trio were separated and the Mooreheads could begin the wholly independent family life they had never known, albeit under curious circumstances.

The *Zola* was a fast, modern ship and sailed alone, eluding attack, and her progress was only slowed when she entered fog off Newfoundland. At last she docked at Halifax and the prisoners were marched ashore to begin their captivity in Canada, while the Mooreheads took the night train to New York.

They arrived towards the end of September, the beginning of the season when life in Manhattan is at its most stimulating. Yet everywhere was an atmosphere of frustration and discontent. The United States had been at war for more than nine months and the Americans wanted visible success and signs that their military and economic strength was turning the tide. True, the United States Navy had won notable victories over the Japanese at the Coral Sea and Midway but everywhere else the enemy seemed to prevail or showed no sign of flagging in offensive vigour. The Japanese had taken most of the Pacific islands west of Hawaii, most of Burma and could still threaten India and Australia. The Germans were at the gates of Egypt, held all of continental Europe that was not cowed and neutral and, in Russia, had reached Stalingrad on the Volga. Only the Italians had been soundly defeated.

Personally, Moorehead's welcome was not what it would have been had he arrived a year earlier, when he would have been lionised. Now, the Americans were more interested in their own war correspondents and first-hand accounts of battles their own troops were fighting – albeit with lack of the expected success – on the island of Guadalcanal in the South Pacific. Everybody seemed to be complaining of the lack of results. Now that their armies were available and the British had had time to re-arm after the disasters in Europe, surely the fighting against the Germans should not be left to the Russians? When was a second front – the counter-invasion of the Continent – going to be opened? In his first report to the *Express*, Moorehead quoted a New Yorker who complained to him, "Nothing ever happens. I guess it would be a good thing if the town were bombed – it would wake the people up and make them realise they are in the war."[1]

His receptive eye recorded the excitements of New York, yet these were not satisfying in the context of unrest and discontent. He went to Washington and found no answers nor any solutions, although it was obvious that, since Churchill's visit in July, a new global strategy was being planned there and in London. Something tremendous was going to happen, and quite soon, but nobody would say what it was. So he toured the war industries, describing manufacturing processes. He visited an aircraft factory at St. Louis, inland shipyards mass-producing prefabricated warships, and toured Pittsburgh steel-mills with the British ambassador, Lord Halifax, noting that he was addressed by their guide as "Your Majesty". His eye for power and colour was caught by the smelting of the iron ore in furnaces which "reduce it in a volcanic heat to a lava flow of pure metal. It hit the rollers like an explosion and burned our faces and blinded our eyes despite the blue glasses we were all wearing. Nothing I have seen on the battlefield yet eclipses the monstrous uproar of this. You have the same uncomfortable feeling that this is something uncontrollable and much bigger than the men who created it."[2]

The gigantic industrial effort bred a new impatience in him, too. Already he was feeling out of the main stream of affairs and hankered after a return. News of the war in American newspapers and on radio bore little relation to what he had known; it was often confused and contradictory and either over-pessimistic or over-optimistic. He had not been there long enough, he said, to "assess the alternative moods that swept the people from one enthusiasm to another with the regularity of the rise and fall of the tide; nor time to probe deep enough and find something" as solid underneath as the sea-bed".[3]

Late in October a cable arrived from the *Daily Express* recalling him urgently to London. He would have to travel by air, leaving Lucy and the baby to stay with friends in New York. He took the train to Montreal and, equipped with a high priority to travel and a thick fleece-lined flying-suit and boots, parachute, life-jacket and oxygen mask, boarded a four-engined Liberator bomber bound for Scotland. There were fifteen other passengers for the crossing of the Atlantic, all priority passengers of importance but treated as cargo, lying prone on the floor of the bomber, side by side, for more than ten hours. They flew all through the night and landed next morning in the clear, fresh Scottish air at Prestwick, where they had a meal and baths and were given sleeping berths on the night train from Glasgow to London.

As soon as he had landed, Moorehead noticed a new mood amongst the British in refreshing contrast to the frustration in America. Here, everybody seemed surprisingly brisk, efficient and friendly and the stuffiness that he remembered in the British character seemed to have been dispelled by war. There seemed to be a new egalitarianism abroad and it appealed to the liberalism – or even socialism – that he and his friends had found so congenial when students. A report on social insurance, prepared by the economist Sir William Beveridge, was about to be presented to the House of Commons and this, it was being said, would put an end to social deprivation. There was talk of Utopian new towns that would be built after the war, and architects' impressions of their sunlit vistas were being published.

The nationalisation of the major industries, the railways and even the banks, was being proposed and not only by Labour Party politicians but by churchmen and members of the professional classes.

This hopefulness was stimulated by the shabbiness of the bombed cities and the shortages of food – most of which was rationed – and consumer goods. It was also being promoted by many journalists, including some who worked for Lord Beaverbrook, including Tom Driberg, who was still writing the "William Hickey" column, Frank Owen, who had given up the editorship of the *Evening Standard* to join the army, Michael Foot, who had taken his place, and many more. At the *Daily Express* office Moorehead was given a hero's welcome and Christiansen told him that he had been recalled to report part of the massive military operations that were about to begin. The first was launched on 23rd October when General Montgomery began his great offensive on the El Alamein front and Moorehead read Alexander Clifford's reports of it in the *Daily Mail*. The second began on 8th November when British and American armies landed in French North Africa. Moorehead was to join the latter when they began to advance eastward to meet the 8th Army and to crush the Afrika Korps between the two. When that happened he could expect to meet Clifford and Buckley again.

He had long talks with Christiansen and Foley about the past two years and about his ambitions. He told them that he did not always want to be a newspaper journalist and hoped to become a "writer"; apart from his book *Mediterranean Front*, he had tried and failed to write a novel and had written a play set in Cairo and the desert as an exercise rather than with expectation of success. He had proved himself as a foreign correspondent, war correspondent and a bureau chief in a major theatre of war and wanted to stretch his abilities more. His superiors made it clear that he was their most highly-prized correspondent; he had brought the war and its military, political and human aspects home to their readers more vividly than ever before. The most important job for a writer in wartime was to report the war and that was why they were sending him back to North Africa.

He whiled away a week or so watching British Army training exercises with troop-carrying gliders and in the new battle-schools while awaiting passage. He had asked that this should be in one of the naval escorts accompanying an Atlantic convoy and he was ordered to Londonderry in Northern Ireland to join the frigate *Exe*, which was bound for Algiers. He had wanted to report more action at sea and was not disappointed, although this was very different

from the spectacular cruise with the Mediterranean Fleet. The sea
was cold, rough and grey, the ship was wet and cramped and alarms
of submarine attack allowed her crew little sleep. But he enjoyed the
easy-going manner of the officers and the informality which recalled
Australian ways and he admired the stoicism of those who spent
most of their year in this discomfort and danger. He was getting
accustomed to the ceaseless plunge, roll and lurch of the little ship
and the jarring explosions of depth-charges when the *Exe* was suddenly ordered back to Londonderry. Rather than take their passenger
with them, Moorehead was transferred to the destroyer *Loyal* in the
frigate's whaler in a sea thought too rough for such boat-work and
scrambled aboard with drenched baggage and an even deeper respect
for seamen.

A few days later the *Loyal* arrived off Algiers, where the gleaming
white modern buildings and the mosques and minarets of the *kasbah*
cast their reflection on the calm blue sea. He landed, booked a room
at the smart Hotel Aletti and found himself immersed more in political
intrigue than the expected demands of war.

This was the first week of 1943. In November, the Anglo-American
landings in French North Africa had been successful although this
had meant cooperation with a regime that had collaborated with the
Germans and had only just been weaned from the control of Vichy.
The flaw in the strategy was that Tunisia had not been occupied
because landings there would have been within range of German
airfields in Sicily. After assembling the new British 1st Army – its
men mostly new to war but armed with the latest weapons – in
Algeria, the overland advance towards Tunisia began. There were
administrative delays and wet weather turned ground that had been
thought suitable for tanks into glutinous mud. The enemy reacted
with customary vigour, flying in airborne troops and reinforcing
them by sea. By the end of the year, the 1st Army and a smaller
American force were literally bogged down before the German
defences in the Tunisian hills. Meanwhile, in Algiers, the senior
French officer and most notorious former collaborator with the
Germans, Admiral Darlan, had been assassinated and replaced by
General Giraud, an elderly officer of high standing, but also one
of those who had failed to defend France in 1940. "Alan Moorehead,
the famous war reporter, has arrived in Tunisia,"[4] announced the
Express over his first despatch from Algiers, a summary of the military and political situation which almost gave the impression that,
with his arrival, the campaign was about to start.

From Algiers, Moorehead set out overland for Tunisia. Professionally, the campaign was to be stimulating for he realised that his readers knew little or nothing of the problems involved or of the terrain, which most thought to be desert, but were avid for news, particularly because the British soldiers involved had so recently been at home. Personally, though, it was depressing: most of the other correspondents were new to war-reporting but had been in North Africa for a couple of months and considered themselves veterans. He missed the company of his former companions though he made friends with Philip Jordan of the *News Chronicle*, who was sophisticated and well connected amongst politicians, but only after a wary first meeting following which Jordan had described him as "that comic little party".[5] He also missed the contrast between the healthy life in the desert and the pleasures of Cairo. Here in Tunisia civilians could be involved as they rarely had been in the desert and were being killed by bombs, shells and mines.

He had been reporting these battles for little more than a fortnight when all the correspondents received orders to return at once to Algiers, no explanation being given. There they were told that they were all to be flown to an undisclosed destination next morning to report important but unspecified news. Such occasions did arise from time to time – secrecy being an obvious necessity – and were usually regarded as a welcome break from reporting in the forward areas. This flight proved otherwise. Some twenty correspondents and conducting officers boarded a Dakota transport, which took off and flew westward along the coast of North Africa. They had no idea of their destination, or of the news they were to report, and so settled down for a pleasantly smooth flight over a calm blue sea. They passed Oran, Ceuta, Gibraltar and Tangier and headed south along beaches where Atlantic rollers broke.

Then the aircraft began to turn as if for landing and, looking down, they saw a town and a port and that, they assumed, was their destination. But, as they sank lower, Moorehead, looking through the Perspex window, could read names on hoardings and shop-fronts and they were Spanish. Just then, as he later wrote, "A bright golden burst of tracer bullets broke through the floor of the cabin. Bullets were flying all round us and now we could clearly hear the rattle of the guns. I stumbled along to the door of the cockpit and shouted to the pilot . . ."[6] Another burst of fire hit the aircraft and several of those on board; one, a Canadian correspondent, was shot through the head. One of the American crew had also been hit but they managed to pull the aircraft away from the gunfire and fly out to sea. Only then did they discover what had happened. The pilot, hoping to land at the French port of Lyautey to refuel, had lost his way and approached the Spanish airfield at Larache instead. There, the anti-aircraft defences were alerted at the approach of the unidentified aircraft and tried to shoot it down. Soon after, the Dakota landed safely at Lyautey, the dead Canadian was removed, the fuel tanks were refilled and they took off for their final destination which proved to be Casablanca.

There they were sworn to secrecy and told that they had been assembled to report a meeting of "the biggest assemblage of high dignitaries ever gathered together since the war began".[7] Who these were was only revealed when the journalists were summoned to a press conference held by Winston Churchill and President Roosevelt with Generals Giraud and de Gaulle and their own commanders-in-chief, chiefs of staff and principal advisers in attendance. It was obvious that decisions of the utmost importance had been taken but nobody would say what they were or anything except that it had been a successful meeting. The only news the correspondents could send was that the conference had taken place at Casablanca.

Churchill and Roosevelt had, as was assumed, discussed the future strategy of the war. What was not known, and could not be suggested in speculation because of censorship, was that it had been decided to confine the next major efforts against Germany to the Mediterranean theatre. The American chiefs of staff had urged an early cross-Channel invasion of Europe from the British Isles, but the British considered this too risky and finally it was decided that, once North Africa was cleared of the enemy, Sicily should be invaded as a preliminary to an attack on Italy itself. The correspondents did not know this and flew back to Algiers frustrated.

It was obvious that the Germans could not be cleared from Tunisia for many weeks until the Allied forces advancing from the west could join with those now arriving from the east. In January, the 8th Army had at last achieved its original aim of driving 1,400 miles through Libya and capturing Tripoli, though Rommel was still resisting fiercely and had prepared two strong defensive systems along two ravines, Wadi Zigzaou and Wadi Akarit in southern Tunisia. Moorehead would have to be there for the junction of the armies – and to meet Clifford, who he knew would be with the vanguard of the 8th Army – but in the intervening period there was an opportunity which he could not bear to miss. He was offered a flight to London in a B17 Flying Fortress bomber on a courier flight for General Eisenhower. It was not that he needed leave so much but that he desperately wanted to resolve his future. This would give him the opportunity to tell Christiansen of his frustrations and ambitions, although he hardly knew what the latter were beyond achieving literary fame and being reunited with his wife and child.

The arrival in London and another hero's welcome was gratifying but he was unhappy. It was not only that he was tired of travelling but by the continual flow of demands from his newspaper for more exclusive news, confirmation of rumours, interviews with those who could not be reached or would not talk and constant pressure for extra efforts which might be neither possible nor necessary. He had come to envy his contemporaries in the armed services, who simply performed as effectively as they could, as George Millar and Geoffrey Cox had. He longed for the rough simplicities of a soldier's life and decided that he would resign from the *Daily Express* and join the army.

He wrote to Lucy in New York, telling her of this decision and of what followed:

I told Christiansen that I would not continue with the *Express* after you had returned to England . . . I worked it out that if I joined the Army I would have at least four months' training in England when I could see you and John fairly constantly. And I would have some machine to which I could attach myself, some security in the world, something more tangible than this fickle irresponsible job. I want the quality of inevitability in my life. Puss, you understand. We have no home anywhere. At least if I were in the Army I would be identified. It would be better for you. You would know that I was in something definite. There would be all the routine to buoy us up. C. said I was mad. I tried to explain and little by little he began to see. He said, "I see it's no use offering you more money" and then a little later, after we had argued all day, he really did see.

I did not attempt to go into all the mental sickness I feel over the Beveridge Report* and over the Darlan politics of North Africa. I suppose I am in something of the same state Geoffrey Cox was at the fall of France – the feeling that I just can't deal in trivialities any more.[8]

* He feared that the social security plan was to be shelved indefinitely.

He was then summoned to spend the weekend with Lord Beaverbrook at Cherkley Court near Leatherhead. At once they argued about
tanks, with the former Minister of Supply – he had resigned early
in 1942 – trying and failing to persuade the war correspondent that
he had been inaccurate and unfair. Then, as he wrote to Lucy:

> We fought all Saturday afternoon about the Beveridge Report
> and the North African politics – and then again on Sunday. He
> told me a lot of secret things and at least appeared to be sincere
> and kindly as he talked. He would, I think, really like to see me
> in a place of some power after the war and he said several times
> he is convinced I can take a big part. He doesn't see that my world
> and his are irreconcilable. He's Right. I am Left. I will not sell out
> and he cannot.
>
> He said he could not presume to advise me if I wanted to
> join the Army – and then said I would be a damn fool.[9]

Beaverbrook and Christiansen had decided that Moorehead must
not be allowed to go. They were aware that other editors would
be bidding for his services – although they did not know that the
editor Gerald Barry had already tried to persuade him to join his
Liberal newspaper, the *News Chronicle* – and so his wishes, and
even whims, must be met. Christiansen at once agreed that he could
fly home on leave when Lucy returned from America. There was no
reason why he should not return to work in the London office for a
while. Beaverbrook offered to move Foley to the *Evening Standard* so
that Moorehead could take his place as foreign editor, but he rejected
this at once as a betrayal of his superior.

Then the managing director, E.J. Robertson, sent for him and
Moorehead quoted his proposals verbatim to Lucy:

> We have never had for years the right kind of foreign editor
> [he told Moorehead], never had anyone who understands foreign
> news. We want to entirely reorganise our foreign staff. We want
> to stop this business of sending people rushing all over the world.
> We want to send off our men for three or four years at a time –
> send them to Moscow with their families, their furniture and tell
> them to make a life there and really get to know the place. We
> want to bind together the staffs of all three papers – the *Express*,
> the *Sunday Express* and the *Standard*. We want someone to re-
> organise the whole thing. Someone who will make the appointments

and then from time to time travel around seeing the correspondents and keeping in touch with what is going on. We think you
will be able to do that. He was talking, of course, vaguely for
the future. But just for a moment I felt enthusiasm again.[10]

Finally, Christiansen told him that Foley himself needed a change.
He would be willing to take Moorehead's place, covering the war
in the Mediterranean theatre, while he occupied the foreign editor's
chair for a spell. Moorehead told Lucy:

> If, darling, in all this I have seemed arrogant and over-confident
> and conceited, then, darling, I do not care. I simply do not care.
> I do not want from them money or praise – I just want to be
> with you and try to become sane again. Really at times now I
> do not think I am sane. In all these negotiations I have always
> thought, "Lucy will agree, Lucy will say yes and support me." I
> am so utterly dependent on you. It is just the same dependence
> that John has and I need you desperately at times.[11]

He was supported by the company of their friends in London.
There was his urbane publisher Hamish Hamilton, now in the
army, who had married their friend from Rome, Contessa Yvonne
Pallavicino; Sidney Bernstein, who had been in the film industry and
was now involved in psychological warfare, and his wife Zoë, who had
worked with Lucy for the *Daily Express*; Noel Monks and his wife
Mary Welsh; Osbert and Karen Lancaster. His second book, *A Year
of Battle*, was doing well; Hamish Hamilton had ordered a first run
of 7,500 copies and had commissioned a third book to cover the
end of the war in Africa; eventually, all three would be published as a
trilogy. Most heartening of all, "Jamie" Hamilton himself was telling
him that, after the war, he would be able to live on his earnings as
an author. "So, even if the *Express* project falls through, my way is
set for after the war," he wrote to Lucy. "I shall have to make the
big decision – Fleet Street or books – I still madly incline to books
but will not decide until I have seen you."[12]

Moorehead was much in demand at dinner parties in London with
everybody anxious to meet him and hear his uncensored views on the
war. In Lucy's absence, he was usually paired with an unattached
woman, whose husband might be serving abroad or who was single,
and he again took up the sport of flirtation without emotional involvement and found it entertaining, harmless and no betrayal of his wife.

There were talks over lunch and dinner in restaurants with politicians, publishers and writers: John Strachey, who was joining the Labour Party; Tom Driberg, who also had political aspirations and was "as active as a flea in the lobbies";[13] Kingsley Martin, the ascetic editor of the *New Statesman*; Vernon Bartlett, the political commentator; Michael Foot, editor of the *Evening Standard*, who "looks so tired".[14] The attractions of a future literary life in London became pleasantly apparent.

He was sensitive to the moods of London and Londoners and wrote in an article about his reactions on his return:

> London to me was always a place where things happened at second hand. Battles were fought here on a map and the gold mines of Peru were worked on a string of figures in the City. The rest of the world flowed by in the newspapers, remote and full of vicarious thrills – and nothing ever happened. The Blitz has changed all that . . . the audience suddenly became the actors.

He sensed, too, that wartime propaganda often struck a false note and that the British knew what rang true. "A small thing most of them did not like was the ringing of the church bells over the Alamein victory," he wrote. "They thought it was a mis-timed gesture, too premature, too optimistic and slightly theatrical into the bargain."[15]

He stayed in London for less than a fortnight. It was agreed that when Lucy returned in April or May, he could change places with Foley for a while and only then would his long-term future be considered. For the moment, thoughts of joining the army – or, as he might have put it in more reflective days, running away from a difficulty – were set aside. He flew back to Algiers in the same aircraft as his new friend Philip Jordan. They stopped in Lisbon – with time to watch a carnival in Estoril – and again at Gibraltar, where the Governor, General Mason-Macfarlane, who was known for his socialist views, took them on a tour of the tunnels linking his headquarters and barracks, magazines, hospitals and fuel tanks dug deep in the Rock. On 10th March, they arrived at Algiers, where there were eight letters from Lucy awaiting him and, before going to bed, he typed a long and anguished letter to her, raking over the talks he had had in London and pouring out his love and need for her:

> I am a bit tired after today's flight, but I must be very lucid because I have a million things to say . . . I do not feel very lucid. Puss, I

am growing old in wanting you. I do not feel able somehow at this moment to write cheerfully when I think of how sad it has been for you. Every word you write makes me see how terrible it has been for you, how lonely, how difficult, how much of a strain. And now that I have achieved everything – have arranged everything for us to be together in May, I am suddenly quite exhausted. May seems an eternity and I am wandering lost in all this impossible interval. I do not *want* to be here. I hate it. I hate everywhere you are not . . . I simply cannot think of anything but meeting you. My dear, it is just that I am so tired. I am not being very lucid. Your letters – they somehow have rushed at me and I have so much emotion I cannot think. It is almost painful to read of John, I want to see him so much. And I am so much in love with you. Well, it's two months more. Surely to God you and John will come safely across the Atlantic. Darling, I will stop this jumble. I feel better now I have made this outburst.[16]

Next morning, rested, he wrote a postscript:

I have had a big sleep, puss, and feel better this morning . . . Dear puss. How did we grow so inter-dependent on one another? "That two souls inter-inanimate may lie" and you remember that time I was saying the rest of the piece to you, saying it was impossible for two people in love not to be together "else a great prince in prison lies".

Darling, I am so steadfast for you, I believe in you so much . . . Twice in your letters you say we will have another baby. I have never altered from wanting that increasingly. I want to now more than ever. If there is nothing else I ever do in the world, I will make you happy and proud in England.[17]

He now had to make the long journey back to Tunisia and the war. There had been heavy fighting as Rommel, who had taken command of all Axis forces there including his Afrika Korps, tried to break either the 1st or the 8th Army, between which he was about to be caught. In February, he had come within sight of success when he broke through the inexperienced American defenders of the Kasserine Pass in Tunisia in an attempt to turn the whole Allied front.

When Moorehead reached the 1st Army front, Rommel's last counter-attack against Montgomery had failed and realising that he was hopelessly outnumbered – his 120,000 men and 200 tanks against more than 500,000 men and 1,800 tanks – he handed over command to General von Arnim and left Tunisia for sick leave in Germany. On 20th March, the 8th Army assaulted the Mareth Line in the south, while the enemy's rear lines of communications were attacked from the west by the United States 2nd Corps under the command of the vigorous and flamboyant General Patton, whom Moorehead described as "a large and gregarious man with a fine weather-beaten face and a pearl-handled revolver strapped to his side".[18] After a week's heavy fighting Montgomery broke through the Mareth defences and, on 11th April, the 1st and 8th Armies met on the coast near Sousse.

Moorehead was with a few other correspondents in the vanguard of the 1st Army, driving through hilly country and wary of ambush. He wrote later:

We had come in off a side road and just for a moment it seemed that we had made a bad mistake. The vehicles running up the main road were all German or Italian. Then, drawing closer, I saw the British troops in the lorries. The British desert soldier looks like a rather rakish and dishevelled Boy Scout, the effect, I suppose, of his bleached khaki shorts and shirt and the paraphernalia of blackened pots and pans and oddments he carries round in his vehicle which is his home. He practically never wears a helmet and he has a careless, loose-limbed way of walking which comes from living on the open plains . . . These youths were burnt incredibly by the sun and they had that quality of brimming health that made them shout and sing as they went along.[19]

This was the vanguard of the 8th Army.

A sand-coloured armoured car approached them, a sergeant leant from its turret and shouted, "Who are you?" "The 1st Army." Then he shouted back, "You can go home now."[20]

Moorehead made for Sousse because he expected to find Clifford in the town where the two armies would formally link. They met in the main street, Clifford and Geoffrey Keating having just arrived. For a moment, Clifford, seeing Moorehead riding down the street in a jeep, had simply recognised his friend. "Then abruptly I remembered that they were all 1st Army correspondents,"[21] he said later, and realised the significance of the meeting. Immediately after the reunion, they all automatically took up the duties that each had performed when they had travelled together in the desert. Moorehead remembered:

147

Within the hour we had broken open and entered a comfortable villa by the sea. One man had gone off to ferret for wine, another to clean the house, a third to cook. I would no more have dreamed of interfering with Clifford's cooking than he would have thought of instructing me on the lighting of the stoves or the unpacking of the trunks. Keating always procured the petrol and the rations, and so it went on.[22]

While Clifford cooked, Moorehead poured two mugs of whisky and then laid out their bedrolls on the floor of an upstairs room. It was not until they had eaten with Keating and others and found themselves alone that, as Moorehead put it, "we took up the conversation that had been broken off in Cairo half a year before."[23]

For the next ten days, Moorehead travelled with the 8th Army, delighting in meeting old friends from the desert. Victory in Africa now seemed in sight but first the Allies had to capture Tunis, Bizerta and Cape Bon, where the enemy would have his back to the sea, and these were defended by a ring of mountain strongholds, the most formidable of which was named Longstop Hill. This could only be taken by a formal, frontal assault and that was launched on 23rd April. The battle ranged over the bare hillsides for three days and the correspondents were often with the forward troops, their despatches sent back by runner, despatch-rider and aircraft to Algiers for transmission.

After the attacks and counter-attacks among the bleak hills, this was a grand, set-piece battle offering the drama and spectacle that Moorehead described so well. More poignantly than any other correspondent he was able to relate this with the soldiers themselves as much as with the strategy that had brought it about. On 27th April, his despatch, typed on the heights of the contested hill, began:

The last Germans were flung off Longstop Hill this morning and this I believe to be the turning-point of the campaign . . . A blinding hot sun blazes down on the scrub and there is a watery heat-haze on each succeeding height. As you tramp upward, you are half-choked with fine white dust from returning ambulances and tanks and then sweat makes runnels through the dust on your arms and face as you go higher and get hotter . . . You reach the top of each ridge only to find another ahead and there you see the front-line infantry . . . Men lie about, half in, half out of the trench, not talking much but smoking, waiting, watching.

Each time a shell comes over, they cock their heads slightly, listen shrewdly to its whine, which gives the direction, and then relax, hardly bothering to look where it falls in billowing smoke – perhaps half a mile away, perhaps 200 yards, but anyway not in the trench.[24]

Amongst the correspondents and, indeed, officers who found themselves commanding troops in action for the first time, Moorehead was regarded as an authority in military matters. His intimacy with the old soldiers of the 8th Army had been noted and his friends among the American correspondents – such as young Drew Middleton of the *New York Times*, who had reported the air fighting that was now known as the Battle of Britain and the Blitz – made a point of telling their fellow countrymen of this. So, particularly in American sectors of the front, it was quite usual for battalion-commanders to explain the current tactical situation and then ask him what he thought the 8th Army would have done.

When Longstop Hill was taken, the way to Tunis lay open and, as the first Allied patrols entered the city on 7th May, street fighting began with snipers and in sudden confrontations with Germans on the streets. Resistance collapsed quickly and the leading British armoured cars drove into the centre of the city, taking it by surprise. Moorehead remarked:

Hundreds of Germans were walking in the streets, some with their girlfriends. Hundreds more were sitting drinking aperitifs in a big pavement café . . . The Germans rose from their seats and stared . . . In the hair-dressing salon next door, more Germans struggled out of the chairs and, with white sheets round their necks and lather on their faces, stood gaping.[25]

After Tunis, the port of Bizerta fell and then there was only the headland of Cape Bon from which the survivors of the German and Italian armies hoped to be evacuated by sea. They were disappointed for there was escape for very few. On 13th May, they surrendered and some 180,000 prisoners were marched away to prison-camps.

With the expulsion of the enemy from Africa, Moorehead saw that more than a geographical phase of the war had ended. He forecast in a long summary of the campaigns:

The war of fast movement is finished. From now on we have to stand and fight on a line and go right on fighting until the line is broken. Mud and mountains, mines and concealed guns, snipers and sabotage – these are the sort of things we have got to break. We might as well say goodbye to the old hectic days of great flanking moves, of massed tank charges, of sudden piratical raids and the old game of bluff . . . Henceforth you can expect us to start battles with aircraft and artillery and finish them with tanks.[26]

Having sent their final despatches, Moorehead and Clifford rummaged through the enemy camps, selecting a Volkswagen car and loading it with loot: wine, cameras, typewriters, binoculars and sheepskin coats. Then they set off for Algiers, three days distant, stopping when the mood took them to swim in the sea. On arrival they were obliged by the military police to surrender their booty but, for Moorehead, any disappointment was forgotten on hearing from London that he was to fly home immediately to meet Lucy and that his place in Algiers was to be taken by Foley.

On 21st May, he arrived in England and the family was reunited. It was not as idyllic as he had expected. After the first delight in meeting, the future clouded over again. Christiansen made it clear to him that the exchange of jobs with Foley was to be brief and that he would return to war-reporting in less than three months' time. He was told that as the newspaper's star correspondent he could not be spared, particularly now that the invasion of the Continent was imminent.

Lucy was appalled. She had arrived in London expecting to set up house with her husband, whose wish had been to be reunited with her and their baby, only to discover that he had agreed to return to the work he had claimed to hate. She was despairing at the prospect of further long separations. Had he been in the armed forces and obeying orders to go overseas again there would have been no choice. What hurt her was that they both knew he could dictate his own terms to the *Daily Express* and take his pick of other well-paid jobs in Fleet Street but he seemed to have put his ambition first. He himself was defensive and abrupt and spoke harshly about the realities of his work. It was not a happy interlude and he flew back to Algiers at the beginning of August, leaving her sad and seeking comfort as the guest of Osbert and Karen Lancaster at their house in Addison Crescent.

Much had happened since he had left for England in May. On

10th July, the Allies had invaded Sicily; the fighting had been far heavier and the cost in casualties higher than expected, but now the campaign seemed almost over, with the two Allied field commanders, Montgomery and Patton, vying with each other for glory. Clifford and Buckley were already in Sicily and Moorehead planned to join them, but he felt none of the contented excitement of the days when he had left Lucy safely in Cairo to drive into the desert for a few weeks before a happy return to their exotic domesticity.

He wrote to her:

Perhaps I have always been a little afraid of you, a little too anxious to live up to you and avoid ridicule. I begin to see that I never acknowledged that you could be dependent on me; and now I feel the damage is done. You came back to England with this feeling of dependence and found that I did not accept it. And so I suppose now you might be in the process of making your own life without me. What can I say? I can't forever ask you to go on and on waiting. You can't, I suppose, live on my ambitions with me absent as well. God knows what you must have thought of me in London. That I was callous and indifferent. Even that it was impossible for us to be together happily. What on earth can I say? I suppose the thing to say is, all right, I behaved atrociously in London and I must pay for it. I should say – I expect that while I am away you will probably grow fonder of someone else and have a love affair and that I have no right to interfere. But it's no use, my darling, I could say that a million times and it would not be true. Whenever I think of you with someone else I simply have this frightening choking feeling and I can't stand it and I will never be able to stand it because it is too much and I am in love with you . . .

I seem to have imaginary terrors all around me about you. Incredible, you who are so true and have accepted so much from me. Well, I am in love with you. God knows that is hardly enough. I have to be with you to put this love into practice and then we see how badly I behaved in England. Why did I? I feel no conscience about it. I know I behaved exactly as I felt compelled. And now I hate myself for all the things I did not do and would do now. It is always like this . . . There is blackmail in all this, of course. I so passionately want you to wait for me now that I am constructing this mental chastity belt in this letter, telling you how I love you so that you will wait.

For my part, I have no will but to get back to you and John and have another baby. I bitterly regret that we did not start a baby before I left. Well, we will . . . How I love you. I am still a little afraid of you and there is a pride in you, a mixture of things, but mostly I love you . . . There is so much pain in being in love with you.[27]

Then he went back to the war.

Chapter Nine

"It was almost heart-breaking"

When Alan Moorehead flew to Sicily in the second week of August, the campaign was nearing its end, and again he seemed to carry his readers with him, showing them the island with fresh eyes:

> I was over the Sicilian Narrows soon after dawn this morning, a calm sea, no Luftwaffe anywhere . . . Suddenly Sicily was below and for some reason I found it a slight shock that the country is so burned up and brown, almost a monotone of brown and a dryness that reminds you of the desert. The air is hot and dry and the dust almost as thick as you will find it anywhere from Tobruk to Tripoli . . .
>
> For twenty miles we flew on over the same brown landscape with its sun-baked ridges and terraced valleys, all locked in the same hard midsummer heat. Even Etna, floating above a lake of clouds, did not look cool. My aircraft put down into an olive-tree-skirted airfield ten times as busy as Croydon was in the old days.[1]

On arrival, he set out to find Alexander Clifford and met him that afternoon at the press camp outside Lentini asleep under a mosquito-net suspended from an orange tree. As Clifford awoke from his siesta, it became apparent that he had changed since their last meeting in North Africa. He looked thinner, pale and tired and, Moorehead noted, now had "a wariness, a certain inward preoccupation. The transition to Europe, he said, had been unexpectedly upsetting. Things were very different from the desert."[2]

There it had been a clear-cut contest between armies with civilians and cities seldom involved. Clifford had not enjoyed the desert and had simply endured its discomforts and dangers. But this was the beginning of Europe with its rich history and here the people and architecture were a product of many European conquerors from Greeks to Normans. Sicily was almost home to an educated European and it was disturbing to see it being ground to ruin between the opposing war machines.

This was illustrated that same evening when an hysterical peasant appealed to them for help: his daughter was being raped by a soldier. The soldier was a North African – a Berber *goum* with the Free French – and, as he was armed and probably dangerous, the two correspondents drove to the nearest French command post for help. Next morning, the peasant, still shocked and not only by his daughter's rape, told them that French soldiers had come, taken the Berber out of his house and shot him.

Yet Clifford also seemed to have gained in self-confidence. During Moorehead's absence from the 8th Army, he had been regarded as its most celebrated correspondent and had responded accordingly. When he had been the only correspondent reporting an operation – like the occupation of the island of Pantellaria – his reports were pooled and had even appeared in the *Daily Express*. He wrote better English and tighter prose than his friend but his despatches lacked the compellingly conversational, button-holing appeal of Moorehead's.

Christopher Buckley had often been with him and he too had won admiration and not only by his reporting. In battle, he had shown himself to be not so much brave as fearless, which seemed all the more remarkable since he had never lost the looks and manner of a middle-aged schoolmaster on holiday. Before the assault landing on the south coast of Sicily, he himself had noted, "I knew that I ought to be feeling frightened. In fact, I felt nothing of the sort, only the tingling sense of excitement that one knows just before the curtain goes up on a new play which you have every reason to believe you are going to enjoy."[3] Since then he had often been with the fighting troops, and in the ferocious battle for the bridge of Prima Sole the infantry officer, who had taken him as far forward as it was possible to go, kept talking about this strange journalist who seemed to have no fear. Indeed, his daring seemed so gratuitous that other correspondents joked that it must give him a masochistic thrill.* In counterpoint to this were his donnish ways. Once, he recorded, he dozed in the shade of a tree just behind the lines one hot afternoon "murmuring such tags of Theocritus and Horace as I could recall and throwing in an occasional polite 18th century pastoral couplet".[4] When asked his opinion of other war-reporting, he was likely to favour that of Thucydides as "the best continuous piece of war correspondence".[5] There was one aspect of land warfare that worried him, however, because human qualities were not directly involved and that was the danger of mines, buried and invisible.

Together again, The Trio set off for an objective that would combine military importance with its reputation for being one of the most beguiling places in Europe. Taormina, overlooking the straits of Messina and Italy beyond, was said to be as beautiful and exotic as anywhere in the Mediterranean and from there they could report, and probably watch, the flight of the enemy to the mainland and the attempt to follow them. So it was that a month after the invasion of Sicily and a week after Moorehead's arrival on the island, the three of them walked along the coastal road towards Taormina, perched amongst its bougainvillea and cypress trees on the cliffs above the sea. Characteristically, Buckley described this view as "like a vision of the Celestial City in a child's illustrated edition of *Pilgrim's Progress*",[6] while Moorehead wrote to Lucy that it was "a glamour resort much like Capri".[7]

The road was ostensibly defended by Italian troops but they had even less heart for fighting since the news on 25th July that Mussolini had been deposed by his own Grand Fascist Council. Italy was still at war with the Allies but it seemed only a matter of time before terms of surrender were agreed and the defenders did not want to die at such a moment. So as the three journalists walked towards Taormina, Italian soldiers came towards them with white flags, their hands above their heads in surrender. "Taormina now was directly above us and it is one of the fairest sights in the Mediterranean," Moorehead reported. "A 1,000-foot cliff laced with vines rises sheer from the sea and along the lip of its dizzy heights stand the great luxury hotels in their flowering gardens."

As the three journalists climbed the flights of stone steps up the face of this cliff more Italian soldiers appeared before them, trying

* The same fearlessness was to be shown by his friend Clare Hollingworth when reporting the wars of the 1960s, as the author remembers from experience.

to surrender, and were told to throw their weapons over the edge. At the top, he wrote, "Girls came out to link arms with us. A stately old man offered us his villa. A French-speaking maitre d'hôtel offered me his whole hotel. There was a look on their faces I can hardly describe – a look of shining joy."[8] Also at the top was Geoffrey Keating, as they might have expected. Now a major and with a command 160-strong, he was still likely to be "swanning" ahead of the vanguard, looking out for the best billet and the most promising source of food and drink.

Soon after their arrival, General Montgomery drove into the town with his operations officer, Brigadier Belchem, in his staff car. He cast an eye over the sumptuous scenery and sniffed the scented gardens, then turned to his companion and said, "We must keep the troops out of this place. It smells of love. It would take their minds off the war."[9] This did not apply to himself, for he set up his own headquarters there; nor did it apply to The Trio, who did likewise. They chose one of the empty hotels with a view along the coast to the smoking volcanic cone of Etna and across the blue straits to the mountains of Italy, and picked the best rooms.

Moorehead wrote to Lucy on 18th August:

Alex and I have a room a thousand feet above the sea and the war for the time being is over. Geoffrey Keating has a villa a little higher up the mountain and we go up there each evening to play bridge. Outside our hotel window we can see Italy very clearly. There is a big moon and we sleep on our balcony with just mosquito nets over us. It is a strange life, very full in talk and things to do but empty somehow without you.[10]

The day before, he wrote, the conquest of Sicily had been completed although most of the defenders – nearly 40,000 Germans and more than 60,000 Italians – had been successfully ferried across to the mainland. There the Germans, at least, would await the next move: the invasion of Italy by the Allies, which everybody now assumed was more likely than any of the other alternatives – landings in the South of France or the Balkans, or even the ultimate counter-offensive across the Channel from England, though that now seemed out of the question for 1943. The main force for the next invasion was to be the new Anglo-American 5th Army now forming in North Africa under its American commander, General Mark Clark. The Trio were outraged to hear that they were not amongst the correspondents

chosen to accompany the assault and would have to remain with
the 8th Army, which would, they understood, be assigned a lesser
and probably diversionary task.

Moorehead wrote to Lucy:

A whole lot of unknown correspondents, who have never seen
a shot fired, have been raked in from London. Possibly the
trouble is the newspapers are against pooling and won't let their
senior correspondents be shared with other papers. This is a nice
conceited view for us to take but we do feel angry, especially as
we are forbidden to leave the island. Any rate I fancy when the
thing starts we will find a way.[11]

They began to find a way by detaching themselves from the 8th
Army's Public Relations officers and attaching themselves to Geoffrey
Keating's Army Film and Photographic Unit, which had plenty of
transport and, through its commanding officer, influence. Keating
had become friends with General Montgomery soon after the latter's
arrival in the Egyptian desert by photographing him in varieties of eye-
catching headgear – finally in the famous black beret with two badges –
so as to make him familiar to his troops and the newspaper-readers of
the world. Clifford and Buckley had got to know him, too, and, soon
after the final conquest of Sicily, Moorehead told Lucy, "Geoffrey
took me and Alex to tea with Montgomery the other day and I must
say I found him very charming indeed."[12] Another friendship had
been struck and a week later he was writing, "Ever since I met him,
I am becoming more attached to Montgomery."[13] A few days after
that he continued:

Have had a number of talks quite privately with Montgomery
now and find him fascinating, a curiously direct missionary, hard-
headed and shrewd and with this gaiety and good humour. He is
very easy to talk to and very quick in conversation. His methods
in meeting the troops are quite brilliant – a mixture of shrewd
showmanship and genuine devotion. Though a much lesser figure,
he is astonishingly like Gandhi, the same painfully thin figure, the
same sort of gaiety and naturalness. He is worshipped.[14]

The general responded by asking for copies of Moorehead's three
books – the third, *The End in Africa*, was about to be published in
London, again by Hamish Hamilton – and suggested that, when the

8th Army crossed the straits to Italy, he and his immediate colleagues might like to accompany him. The general's staff officers, most of them old friends from the desert, were always helpful and hospitable, notably his chief of staff, Major-General "Freddie" de Guingand, a South African who found an affinity with the Australian journalist and had taken a particular liking to the dashing Geoffrey Keating; and Major Bill Williams, his Intelligence officer, who had been a history don at Oxford and so had much in common with Christopher Buckley.

There was now a lull while the 5th Army prepared to sail from North African ports and the 8th to spring across the straits but none of the journalists in Sicily knew whether it would last days or weeks. Meanwhile they enjoyed an extraordinary holiday from stress. Clifford had gone to Cairo for a fortnight's leave, so Moorehead and several others moved into a villa near Keating's and established what they later described as their "Taormina Summer School". As Moorehead described it in a letter to his wife:

> While we wait, we are drifting into a sort of holiday atmosphere of bridge and swimming and mild parties. All far too masculine. Really Taormina is heavenly, one bright hot day after another. Sometimes I take a car down to the sea and gather baskets of grapes and plums. Dear puss, does it madden you to hear of all these good things? We had perfect gins and french last night and I thought madly of you. Geoffrey and I took a jeep yesterday and drove for miles through the higher villages around Etna. All the time the Italian mainland is plainly in view. It is as though one was looking from one bank of the Thames to another.[15]

The life was even more idyllic than he described it to her. He was to recall with relish the succession of blissful days. How he slept on the terrace and was woken by the sun "hitting Taormina full in the face. Everything – the ravines that tumbled down to the sea, the houses perching on the crests, the pine trees outside and even the wine bottles left on the terrace from the previous night – was cast into full light or full shadow."[16] There would be swimming in the transparent sea during the morning, then lunch on the terrace in the shade of palm leaves spread as an awning, trying a new chilled white wine, often in the company of two beautiful young Italian girls, who lived next door and whose mother would allow them to visit during the lunch hour but would, together with her husband, chaperone them when they were invited to dine.

"There were always guests for lunch, young soldiers we had known for months or years in Africa," he remembered. "In half an hour, they came under the spell of the sun and the wine and the food. All the desire for talk, talk for its own sake, that had been bottled up through the campaign, began to come out."

Then there would be a siesta and a later afternoon excursion before the evening's entertainment at the villa. He wrote later:

It was towards the end of dinner at the villa that the real arguments used to rage. The atmosphere was more than a little undergraduate. Topics began with violent generalizations and ran quickly into abstracts . . . We made a hundred extravagant sublimations on any theme – food and chess, paintings and gambling, books and wine, music and clothes . . . And now this villa, full of wine and talk and comfort, became an unreal and child-like fantasy and its warm and excited atmosphere was that which children feel at the height of a Christmas or birthday party. It was an intimacy created by three years of the war, but well apart from the war . . .

The moon coming over Italy turned Taormina into a series of tossing crests and rocky spikes, and here we sat on our own crest, nothing but lighted empty space around us.[17]

Sometimes they would wander down to the piazza with the Italian girls and their parents and sit at a café table, drinking more wine while being serenaded by a tenor accompanied by mandolins. Sometimes they discussed the war as it would affect their own lives. They would complain about their exclusion from the main invasion and accord grudging admiration to Moorehead's old friend Noel Monks, who had made his way to Algiers and managed to become accredited to the United States Army, who were said to be lavish with their transport and communications. They talked about their aspirations and Moorehead announced that, once France was liberated, he would like to stay in Paris as his newspaper's senior correspondent there until the war ended. He was so taken with the idea that he wrote to Foley, who was now back at his desk in London, suggesting it. Those who were married talked about their wives and children: several knew Lucy and spoke about her with admiration and the *Manchester Guardian* correspondent, Evelyn Montague, who was soon to be sent home with tuberculosis and whose judgement Moorehead trusted, said that he must send John to an English public school and then they must settle in England. "Well, I don't know," remarked Moorehead, in the letter reporting this to Lucy, "you must have some sunshine first."[18]

At the beginning of September, it was obvious that the invasion of Italy was imminent. Clifford returned from leave and General Montgomery invited them to his headquarters near Messina to make arrangements. The straits were to be crossed on the fourth anniversary of the declaration of war and, on the night of 2nd September, The Trio drove through the darkness to the hillsides where five hundred guns of the 8th Army were to open the campaign with a bombardment of Italy.

The guns fired an hour before dawn, lighting the rocks and olive groves with their flashes. Half an hour later, they stopped and the invasion had begun. At his headquarters, Montgomery showed the correspondents the points on the map where his soldiers had landed and invited them to accompany him in a naval launch in their wake. Stepping ashore in Italy, they followed the general on a brief tour of inspection for it had become apparent that the coast was undefended: the Germans had gone and what Italian soldiers there were did not want to fight. Moorehead had already seen the effect of Montgomery's strange personality on his troops and the confidence his little lectures on simple certainties inspired. Following the general's car in a jeep, he noted, as he told Lucy, "The troops in Italy when we landed kept cheering, their faces lighting up, along the roads – it was almost heart-breaking."[19]

Other landings had been made along the southern shores of Italy and it became apparent that there would be no serious fighting. Presumably the Germans were concentrating their own forces to meet the landing of the 5th Army and would place no reliance on the Italians who were by this time their allies in name only. This attack, Moorehead now knew, was to follow a week later and was to coincide with the declaration of an armistice between Italy and the Allies. The landing was to be on the wide beaches to the south of Salerno and it was hoped that the Germans would hear that the Italians had abandoned them as the landing-craft approached and would themselves withdraw. In the event of an unforeseen disaster to the Allied plans, the 8th Army was already ashore in the far south and their beach-head could eventually become the main thrust into Italy instead of a diversion.

The assault on the Salerno beaches began in the early hours of 9th September. Seven hundred ships and landing-craft put ashore 55,000 British and American troops – more than half of them British – who were to be followed by a further 115,000, far outnumbering the

German divisions that were being hurriedly deployed to oppose
them. The Italians had laid down their arms in accordance with the
armistice, which had been declared, as planned, to coincide with the
landings, but the defence was vigorous and soon the Allies were in
danger of being split by armoured attacks and driven into the sea.
For the correspondents with the 8th Army in the peaceful south of
the country it was frustrating to hear news of this without being
able to report it, and to know that only one British newspaper
correspondent had been allowed to accompany the British troops to
Salerno. Several, including Moorehead and Clifford, decided to act
without permission and attempt to reach the 5th Army overland,
although this would mean travelling through country occupied by
the enemy.

Two small parties of correspondents – one of them including
Buckley – set out in the hope of reaching the Salerno beach-head
overland, followed by Moorehead and Clifford in one of Keating's
fifteen-hundredweight trucks. They were known throughout the 8th
Army and had no difficulty reaching the most forward and northerly
positions but there they were told that they would henceforth be
on their own, that the Germans had blown the bridges and were
patrolling with armoured cars. The two jeeps had gone ahead and
not necessarily by the same route so the truck headed blindly up
the road winding two hundred miles to Paestum, where they had
heard General Clark had set up his headquarters. They kept to the
coast road, with the sea to their left and the bare, brown hills to
their right, and the unknown ahead. At each village they reached,
Clifford would ask in Italian for news of the enemy and usually be
told that they had departed the night before or even that the patrols
had been seen that day. Sometimes Clifford would telephone to the
next *carabinieri* post to ask if the road ahead was clear of Germans.
When he heard that it was not, they turned into the hills.

Danger came not only from the Germans. The other party of
correspondents was ahead on the same inland road and, when
halted in a village, they heard the sound of an engine behind them,
expected it to be a German armoured car and laid an ambush. Just
in time, they recognised an 8th Army truck and held their fire. All
were now together amongst the enemy and narrowly escaped capture
when a patrol passed by a monastery where they were sleeping and
had parked their transport in the courtyard. Finally, when they were
within twenty miles of their destination, they found that the bridges
had been blown, but not by Germans, for the empty food-cans and

packets of cigarettes were American. After many detours they came upon a bridge where soldiers in khaki could be seen preparing demolition charges. They were engineers of the 5th Army.

At General Clark's headquarters, the correspondents were welcomed, as was their news that the country between the two Allied armies was almost clear of the enemy and there was nothing to prevent a junction. However, the beach-head was under heavy attack and there was no possibility of attempting that for the moment. Although the Germans had so far committed less than the Allies' force of seven divisions at Salerno, they held the initiative with their counter-attacks, but the morale of the Anglo-American troops, facing this unexpected and fierce opposition, was low. It was suddenly enhanced that day – 15th September – by the arrival of the unruffled General Alexander in the beach-head, the appearance of two British battleships with their tremendous broadsides of 15-inch guns off-shore and the arrival overland of Moorehead and his companions, which proved that there was now nothing to prevent the 8th Army launching its own offensive against the enemy's flank. This was the turning-point of the battle for the Salerno beaches and the road for Naples and Rome.

On 15th September, the German counter-attacks wilted under bombing and naval bombardment and the 5th Army again began to push inland. But the nine correspondents and their conducting officer – a buccaneering extrovert of White Russian descent – had won no credit for their feat in linking the two Allied armies; indeed they were told by a staff officer that it had been of no military significance and were ordered back to the 8th Army. Moorehead wrote furiously to Christiansen, "The situation was farcical. Here was a large British army fighting a vital battle for Naples – the only battle in the peninsula. Here were the British correspondents on the spot ready to report it. Here was a chance of balancing the grossly unfair number of American correspondents reporting the battle. But we were compelled to leave."[20] Equally mortifying was Moorehead's discovery that his long and dramatic account of their adventure had been mislaid before transmission and that, instead, the *Daily Express* had published the report of another member of their party and another Australian, Ronald Monson. Moorehead wrote to Lucy on their return to their own press camp:

At the moment we are at a pretty low ebb. Either through design or stupidity, the Americans, who are in charge, will not let us report the battle . . . This means, of course, that we have virtually nothing to do and that we shall almost certainly be unable to report the fall of either Naples or Rome . . . I feel baulked and restless and very much like throwing the whole thing in. Yet I suppose one simply must condition oneself to a war that is run politically. We have had a thousand arguments. The whole thing, almost from the moment I left England, has brought me only a feeling of distress and irritation. It is not at all what I imagined it would be.[21]

This tension was to break out in an angry, petty quarrel a week later. The Adriatic port of Bari had fallen to the 8th Army and, on entering the city, the correspondents looked for an hotel that would be suitable as a base. Hitherto, it had only been necessary to choose one and announce that it had been commandeered; formalities could be completed later. But, since the armistice, such high-handed behaviour was not permissible. So, again and again, they were told that the hotel of their choice was fully booked and occupied by Italians. They were tired and, after several unsuccessful attempts to find rooms, showed their irritation at another reception desk. At this, a young Italian-American lieutenant of the US Army's Psychological Warfare Division overheard them and said, "It's all changed. It's all under political control now." Moorehead remarked tartly that the 8th Army had been fighting to capture the town, and a quarrel broke out, culminating in a fist-fight between the American and a British correspondent. The combatants were separated but Moorehead and Clifford continued the argument. "Get out of the hotel," ordered the lieutenant, at which Clifford removed his spectacles and said quietly, "Just try and do it." Moorehead sought and found the American's superior officer – a former secretary at the United States Embassy in Rome, whom he had known – but whose attitude was just the same. Finally, an American correspondent, Ed Kennedy of the Associated Press, took the British side, announcing that he would report the incident. Moorehead wrote to Lucy:

It's all so trivial but it's one of those trivial things that give point to the whole situation. I see that armies cannot rule and that there must be political control. But to betray in this way the things that everyone imagined he was fighting for . . . This new brood of amateur politicians has insolence and a technique in place of courage; they batten like vultures on the soldiers, who have risked everything, where they risked nothing.[22]

To him this was political expediency just as it had been in
Algiers. There, the Allies had made use of the senior French
officers and officials, who had recently collaborated with the
enemy through their masters in Vichy. Here, the Italians seemed
to have been forgiven overnight and those who had supported
Mussolini were often regarded as allies by those involved with
the civil authorities.

After the occupation of Bari, Foggia fell and with it the airfields
on the surrounding plain from which Allied bombers would be able
to range over southern Europe. Moorehead reported this but there was
little serious fighting on the 8th Army front and his main contribution
to his newspaper was an interview with the elderly Marshal Badoglio,
the new prime minister of post-Mussolini Italy, who, on 13th October,
declared war on Germany. All the action worth reporting was on the
5th Army front and there, at the end of September, two British
correspondents and one Australian were killed by a German tank.
Moorehead was particularly distressed about one of them – Austin of
the *Daily Herald* – whom he had persuaded to come with him to the
Mediterranean and who had been the only British newspaper reporter
to cover the British landings at Salerno. Soon afterwards, Moorehead
told Lucy, there was "a dirty crack going around the correspondents
– 'Clifford and Moorehead are jealous because they were not the first
correspondents to get killed.' "23

Even though they had been turned away from Italian hotels,
military regulations allowed them to requisition a house and they
did so, taking some mischievous satisfaction in choosing a handsome
villa near Bari belonging to a rich old woman who declared that she
deplored the departure of the Germans, whose behaviour had been
so correct. There The Trio were reunited and Moorehead wrote to
Lucy:

Christopher Buckley has joined Alex and myself and he casts a
pleasant Victorian glow over the whole absurd charade. But for
the fact that we know we are wasting a good deal of our time
as war correspondents, it would be most agreeable. For the past
week we have been living just outside the thriving city of Bari. We
requisitioned the Villa Aurora, full of painted ceilings and plush
and gold-painted furniture. The Countess Sabini wrung her hands
and had a fit when I took the key from her – for four years she
has had tremendous wealth and security and privilege. We sleep
on the verandah. We write our stories before breakfast in the mess

in the main salon, then shave and open a bottle of champagne at ten. Then we go out for the day and in the evening drive into one of Bari's restaurants for dinner. Of the war, nothing.[24]

But for the frustration of knowing that serious warfare was in progress on the 5th Army front and across the Adriatic in Yugoslavia, this would have been another gentle interlude like that at Taormina. Long conversations late at night turned to the most intimate matters, amongst them love and sex, just as they had in the desert. He confided in a letter to Lucy:

Alex doesn't need a woman as I do, and especially you, so on the whole he is happy and he gets nearly all he wants by this absurd scene around us and in being with me and the others . . . He does not want to return to England but looks forward to taking over the Berlin or Paris bureau after the war.

Moorehead knew that Clifford had had two love affairs: one in Spain and Berlin; the other with a music-teacher in England. He had often wondered about the exact relationship between Clifford and Lucy. Although sure of her fidelity, he knew that the friendship between them was – like that between Clifford and himself – a form of love. Only now did he feel able to ask outright about it and wrote to Lucy:

Please never mention it to him but when at the end of a long conversation the other day I asked him if he would have married you, he said, "Yes, I think I would"; but he added that he did not think you would have married him. Dear puss, I can't help thinking he would have made you happier in many little things than I have. You would have been spared the egocentric hysterics. But will Alex ever marry anyone? If only you were here I think he would be content.

He told her proudly of Clifford's prowess as a linguist. They had just visited a camp and hospital for refugees from Yugoslavia and, he wrote, "He carried on a simultaneous conversation in English, French, German, Italian and bits of Russian";[25] and when he met priests who could converse only in Serbo-Croat, interviewed them in Latin. From the Yugoslavs – amongst them girls who had been wounded in action when fighting as partisans – he heard of the ferocity of the guerrilla war across the Adriatic. In another part of Italy, there was action, too, and, at the beginning of October, Naples fell to the 5th Army and the event was reported at length in the *Daily Express* by one of their less-celebrated correspondents. Soon after, however, The Trio were given permission to drive across the Apennines to visit the 5th Army. In the three weeks since the landing at Salerno, it had suffered some 12,000 casualties – more than half of them British – in fighting its way inland and around the base of the Sorrento peninsula and past Vesuvius into the great city.

Naples reflected Cairo in the contrast between the louche living it could offer, the occasional splendour of its architecture and of its past and the squalor of its streets and the miseries being endured by the soldiers on the battlefields up the road. It was obvious that the inability of the Allies to seize the opportunity of Italy's surrender and take most, if not all, of the country had been a disaster. The Germans, with their extraordinary powers of recovery and initiative, had rushed troops southward and were manning defences on the line of the Volturno river just to the north of Naples. On 12th October, the 5th Army attacked in rain and mud and after three days the enemy withdrew. But this was a planned move to far stronger defences being prepared on what was called the Gustav Line based upon the Garigliano, Rapido and Liri rivers. This was where the road to Rome was to be barred.

Moorehead and his companions reported the apparent success of the Volturno offensive and returned to Naples, where he wrote to Lucy:

Alex, Christopher and myself have crossed from Bari to Naples, which is much livelier and here we stay for a fortnight covering the Volturno fighting and then return to the 8th Army. We lunched first at Amalfi and then, coming over the mountains of the Sorrento peninsula, saw Vesuvius and Naples again and I could think of nothing but you . . .

Naples has been mauled about but how lovely it is still . . . Outside the town, Nigel Dugdale, the PR major, had got a marvellous villa and two Viennese cooks and here we live. Alex and Christopher have gone into a mania of shopping. They spend days and days at it. Once Christopher offered a man £20 for a white and gilt hearse, which he wanted to use as a trailer behind the jeep and I only stopped the deal at the last minute. At this minute I am trying to stop Alex from paying £600 for a vineyard we visited on

Anacapri. It produces twenty-four barrels of wine a year and Alex wants his architect brother to come and build a villa on it after the war. The visit to Capri was sheer craziness. We went over on a naval launch with no luggage or food intending to stay an hour and instead lingered two days. We sat in the square in the sun, dined out in villas, visited the Piccolo Marina and fell into a daze of laziness I have not had for years.[26]

He wrote later of Capri having remained

a curious little nodule of lotus-eating throughout the war. The same international society, a little diminished, had continued somehow throughout the trouble, although with the slightly beaten air of a worn-out roué. On the island I met British residents who had continued in their villas unmolested . . . It was as though someone had placed a glass bowl over the whole confection in 1939 and, now that the bowl was lifted again, the people came out, a little jaded, like a railway sandwich, but quite genuine Capri stock.[27]

As winter set in there was comparatively little fighting to report, since tanks and guns were bogged down, and the correspondents were grateful for the comforts of Naples. Moorehead accepted that the new influx of correspondents would be given priority when reporting the 5th Army front and that the 8th Army, where The Trio were held in high regard, had been relegated to the less dramatic role of fighting its way up the Adriatic coast, where they would capture no famous city before they reached Venice. He decided to enjoy an undemanding regime and look forward to the day when he could return to London before reporting the coming invasion of France across the Channel.

Moorehead's fantasy was to settle down after the war with Lucy, John and two more children at St.-Jean-de-Luz:

We must get to St. Jean quickly and pick a nice villa above the village. John must grow up in the country and by the sea . . . From St. Jean you will go often to Paris and London and New York to buy hats. I know I will live fine with children if they can be as they should be, out of doors all day. It's only the trying to write cooped up in a tiny apartment that has made the trouble before. I have this passion to write always and will never be content until you are with me and John because I always write better when I am with you and relax in the writing with you. Puss, it really can be done.[28]

Meanwhile they had moved northward from Bari to be ready for Montgomery's offensive across the Sangro at the beginning of November. Again they found that life behind the lines was more absorbing than on the line of battle. He wrote to Lucy:

> We are living in a kind of mad palazzo in the village of Lucera outside Foggia and close to the Adriatic. God knows we have camped in some weird places but this is straight surrealism. There is an enormous old lady who runs the place with half a dozen servants, a family of Neapolitan refugees and about a dozen others with walking-on parts.
>
> We arrived in the village and asked the AMGOT [Allied Military Government of Occupied Territories] people for a billet. A stooge led us through the usual appallingly squalid streets and we banged on the double doors of a courtyard until the gates were opened. The countess who owns the place screamed that this was not an hotel and the Neapolitans screamed. Eventually we got in and ever since we have been roaming through these acres of Vatican-like rooms. It seems that four English chorus girls touring with an ENSA [Entertainments National Service Association] show for the troops were here last week and made such a bloody nuisance of themselves (*"Dio mio*, five meals a day!") that the old party did not want any more. But she has fallen in love with us. We have clean sheets and towels, electric light and four servants. She gives us thirty-years-old wine and last night threw a banquet with a turkey . . .[29]

The chorus girls returned, and almost at once he described a scene when they were denounced by the housekeeper as prostitutes for inviting an army officer to their part of the palace, which, thought Moorehead, "seemed a bit hard since it was only five in the afternoon and the major stayed only long enough to drink half a glass of kitchen wine". He was confined indoors with a cold, miserably telling Lucy, "It is strange to be alone. One is a little afraid of it. I sit surrounded by mahogany cabinets and the ceiling is a great domed, painted affair."[30] He had more than enough time to brood about his writing career, his marriage and let his thoughts stray to Australia, which they seldom did, deciding to post his sister Phyllis a handsome cheque for Christmas and, when writing to ask Lucy to send this, adding, with some malicious glee, news of his well-to-do relations in Melbourne:

"To my intense delight, two of my male cousins, the Carnegies, are getting divorces from their prim little wives and marrying shopgirls."[31]

Despite occasional drinking and gambling parties in the palazzo, they were depressed. He told Lucy:

We are all feeling rather low-spirited. Alex is getting recurring bouts of melancholy . . . The three of us being together all day and all night argue endlessly on about six main topics – women, Christianity (especially on the Trinity and the Immaculate Conception), the war, after the war, Marxism, writing and fifth-century philosophy. It's all very undergraduate and smug, especially as we speak in American jargon, putting the obscene words of the Army into long Latin sentences. How childish and ridiculous men are when they have no women. All we are doing is airing an enormous amount of rather dusty and out of date schoolboy knowledge. Christopher rumbles in Latin and Greek, Alex flits about from one language to another. We laugh a good deal at one another's obscure jokes.[32]

He found some relief in reading:

I continue with *War and Peace* and it is much more real to me than the present war. Yesterday as we were driving up to the Campobasso front I developed an argument with Alex and Christopher, saying that no one in England was going to read little tactical pieces about the fighting – a village taken here and a river crossed there. All this, I said, was a bore. The thing to do was to write of such things as the psychological feelings of the troops . . . The argument seemed to have terrific effect. Alex and I sat down and wrote most moony pieces, poor Christopher wrestled half the night and finally rose at six this morning and tore up the whole thing, substituting a few cracks from Horace and a picture of an Englishman at bay. We are all very tired of the war and cannot really write it straight any longer.[33]

Nor did they want to write articles about the war for American magazines – despite offers of high fees – or even books about it. Moorehead speculated about how much money Hamish Hamilton had made out of his three books and whether he would be willing to give him a contract for that amount for three years' work after the war. Increasingly he had been sending the *Express* discursive articles about Italian affairs and European politics instead of war despatches. Visits to the fighting were no longer the exciting expeditions they once had been. "Alex, Christopher and myself go very slowly now," he told Lucy, "always making sure we have wine with us. All of us are so bored with doing straight reporting on the war, we are resorting to trick writing and God knows what they think of it at home."[34] They soon knew when both Moorehead and Clifford received terse cables from their editors once again complaining that they were sending "the same sort of stuff". They were, he confessed, "barracks happy" and, at the end of November, would "only with enormous effort set off for the front".

Depression usually lifted when they were back among fighting soldiers but sometimes sadness joined the other emotions. Returning from the battlefields to Naples and the luxury of Major Dugdale's mess, Moorehead wrote to Lucy:

God, if you could only see the wizened little London boys tramping through the awful mud and mortar fire. They have a tremendous dignity in the stark staring madness of the fighting. When you watch them going forward you suddenly think – *they* have no plans for the future. By this evening they are going to put themselves in the way of death . . . Everyone who has not experienced this feeling again and again, the feeling of going up to It is quite unable to understand the soldiers. All war is bad for any purpose whatever except for this one thing – the wonderful, majestic fullness of the soldier walking up to the precipice to look over at the unknown and coming away again. I think that a woman having a child has this experience and her love for the child after-wards comes greatly from the fact that it was something that came from the moment she walked up to the unknown.

One is not a human being unless one has experienced this mystery and the whole tragedy of the war is that the soldiers and the airmen are obliged to experience it far too often. Consequently they become haggard and coarse and careless like a woman who has had too many children . . .

The few, who every once in a while risk everything, have a sense of fulfilment which is possibly better than the ordinary surface pleasures. And so, my dear, all this dismal, dark waiting and struggling you are undergoing is not all hopelessly bad . . . Once you have in your heart accepted what I am writing here, everything will be easier for you.[35]

Increasingly, The Trio were spending more time with the 5th Army than with the 8th, both because, with the relative proximity of Rome, there was likely to be more news on that front and also because life in Naples was more amusing than in Foggia or Bari. Major Dugdale's mess was the envy of all for its comfort, entertaining company and profusion of delicious food, which was so rich that a cold table of plain beef and ham was kept for those with simpler tastes. The mess secretary, Captain David Heneker, was not only a gourmet himself but an entertainer, a composer of popular songs and a pianist who would sing and play after dinner. But early in December, Geoffrey Keating acquired a twelve-room apartment on the Naples waterfront and The Trio moved there together with the war artist Edward Ardizzone. There was room for others, too, and they engaged a cook, a waiter and a girl – Erminia by name – to act as housekeeper. "I hope to God we can keep the place and spend Christmas here as we are all pathetically pining for a home of some sort," Moorehead told Lucy, explaining that they tried to make the flat with its gilded salon and terrace overlooking the Bay of Naples homely with "a few things we cart around wherever we go – Buckley's 19th century fashion plates, Alex's Japanese prints and my cuts from the German magazine *Signal* (including a nude that has become famous)."[36]

It was a continuation of their former life behind the lines. He continued a week later:

We loiter in Naples, doing nothing but live in our flat, talking, drinking, driving idly about. Buckley could not stand it and went off to the 8th Army and Geoffrey goes off today. But Alex, Ted Ardizzone and me – we hang on and wait for something to move us. Every day people gather here for luncheon or in the evening. Sometimes we drive down to the opera or wander through the shops. Sometimes American nurses and Neapolitan girls are brought in but there is something in the house that precludes vice, or, at any rate, no one makes passes at them. Ted paints away restlessly unable to fix his mind on anything.[37]

They had literary evenings, too, and he recounted:

We have all been reading John Donne at a great rate and I have been elected chief reader. The readings usually break out after dinner. The night before last, Geoffrey insisted in bringing all the available 8th Army brigadiers for the reading. After each verse we have a discussion of the meaning and the syntax. Alex and the more classically-educated brigadiers explore the word "roots", Ted discusses the artistic balances of such lines as "Else a great prince in prison lies" and "Now good morrow to our waking souls". And I usually find myself discussing the lust content. *On Going to Bed* is our favourite elegy. We have also had a succession of first-class piano-players at the flat and there is often a concert after Donne.[38]

Such scenes were described by Ardizzone in his diary:

Some good talk. Alan being Tolstoyan, gloomy conclusions. . . My gloom of yesterday not altogether lifted, however produced a small drawing (a gay one of a corpse) . . . The squalor of the streets and a people completely lacking in pride. I hate Naples. Afternoon spent in preparing for a party we gave in the evening, then to a short concert of chamber music . . . Return to find the party in full swing . . . To the Opera House in the afternoon to hear a concert. Return to find Erminia prancing about the flat in Geoffrey's dressing-gown and looking very gay and guttersnipish. She had brought with her a pretty little girl who looked about sixteen and was almost prostrate and trembling with fright and shyness. The idea being that she should be Alan's mistress. She was without a job and hungry and it was Erminia's idea of being of service to both of them (Erminia, of course, having no intention of lying with anybody). What could one do but send the wretched child away loaded with bread and tinned meat . . .

A big crowd here . . . a pleasant American Red Cross girl to dinner. Alan reads Donne to her and puts her considerably on heat . . . Erminia sad, confesses to me that she loves Geoffrey, who won't have anything to do with her. Suggest that Alan might do instead but she scorns the idea as he is married . . . Erminia makes much of Alex on the rebound.[39]

Moorehead avoided serious sexual attachments but, like many men of strong libido, enjoyed flirtation and sometimes went much further when away from home, regarding this as only marginally more reprehensible than indulging the other appetites.

In this unsettled state – moody, quarrelsome, alternately elated with hopes for the future, depressed by the inactivity of the present and, as he put it, feeling "well and irresponsible" – Moorehead and his friends prepared for Christmas. They bought a live turkey, cheeses,

fruit and almonds and large quantities of alcohol, including seventy
bottles of wine. On Christmas Eve they tried to attend a midnight
Mass but could not find a church that was open. On Christmas Day,
drinking began on the terrace at noon, and they drove up Vesuvius in
the rain during the afternoon to clear their heads before the feast that
Clifford had prepared. "Alex's tremendous dinner raged until two in
the morning,"[40] Moorehead reported to Lucy, adding that over the
three days of Christmas they must have entertained two hundred
guests. Even Clifford had lost his usual inhibitions and, towards the
end of the carousings, "Alex's behaviour became extraordinary when
he made a pass at Erminia, our blonde, twenty-year-old housekeeper,
and no small pass at that. He pursued her, roaring, down the passage."[41]

The life had acquired even greater importance than the work
and, sometimes, even the war. He told Lucy:

I have an idea for the next book so fragile and reeking that I
scarcely dare to write about it. It's a book about our summer school
in Taormina and our winter school in Naples. Alex and Geoffrey
and I have really succeeded in setting up two extraordinary salons
in these two places in these six months. While the front was only
an hour away and we were constantly going to it, we had, and still
have, an extraordinary concourse of people coming to the house.
Tomorrow at dinner there are only to be admirals. Yesterday they
were infantry and whores. Ted paints in one room, Geoffrey
photographs in another, Alex and I write. People start arriving
at ten in the morning and keep on arriving until midnight. The
wine is really good and so is the conversation. Every day or two
we drift away, some to the front, some to London and New York,
some to India and so on. It is not quite so phoney as it sounds. It
is a compression and a cross-section of the war . . . The book must
begin quietly with us walking ahead of the Army into Taormina and
then I have all my characters and situations ready made. I want to
write it.[42]

But now a new preoccupation arose. It was announced that General
Montgomery was returning to London before taking command of
the forces engaged in future offensive operations against Germany
under the supreme command of General Eisenhower. This would
be the long-awaited Second Front and The Trio were determined
to be there. During the first days of 1944, they were told in secrecy

that there was to be an important amphibious operation in the Mediterranean and they had been chosen to accompany it. They refused, knowing that something far more important than whatever that might prove to be was being mounted in Britain. Optimistically, Moorehead ended a cable to Lucy about delays in the mail with the promise, "Alex myself planning take you John and new baby to France next year my poor darling eye was never so much in love with you as eye am now."[43]*

At last, on 1st January, 1944, Moorehead wrote to Lucy, "My treasure. I am coming home. Christiansen cabled today."[44] Clifford was also to return to report the Second Front and the round of farewell parties began. There was also a final visit to the battlefront and on the 9th Moorehead wrote a despatch about the beginning of what promised to be the difficult and spectacular battle by the 5th Army to force its way past Monte Cassino, the fortified mountain crowned by the vast Benedictine monastery which barred the road to Rome. It was his last report from Italy. A week later he and Clifford were in Algiers, where they were offered a flight home in General Eisenhower's own Flying Fortress.

First they flew to Gibraltar and passed a day at the Rock Hotel, where they were surprised to hear that a civilian was asking for Moorehead at the reception desk. He was a handsome young man in ill-fitting clothes but the face was familiar; it was George Millar, last seen in Paris, taken prisoner in the desert and thought to be in a German prison camp. On the terrace of the hotel he told them how he had escaped by jumping from a train, then crossed Germany into France and in Paris had sought and been given the help of Mara Scherbatoff. From there he had made his way to the Pyrenees, reached Madrid and been smuggled out of Spain to Gibraltar. But why had he asked the receptionist for Moorehead when he could have had no idea that he would be there? "I had this feeling of certainty that I would meet you here,"[45] was his reply.

While Millar awaited his own flight home, Moorehead and Clifford took off again in Eisenhower's bomber. On the long journey, the worries and frustrations, the doubts and self-absorption drained away from Moorehead. He was soon to be with Lucy again. He would shortly report the greatest event of their lifetime. Even his plan to run away from Fleet Street and become a famous author

* In cable language, "eye" meant the first person singular to avoid confusion with the numeral "one".

had been put in its place. A letter had reached him recently from his friend Evelyn Montague of the *Manchester Guardian* who had been invalided home. Montague had been reading *The End in Africa* and had written his candid opinion of it. Moorehead had written to Lucy just before leaving Naples:

I have just had a shattering letter from Evelyn from his bed in an Aberdeenshire hospital where they say he cannot live much longer. He writes, "Your first book was plain but good; your second was sophisticated, amusing and not so good; this one is fretful, worried, patchily brilliant and bad. I've watched your work going off nearly all this year; do come home and *not* write a book – get the tangles out of yourself, give yourself time to relax and take stock and get your ideas sorted and your nerves in some sort of shape and then, when you do write something, don't rush it."

Well. I've been found out at last . . . I am concerned to write and this clean, sharp kick in the guts, which left me winded last night, has suddenly made a tremendous load of worry roll off my mind this morning. I feel as though I have been to confession. Someone else understands at last. You understand, but I needed to get it straight from someone like Evelyn, who writes beautifully, who is utterly honest in his mind and who now thinks as clearly as some sensitive men do when they are dying of tuberculosis. Underneath the irritability and frustration, puss, you too see that he is right. And so I am coming home, dear, not, as I half planned, to a book; but to you.[46]

Chapter Ten

"The ruin of nearly every normal thing"

Yet Alan Moorehead returned to London as a successful author as well as a celebrated journalist. All three of his books – *Mediterranean Front*, *A Year of Battle* and *The End in Africa* – had sold well and Hamish Hamilton was planning a first print-order of 10,000 copies of them published in one volume as *African Trilogy*, which would, he declared, become the most important book of the war. There would now be a sequel covering the invasion of the Continent and the subsequent destruction of Germany. This could begin with the Sicilian and Italian campaigns and, indeed, open with the walk into Taormina, but all thought of writing about their social life there and in Naples evaporated in the excited atmosphere of London on the eve of the greatest battle of the war.

In the tense months before the expected invasion was launched, the reassurance of those with experience of victory was needed. General Montgomery, touring army camps and munitions factories, provided it on a national scale. Moorehead, arriving in London, gave it to those he met in Fleet Street, the BBC and all those connected with presenting news of the war to the public.

He was a confident, charismatic person now. Arthur Christiansen found him far more self-confident, putting this down to Lucy rather than active service, and Hamish Hamilton found him "loads of fun".[1] He was eye-catching, too. Cyril Ray, who had relieved the sick Evelyn Montague as war correspondent in Italy, noticed that, although short, he was "well put-together and a neat mover, like a dancer".[2] Tom Driberg, the *Daily Express* columnist and aspiring politician, described him as "a trim, slight figure, dark and jaunty, with steady eyes, a scornful, passionate lip and a certain ruthless charm".[3] John Redfern, who had also been reporting for the *Express* in the Mediterranean, called him "the prince of war correspondents".[4]

His reunion with Lucy was all that he had hoped. Soon after his return, when they were apart for a couple of days, he wrote to her:

> You are the most beautiful woman I have seen . . . I did not quite see before this mixture other people saw in you of distinction and elegance like a greyhound. Had I never married you or met you and for the first time saw you today I would be in the state men get into when they see women who look like models in *Vogue*. Strange atmosphere of always wearing orchids and expensive furs . . . You have it natural. You should be married to a belted earl because you have the atmosphere of a remote and beautiful hostess and the instincts of a mistress. You are the only mistress I know who is also able to have children . . . You are liked by more men of good taste and applied intelligence than any other woman I know in London, namely Lancaster, Clifford, Millar, Bernstein, Betjeman and me with many others who talk of my beautiful wife.[5]

Christiansen suggested that he should occupy his time before the invasion began by writing a weekly column called "Alan Moorehead's London", or simply "Alan Moorehead" if he went elsewhere, and for this he should involve himself in the life of the capital. It was published every Friday, covering much of the leader-page, and ranged from strategic forecasts ("I am convinced that the Germans will not let an Allied army cross the German border before they come to terms")[6] to the arrival of Algerian wine in restaurants.

The sight of young soldiers at a railway station prompted him to recall, "Something happens to the boys' faces when they come out of the line, a stiffness about the mouth and, instead of modesty, a certain casual assurance. And, as the months go by, their eyes become steadier, their movements more definite, their talk tougher but quieter. I have seen boys grow from adolescence to adulthood in three months."[7] And he remarked upon the difference between the bombing of London and elsewhere: "Perhaps it is the damp air, perhaps the size of the city but the lights are different, the noises different, the tempo different . . . Here in London all things seem to be anticipated and, once the raid has started, it is reduced to a pattern. You do not see people quietly going off to their posts anywhere else I have been."[8]

It was a stimulating place to be. "Bombs or no bombs, London is the capital of the world," he wrote. "The price of being the world's capital is always over-crowding and sometimes bombs. But where else would you rather be at such a decisive and exultant moment as this?"[9]

Instead of the menagerie of soldiers, Neapolitans, camp-followers, pretty women and journalists who had made up his circle so recently he mixed with those whose names were already well known to him and to whom he was introduced by successful friends, notably Osbert Lancaster, Sidney Bernstein and Hamish Hamilton. These included writers – J.B. Priestley, James Agate, Eric Linklater, William Saroyan and John Betjeman amongst them – and politicians – Ernest Bevin, the Minister of Labour, and the urbane Harold Nicolson – and the coteries based upon the BBC, Bloomsbury and the theatres of Shaftesbury Avenue. He and Lucy were entertained at the best restaurants – The Ivy, the Mirabelle, the Savoy Grill and at the Connaught Hotel – and taken to the theatre. All this he began to record in an occasional journal, even noting snatches of conversation in notes such as: "Met J.B. Priestley who said, 'I hate war correspondents.' I – 'The war's worse.' P. – 'There is not much to choose between them.' But thought my last 3 chapters had 'epic quality'. Nuts."[10]

They lunched with his ubiquitous Australian friend Noel Monks, who was also waiting to report the invasion, and his wife, Lucy's friend, Mary Welsh, who was now working for the American magazines *Time* and *Life*. Mary, the attractive American blonde, now thirty-six, led a busy social life during her husband's frequent absences abroad – counting General Eisenhower among her escorts – and soon after this meeting was telling Lucy that she had been introduced to Ernest Hemingway who had invited her out to dinner. The celebrated author's wife Martha Gellhorn, also a journalist, blonde and beautiful, was on her way across the Atlantic to become a war correspondent like her husband.

London was being bombed again, several of the raids being heavier than anything experienced in the Blitz three years before. On 11th February, Moorehead wrote in his journal:

Queer experience going to the Lynne Fontanne, Alfred Lunt show *There Shall Be No Night* during a raid. Robert Sherwood's play,

18 Writers together, Ernest Hemingway entertains Alan Moorehead while
Mary Hemingway serves at lunch in Cuba, 1956.

19 The happy family: Alan Moorehead with John and Caroline in Italy during the 1950s.

20 The great traveller: Alan Moorehead with the painter, Sidney (now Sir Sidney) Nolan during their expedition to the Antarctic in 1964.

now rewritten around the Great War, is a sincere and talkative piece depending heavily on the artistry of its 2 stars. Around the time the stage guns began to sound the little light above the orchestra pit lit up the word "Alert" and the sirens started wailing in the Strand. From then on I was quite unable to distinguish between what were stage effects and what was the real thing outside. Even Lunt paused to grin at one moment. But what a comment on this brilliant civilisation: a sophisticated theatre, two of the best players of our time, a sensitive audience packing the red plush seats – and a little light warning them that the whole thing might be reduced to dust by a stray bomb. No one moved from the theatre I noticed.[11]

More distant gunfire was finding an echo in the news from Italy, where an Anglo-American force had made a landing on the beaches around Anzio and Nettuno in the major amphibious operation to outflank the German stand at Monte Cassino, which The Trio had been invited to report. It was not going well for the Germans had again reacted quickly and effectively and the Allies were suffering heavily. "Nettuno bridgehead crisis makes me feel guilty," he wrote in his journal. "Missed two Wavell retreats, Greece, Crete, Tobruk, Singapore, Norway, Dunkirk, even Kasserine. You war correspondents go everywhere. Do we?"[12]

He soon would at least be going across the sea to the Continent and doing so as no ordinary correspondent. He now regarded himself as a friend of General Montgomery, who would command the assaulting armies, and, two days after his evening at the theatre, they lunched together:

He seemed just as lively, quite unawed by the Cabinet Ministers whom he said he was meeting for the first time. As usual, filled me with confidence, a sense of direction and certainty for the chaos ahead. He clearly thinks he will succeed. He made a great thing of "getting to know soldiers so we can put our trust in one another". I like him and trust him. But God knows what this continued adulation will do: maybe his simplicity will save him. His vanity is still not complex – pleased at pictures and books and great sums offered for his writing . . .

His portrait being painted by Augustus John. Says diary unprintable as puts down exactly what he thinks and would injure too many people. But it could be used to make a story. Also agreeable to biography. Harraps offered him £25,000 for a contract: refused.

At this, Moorehead had pricked up his ears as it occurred to him that he might be the biographer. Already he had written a three-part series of articles about Montgomery for the *Daily Express* and had established a closer relationship with him than any other journalist, so he should try to see more of his subject before the invasion began. He noted:

> Monty at present travelling round in special train. Will have seen every soldier committed to Second Front by end of this month . . . Agrees my view that war in Europe can be concluded this year, provided make no mistakes as in past. People should be told this so as to enthuse them – they certainly will not be enthused by being told there grim fight ahead and war will drag on for years . . . Monty going to address railway workers, stevedores, etc., to stir them up. Says there no one to enthuse people in England, who tired. Cabinet Ministers and Service chiefs meet every morning, rush off to office to sign papers. They been overworked and bound to routine for 4 years and they go to bed at midnight exhausted. Winston very frail. To go out in weather like this would kill him. Cabinet Ministers, etc., should work with a Chief of Staff as he does (Freddie de Guignand sees everyone). "If ever I were Prime Minister of this country, which God forbid, that is what I should do."[13]

Inspired by their conversation, Moorehead readily accepted Montgomery's invitation to accompany him on a tour of army camps in the south-east of England a fortnight later. At each, he gathered the men around them and spoke in simple, confident terms of the prospect ahead, just as he had in Sicily before the crossing to Italy. "The scene is almost reduced to a schoolroom atmosphere," Moorehead reported in the *Express*, "the men sitting on the grass at his feet and looking upward tensely . . . within five minutes they are laughing, the tenseness goes . . . Montgomery winds up with a serious word about what still has to be done for the winning of the war."[14]

On his return, Moorehead wrote:

> Much impressed to see how M. grows more and more like Gandhi, especially when he puts glasses on that thin peaked face. The same cold, bright, steady eye with the fanatical gleam in. Same dry, precise, half-amused conversation full of obiter dicta and positive pronouncements, the utter conviction that what they say is right.

Both enjoy adoration of masses, both politicians, both non-smokers, non-drinkers and contempt for bodily weaknesses. Both simple, practical and with religious faith which is inverted, turned inward upon themselves and supported every day with worship of disciples and masses around them. One, man of peace; the other, man of war.

M. is undoubtedly a careerist, moving rapidly on from step to step in wonderment at himself but profoundly believing he has a mission, that he is being impelled onward as a leader of erring humanity. He is what he is. Everything is "perfectly simple, perfectly easy" if you know how. And he knows how. Others do not. So he can look with amused tolerance on his rivals. He has Gandhi's naivety and simplicity. G.'s gift for sleeping soundly and regularly, of relaxing at will.

Was intrigued to get reluctant admission from Major Carver* (his stepson, who has just escaped from PoW camp in Italy) as we drove along in wake of M.'s Rolls Royce through forest said that M. has changed recently and now has political ambitions. He has been "angled for" by political parties already. He "always had interest in getting fair deal for working man". He would "step in if there were domestic troubles in England after war". As Minister of Defence perhaps . . . Carver kept comparing him to Duke of Wellington.

Almost as fascinating as the general himself were his comments on the celebrities he had been meeting since his return from Italy and these Moorehead noted, too. Of Churchill he had said:

Been seeing him a lot. Last week had found him slouched dully at his desk, usual glass of whisky at his right hand, cigar, pasty faced, frail. Then suddenly banged the table, sat up, cried, "I'm Hitler." Played game of what Hitler would do. Told M. he must attend important war conference at 10.30 pm. M. "Look here, sir, I go to bed at 9.30." C., "So you do, General. I forgot." "And, you know, he let me off."

He talked of Augustus John, who was painting his portrait at his Chelsea studio and how he kept "lurching about, dropping

* Major Richard Carver.

cigarette ash into the paints". To save time, Montgomery had sent a staff officer of his own build to the studio, wearing his own uniform so that the outline of the figure and details of the clothes could be painted without his presence. When Montgomery himself sat, he was critical of the portrait, telling Moorehead, "I complained my right ear was not in the right place. He rubbed it out and fixed it on two inches further back. I pointed out that the portrait was getting less and less like me and asked if the alcoholic blue cloud that was developing over the portrait was a desert sand storm . . . Still, he must paint what he sees – blue cloud and all."[15]

Because of the bombing, the Mooreheads decided to take John away from London and look for a cottage to rent in the country. This would be important for Lucy, too, because to their delight they discovered early that spring that she was pregnant. Moorehead was convinced that they would have a daughter and would talk of "the girl" instead of "the baby". They decided on Sussex because it would be close both to London and to what presumably would be the ports from which the invasion would be launched. Finally they picked one at Jevington near Brighton from which it was a quick journey by train to London and the multiplying excitements there. Moorehead was invited to address luncheon clubs and to broadcast, which he disliked, and to brief politicians on the war in the Mediterranean. He had become increasingly optimistic but others were more so, John Strachey, another aspiring politician, forecasting that the war might be won by July.

Everybody knew that the invasion must be imminent and, although speculative maps in the newspapers always showed the "invasion coast" as running from Brittany to Denmark, everybody assumed it would be in France and other maps showed the concentration of Allied bombing in the Pas de Calais. In mid-May, the *Express* was forecasting that the landings – known to all as D-Day – would be within three weeks and Moorehead reported that the German defenders of the "Atlantic Wall" along the French coast had been put on full alert. At the end of the month he wrote a farewell to England listing its attributes that he would miss, amongst them the spring weather, books, girls and draught beer and "the best of all is this: a sense of security, a sense of permanence and rest, a sense of things being preserved and not destroyed."

He himself felt the need to go if only to release the increasing tensions of expectancy. "I have the impression that the average soldier will not be altogether reluctant to go," he wrote in the *Express*. "They want to finish with the war once and for all and when they next come home they want to come home for good . . . And now (with apology to Mr Fitzpatrick's movie travelogue) it is with this thought that we shall say farewell to England, or merely au revoir."[16]

On 4th June, news came from Italy that the 5th Army had entered Rome but there was no comment upon this from Moorehead in the *Express* because he had already left London. On 30th May, the war correspondents had been summoned to a Public Relations office of the Supreme Headquarters Allied Expeditionary Force in Egerton Gardens and collected their field equipment from the Duke of York's Headquarters in Chelsea. They were then summoned to a final briefing at the Wentworth Golf Club near Virginia Water, now a military communications centre and one of the alternative seats of government outside London. There they were to be told which units of the invasion force they were to join, although they would not be told the date of D-Day or where the landings would be made.

Dozens of olive-drab jeeps and staff cars filled the drive outside the rambling castellated club-house as scores of correspondents filed into the lecture hall to learn their fate. Moorehead recognised many old friends: Buckley was there, but Clifford was ill with jaundice and would not be able to join them until later; there was David Woodward and Chester Wilmot, Desmond Tighe and Richard McMillan; the Amercians, Drew Middleton and Ed Kennedy, and many more from the battlefields of Africa, the Middle East and the Mediterranean. Not all would be able to cross on D-Day; some would have to wait a week or more before Public Relations could house them and handle their despatches. Brigadier Williams, Montgomery's Intelligence staff officer, was on the platform and tried to placate those who would be delayed. One complained, "But this is the biggest story since the Crucifixion!" and he replied, "Yes, but they managed very well with four correspondents."[17]

After the long list of names and units had been read out, they trooped into the garden with mugs of tea and sat or strolled on the lawn in the late afternoon sunlight, discussing the immediate future. David Woodward and Chester Wilmot – now with the *Manchester Guardian* and the BBC respectively – were deep in conversation, for the former had dreaded the possibility of having to go to war by glider; his name had not been read out during the briefing and when he had got up and asked if there had been some mistake, the briefing officer had apologised and said that yes, of course, he was going – by glider. Now Wilmot, who was also to travel that way, was calmly reassuring him and they were finding comfort in one another's company. Leonard Mosley – another friend from the Italian front – was amongst the few dropping by parachute; Desmond Tighe would be in a destroyer bombarding the beaches; most would be with numbered army units, Moorehead himself with the 30th Division, which he had known in the 8th Army. At least he would be among friends.

That evening they dispersed to the various camps around southern England from which they would leave for embarkation; Moorehead's in the suburbs of Southampton. Once within the surrounding barbed wire, all – soldiers and correspondents alike – were isolated from the world outside and committed to the assault. The fighting men lay on their beds, waited in the long lines of tents and Nissen huts, packed and repacked their kits and constantly rearranged the balance of the equipment they would wear and the weapons they would carry. The tension of the past weeks reached a new intensity. Then they were issued with foreign currency: francs – so it *was* to be France. Next they were shown maps of the beach where they were to land: it bore no names – for its identity was still secret – except for its codename, "King Beach" – but at least it looked like a real place with a shore, buildings and roads. Finally the time arrived to board the trucks and jeeps and join the long columns of military traffic moving slowly towards the coast. Somewhere in Southampton, Moorehead's column stopped and there was another interminable wait. The soldiers stared moodily at the civilians with whom they could not converse, cheered a girl on a bicycle and were entertained by a sniper, who, peering through the telescopic sights of his rifle, delivered a lewd commentary on the activities of embracing lovers he had picked out in the distance.

Late at night they rolled on to a concrete hard where the open doors of landing-ships gaped and they drove into the lighted interiors. Next morning they were anchored out in the Solent but the wind had got up, the sea had roughened, sailing was delayed and then postponed for twenty-four hours. Then, on the next afternoon, Moorehead entered on the page for 5th June in his pocket diary, "Sail for France." Dusk fell and, all around them, an array of ships steamed south, their balloon barrage floating above. On the bridge, Moorehead, looking around, began jotting staccato notes with a pencil in a tiny notebook:

Out in open sea, line astern. Barges in flocks. A cold and choppy green sea, tho' no whitehorses. Leaden clouds. Being joined by destroyers and Hqtrs ship flying Admiral's flag. Myriad ships. Converted Thames barges. Lines of tensing khaki at rail and faces peering. No bands, no flags. The fleet is stone grey, hard and cold. In distance ships are series grey smudges now. Balloons like dancing silver insects – hundreds of them. It's piercing cold. We now in lane of warships – an escort unseen above. Sudd. feel v. glad here . . .

There was little sleep that night and the soldiers were called before first light. At five o'clock that morning, Moorehead entered in his diary, "D-Day" and began jotting more notes:

Been ideal night for approach. Green and white flares to starboard. AA and sound of bombs. Now morn coming. Wind dropped. Clouds parting. One by one other ships dissolve from mist. 6 am – 500 Liberators and fighters. 8.24 – Assault of reserve. Landed. Resistance appears slight. 11 – All going to plan but slowly. Mines. Aircraft. 12 – Now shore clear with uncounted ships. Cruiser firing salvoes. Yellow cordite blowing inshore on to grey cliffs. Smoke cols from beach. Explosion on beach. Beached ships over spikes. Destroyers shelling gun on cliff . . .

He had hoped to get ashore immediately, once the great Rhino-powered raft, which they had towed across the Channel, could be brought round to the landing ship's open doors and the jeep got aboard. But the Rhino had broken adrift in the rough sea and floated away; they had launched a motor-boat but that had quickly filled and sunk. So he resigned himself to waiting and watching and hoping for some means of reaching the shore only five hundred yards away. He began to compose the polished prose with which he would later describe the scene around him:

Cruisers and battleships were standing off-shore and firing on to the heights above the cliffs . . . Four or five ships were alight and burning brightly, throwing out shells and explosives . . . German shells were falling in little puffs of grey smoke but the whole scene looked at from this distance was toy-like and unreal. It lacked the element of danger or excitement, even of movement. Behind us more and more ships were coasting in until the whole horizon towards England was blocked by a jagged line of tossing silhouettes.

So Moorehead spent D-Day on board his American landing ship, listening to swing music broadcast to her sailors and watching the dreamlike panorama around him. It was not until next day that he got ashore and was immersed in the sights, sounds and smells of the battle. He went on making notes: "Sgt. and sniper. Tanks up to turrets. 2 Normandy peasants – *Les salles Boches* – the old cry. 4 dead Gers., 2 Brit. in wheat, livid green. Snipers about. Throwing bits of waterproofing off tanks. Tanks jamming roads. Flowers in Bayeux."[18]

On arrival at Bayeux, which surprisingly had scarcely been touched by bombs or shells, he made for the Lion d'Or hotel where the correspondents would be staying and typed out his first despatch based on his notes. He described how a British sergeant had spotted a sniper in a tree and ordered him to come down in English; how tanks had sunk up to their turrets in the soft beach; how dead Germans and British soldiers still lay around the bunker in the wheat where they had fought; and how the French were welcoming their liberators.

At the hotel he heard news of the others. No correspondent had been killed but David Woodward had been slightly wounded almost immediately after leaving his glider in the Normandy countryside before dawn on D-Day and had been shipped back to England carrying some of the others' despatches. Although there was fighting outside Bayeux and German tanks tried and failed to break into the town, life at the Lion d'Or continued normally and, as it was a Wednesday, the madame and girls of the nearby brothel trooped into the dining-room for their weekly luncheon there. The food was excellent and the *patron* promised that, once it was possible to get down to the shore again, his celebrated lobster omelette would be back on the menu.

Jeeps took correspondents the short distance out of the town to watch the fighting but their first despatches were often delayed and the *Express* had to publish a collection of Moorehead's, which had arrived together, on 10th June. There was much to report in the fierce fighting through the close country of the *bocage*, which favoured the defenders and was the antithesis of the desert warfare in which many of the tank commanders had been trained, particularly those of the 7th Armoured Division. As the beach-head was expanded the British were held outside Caen and, although nearly a million British and American troops were now ashore, it was not until the end of July that the German line began to crack.

Moorehead roamed the beach-head with Buckley and, when

Clifford rejoined them, The Trio was complete again. While other correspondents had to request interviews with senior officers through Public Relations, they knew most of them and could call at Montgomery's headquarters whenever they chose. "They form a close and formidable caravan," wrote Tom Driberg, "Brigadiers tremble at their frown, they live and move *en prince* and genuine danger and discomfort . . . may be mitigated by captured German delicacies and mysteriously-conjured champagne. They talk on terms of equality with the highest; more secrets are entrusted to them – and safely – than to most serving officers."[19] The Reuter correspondent Doon Campbell, who, at the age of twenty-four, was the youngest reporter in Normandy, said later that he considered Moorehead to be "the king of the correspondents – and he showed it in his bearing". When the other correspondents were summoned to a briefing by a senior officer, they sometimes saw The Trio leaving his headquarters as they arrived. "They made an interesting jeep-load," noted Campbell, "Moorehead short, neat, compact like a coiled spring; Clifford, square-shouldered, shy, detached, peering uncompromisingly through his glasses; Buckley, tall, rangy, never looking too comfortable in battledress, unstuffily schoolmasterish with a twinkle or chuckle."[20] Their admirers said that, such was their military expertise, each of them could be given command of a brigade, while their critics envied their privileges.

Their standing was reflected in their social life and soon Clifford was writing in a letter home, "In the evenings, Alan and I have a regular table at a little restaurant we have found where the food is brilliant and the service is terrible. We have some very distinguished and useful guests because we both know very well the old members of the 8th Army who have worked their way up and now form Montgomery's personal staff."[21]

Moorehead was gratified to see his forecasts vindicated. On 23rd June, he reported on the opening phase: "Sum it all up – this historic fortnight – and I think you get this: We started this campaign in a mood of risk and high adventure . . . Now we are entering a rather conventional and unimaginative battle which will depend on the weight of our arms but mostly on the courage of the men." Nor had he forgotten his dispute with Beaverbrook over the respective qualities of British and German tanks. On 7th June, the *Daily Express* had printed the huge headline across its front page "TANKS 10 MILES IN" with an eye to the proprietor's approval. But now its principal war correspondent reported from the battlefield,

"It boils down to this – we have more tanks but they have better ones."[22]

At and behind the front, events began to overtake each other in mid-July. On the 9th, the bombed ruins of Caen were at last occupied by the British but although the German defences were still holding, Hitler was dissatisfied and replaced Field Marshal von Runstedt with Field Marshal von Kluge from the Russian front. Then, on the 17th, the brilliant Rommel was wounded when his staff car was attacked by Allied fighters. Three days later came the abortive attempt on Hitler's life and the uncovering of the plot which implicated many of the most experienced officers of the professional *Wehrmacht*.

Moorehead was in Caen to watch the *Tricolore* being hoisted above the still-smoking rubble while British infantrymen presented arms. "They did not do it very well," he reported, "because they are cluttered up with hand-grenades they are going to be throwing presently at the Germans at the other end of the street."[23] A week later, he watched the massed British armour move across the open cornfields beyond Caen in a major offensive codenamed "Goodwood". It was a disaster, the British losing more than four hundred tanks. Yet Montgomery held an optimistic press conference during which his Intelligence staff officer, Brigadier Williams, noticed "the unbelieving Australian expression"[24] on Moorehead's face. But he reported the occasion without comment and even echoed a little optimism himself, writing that "it is just possible that Montgomery has achieved a major stroke".[25] Frank reporting of the failure was prevented by strict censorship in Normandy and London and by his own loyalty to Montgomery so he confined himself to claiming that the German line had been "shaken and loosened along its whole length"[26] and then describing the aftermath for his readers:

I crossed on to the battlefield today . . . and perhaps I can take you along with me for a bit on the journey . . . At nine the wet and milky mist was dissipating but another mist came up composed of fine grey dust and thick enough to compare with a desert *khamseen*. You twist and turn about under fallen railway bridges and piles of stones and finally you bump out into the open . . .

The farmers' machinery which was beginning to harvest the wheat has been abruptly abandoned. In its place, tanks are moving about with heavy guns firing over them. Then you come on the burned-out tanks and lorries, scores of them, with

the grey paint burned to a shade of bright brown and the graves
of the crew alongside – usually a mound of earth, a wooden stick
and a helmet on the top.[27]

His descriptive despatches from Normandy reached the same heights
of drama that he had first achieved in the desert four years before,
and they reached a climax when he reported the destruction of the
retreating German columns, caught between the two Allied thrusts
at Falaise:

If I were to be allowed just one more despatch from this
front, this would be it, because we have begun to see the
end of Germany here in this village of St. Lambert today.

The best of von Kluge's army came here *en masse* forty-eight
hours ago. They converged upon the village to fight their way
out; long caravans of horses and gun-carts, tanks and half-tracks,
hospitals and workshops, artillery and infantry. It was the sort of
panzer battle array that the Germans have used to terrorise Europe
for four years. We knew no combination to stand against it.

And now, here in the apple orchards and in the village streets,
one turns sick to see what has happened to them. They met the
British and Allied troops head on and they were just obliterated.
Until now, I had no conception of what trained artillerymen and
infantry can do and certainly this is the most awful sight that has
come my way since the war began . . .[28]

He knew that the breakout from the Normandy beach-head would
not be the last battle. There might be another stand on the Seine
and then perhaps on the Rhine but he did not think that the Germans would continue to fight within their own country for long and
expected the war to be won by the end of the year. So he thought
of his own future plans. Now that there were several *Daily Express*
correspondents in France and he knew that he, as the senior, could
pick and choose his assignments, one that he would demand would
be the liberation of Paris. Already he wanted to begin disengaging
from Fleet Street and early in June wrote to Christiansen:

Unless some major crisis develops I would like to return to
England in early September for five or six weeks' leave, partly
for the arrival of the new baby and partly to write a book. In the
book I want to describe the collapse of Europe as we have seen it

in France and Italy and put in all the things for which at present you have no space and which one could not properly digest at the time.[29]

The editor replied sympathetically but reminded him that daily news was what now mattered and that books could wait. To this he answered:

> But, Chris, what a story it is. We can't get it into a newspaper entirely, it's too big, it needs a fuller pattern, so much solid, tight writing that can't be done from the back seat of a jeep bumping round the beach-head every day . . . Now where is the story in all this? That wonderful real stuff that is always there – and that you know is there and want to have – gets lost in a forest of quick clichés half the time. And so some of us say, "Can I write a book? I never had time to tell the story."
>
> Heavens if you knew how galling it was to see that landing in France and not get a story back for four days. And then begin to see the pattern – or think you see the pattern – of the whole break-up of Europe. The only answer is: a book, leisure to think and write.[30]

Christiansen's counter-proposal shrewdly attempted to harness his restless correspondent's aspirations. "Do you think you could get yourself fixed up as General Montgomery's biographer," he wrote in August, "with, of course, the idea of such extracts as would be newsy for the *Daily Express*?"[31] He also suggested that as soon as the war ended Moorehead would become the senior correspondent in Paris and that under a new three-year contract his annual salary would be £3,100 and be increased by £500 at the end of each year.

Moorehead responded with a proposal for "a much looser contract" under which he would contribute fifty articles a year to the *Express* at a salary of £2,500 for three years, leaving him free to write his books. "As for the Montgomery biography," he added, "I have arranged to collaborate with Colonel Ewart, his Intelligence officer, and I approached Montgomery himself about it this week; he seemed favourably inclined."[32] He no longer wanted to be the newspaper's Paris correspondent, although he might well decide to live there. Yet that was what he was about to become, if only for a fortnight.

At the end of the third week of August it was obvious that

the capital was about to fall to the Americans and the Free French division. Correspondents accredited to the 21st Army Group would not be expected to report the event so that it would be a matter of taking the initiative – without authority if necessary – and simply going there. So, early on the morning of the 24th The Trio, accompanied by David Woodward, who was now recovered from his wounds, set out for Paris. In the outskirts they were stopped and turned back at a Free French check-point with orders to allow only the Free French division commanded by General Leclerc the honour of entering their capital. The correspondents were not deterred, took side-turnings and soon Moorehead found himself in the streets he knew so well.

There were no communications with London, so he had to store his impressions for later writing:

Nothing was changed, nothing really altered. The cobblestones. The flapping signs in red and gold over the pavement cafés. *Pâtisserie*. *Charcuterie*. Three golden horses' heads over the horse butcher. The newspaper kiosk on the corner. *Café des Sports*. The Metro maps with the broad blue lines. The *flicks* with their flat blue *képis*. *Apartements à louer* under the mansard roofs. A battered green bus beside the road. Two priests who stood, gesticulating. A girl with piled-up hair, intensely and unnaturally blonde. The racing, changing colours of the city, the uplift of a Paris street.[33]

There were cheering crowds along the pavements. Then at the Lion of Belfort monument at the Place Denfert-Rochereau they scattered; there was shooting and the correspondents took shelter behind the big green lion itself. Then on into the heart of the city. Moorehead's party headed straight for the Hotel Scribe near the Place de l'Opéra, which they had heard was to be the correspondents' quarters. Others, who had also made their way past the Free French check-points, headed for particular objectives. Moorehead's old friend from Melbourne University, Sam White – now a war correspondent for an Australian news-agency – went straight to La Coupole, the brasserie in Montparnasse which he had heard was where bohemians met (for he himself had been expelled from the Communist Party when an undergraduate for "bourgeois bohemianism"). A large, bearded figure, armed to the teeth and at the head of a gang of Resistance fighters, appeared in the Place Vendôme to "liberate" the Ritz Hotel. This was Ernest Hemingway, who had engineered a war correspondent's licence as a contributor to *Collier's Magazine* but had discarded his insignia – and broken the Geneva Convention – by taking up arms as a self-appointed guerrilla. To most, however, he seemed to be acting out his own fantasies, for only about half the adventures he liked to boast about seemed to be true. Indeed, John Pudney, the poet who was now an RAF officer in Public Relations, was dismissive of him as "a fellow obsessed with playing the part of Ernest Hemingway . . . A sentimental 19th century actor called upon to act the part of a 20th century tough-guy. Set beside . . . a crowd of young men who walked so modestly and stylishly with Death, he seemed a bizarre cardboard figure."[34]

Moorehead himself was mocked by another correspondent who described how on arrival in Paris, he had gazed over the roof-tops, flung wide his arms and exclaimed, "My city!"[35] Although his first despatches did not reach London in time for publication, he now began a flow of colourful reports and showed increasing interest in the impact of the Free French and their leader General de Gaulle upon the political scene.

"Paris tonight is a French city," he reported at the beginning of September. "At the intersections the gendarmes twirl their batons once more and the tanks and the jeeps and bicycles flow down the boulevards towards Montmartre where the night clubs are just beginning to open up again beneath the Sacré Coeur. At the Hôtel de Ville there is a much more serious air. Here is the heart of French Resistance, which has made a political wedding with de Gaulle . . ."[36]

Less appealing was the start of a flow of cables from Fleet Street demanding that he enquire urgently into this or that rumour. One from Christiansen ran, "Want thorough investigation of Gestapo activities et atrocities Paris stop also real story death Maurice Chevalier et arrest Sacha Guitry stop."[37] It was just as it had been when he was in the Paris office working for Geoffrey Cox, and he no longer wanted to be fussed like that. Yet Paris still beguiled and he lingered there so long that he missed the fall of Brussels, arriving there as the tumultuous welcome to Montgomery's British troops died down. The next major news would be the advance to the Rhine and the invasion of Germany.

With the liberation of the French and Belgian capitals, a new dimension entered the correspondents' lives. The former was the American playground; the latter, the British; they were served by Dakota transports flying from the airfields at Northolt and Croydon outside London, respectively. In Paris, their base was the Scribe; in Brussels, the small but comfortable Hotel Canterbury, deep in a raffish quarter of bars and night-clubs off the Boulevard Adolphe Max. The familiar faces from the early days at the Lion d'Or were now joined by many who would never have been allowed near the fighting hitherto. The Americans had always been more ready to accredit women journalists, magazine writers, artists and even cartoonists and now the British were granting temporary war correspondents' licences to these. Sometimes the new press camps seemed like an extension of social circles in Manhattan and Mayfair.

In Paris, two veteran correspondents, Richard McMillan and Noel Monks, were crossing the Place Vendôme when a trim figure in uniform emerged from the Ritz, joined them and began talking to Monks in a low voice. It was Mary Welsh. When she turned back towards the hotel, he said to McMillan, "I hope she'll be all right."[38] He had just been told that she was leaving him for Ernest Hemingway, whose estranged wife, Martha Gellhorn, was also a war correspondent on the Continent.

In Brussels, the forming of new relationships was less fraught. David Woodward had fallen in love with a charming English girl at the British Embassy, whom he had first met before the war when reporting the League of Nations in Geneva. Among the early arrivals was a young officer in the Women's Auxiliary Air Force, working for Public Relations. She was attractive, self-assured, talked loudly and those who escorted her to night-clubs were impressed by the sensuality with which she danced cheek-to-cheek. At first she seemed drawn to Moorehead but soon realised that, despite his enjoyment of flirtation, he was devoted to his absent wife and she turned her attention to the handsome but unattached Clifford.

Moorehead watched their developing relationship with fascination, finding it "the least predictable of attachments and the most inevitable". To the shy Clifford her "touch of recklessness and eagerness for life" were, he saw, irresistible and his friend remarked, "Alex rose from the depths like a leaping trout."[39] At the end of December, Clifford wrote to his mother, "I have some news for you, though I am sure I don't know if you are going to like it. The fact is I am proposing to get married . . . The girl in question is Jenny Nicholson. She is the daughter of Robert Graves, who wrote *I, Claudius* and a whole lot of other books. Her grandfather on the other side is Sir William Nicholson, the painter, and she has a whole lot of painting aunts and uncles such as Ben Nicholson. She is called Nicholson because her mother refused to take her father's name and called her sons Graves and her daughters Nicholson. She is 26 years old and has had a bizarre and curiously unsuitable career. She has, in fact, been one of Mr Cochran's Young Ladies,* a ballet dancer, a chorus girl, an actress, a radio writer for the BBC and lots of other things. Since the war, she has been in the WAAF and is an officer."[40] His friends in Brussels were delighted for him, if a little apprehensive.

Dalliance behind the lines was interrupted by the breaching of the German frontier and, a week later, the great offensive that was designed to win the war by the end of the year. This was Operation Market Garden, the culmination of the long debate between the Supreme Commander and the newly-promoted Field Marshal Montgomery. General Eisenhower planned a general advance along the whole Allied front, which could meet any contingency that arose on any sector, and would allow the Russians the honour of capturing Berlin. But Montgomery wanted a powerful thrust across the plains of Holland and North Germany by his own armies to finish the war quickly and reach Berlin before the Russians. What transpired was a compromise: the three Allied airborne divisions – two American, one British – which were still held in reserve, would seize a succession of waterway-crossings in Holland and Montgomery's armoured spearhead would plunge across these, outflank the Ruhr and break out into the heartland of Germany.

Only one newspaper correspondent – Alan Wood of the *Daily Express* – was to accompany the British 1st Airborne Division in its assault on the river-crossing at Arnhem, while Moorehead and the others accompanied the relief force which tried to fight its way up a single road across the soft Dutch polderland which could not support the weight of tanks. The attack was launched on 17th September and, while the two American airborne divisions seized their objectives, the British had – as was memorably said at the time – attempted to take a bridge too far. Montgomery's armour never reached them and only a quarter of the original 10,000 men who had attacked Arnhem fought their way back across the river to safety. Despite the censorship, Moorehead was able to comment frankly, "It must be perfectly obvious now that parachutists must get support within 48 hours . . . It is highly dangerous to depend on a single road for supplies.

"Its implications must be faced. The Germans have held off our main thrust into the Reich. Another set battle must be mounted and fought."[41]

* A cabaret troupe of dancers and soubrettes recruited by the impresario C.B. Cochran in the 1930s.

The disaster would mean a regrouping of the armies, for there was now no chance of ending the war in 1944 and Moorehead was speculating that it would probably continue until the following August. There was nothing to prevent him returning to London to be with Lucy for the birth of their second child. The daughter he had so confidently expected was born on 28th October. When the news reached Clifford, he wrote to Lucy, "A daughter was the thing to have. I shall be fascinated to know what you intend to call her. Christopher Buckley sends a message to say he would like the child to be called Alamein (which is, after all, very pretty)." In the event she was named Caroline.

The battlefront seemed to have settled down for the winter. Clifford's letter to Lucy continued:

Here it is all damp and bleak and dreary, and my blood runs cold at the thought of the winter. The stories don't seem very big and you have to drive an awful long way to get them. I confess I feel horribly stale. Thank God my winter clothing arrangements seem pretty good. I have got a leather waistcoat and a very fine pair of gloves and Jenny has sent me the most superb pair of top boots in which I can plod about in the mud quite unscathed.[42]

Most of the time the correspondents could live comfortably in Brussels with short visits to the front when occasion demanded, until 19th December. Then through the freezing mist in the quiet hills of the Ardennes on that morning erupted the German counter-offensive. It burst through the weakly-held American lines, heading for the base areas of the 21st Army Group and the newly-opened port of Antwerp. The Allied predicament was desperate and urgent and in secrecy Montgomery was given command of the northern flank of the expanding enemy salient while British troops were rushed to help the Americans.

In snow and fog, the armies fought; Christmas and New Year passed and gradually the strength of the Allies' armoury began to tell. It was not until 5th January, a fortnight after Montgomery's appointment, that news of this could be made public and the correspondents were told it was important not to interpret this as any lack of confidence in the American generals. Yet in writing of Montgomery's part in the battle Moorehead admitted that when he had first heard, "it seemed to justify taking a more optimistic line in messages, even before Christmas."[43] Two days later, Montgomery himself held a press conference and, while paying tribute to the Americans, spoke with self-satisfaction, saying, as Moorehead reported, "I busied myself in getting the area sorted out, in getting a balance, in putting reserves in the right place. I regrouped the whole show. It has been one of the most interesting battles I have ever fought."[44] This did not endear him to the Americans and, although Moorehead was privately appalled by his patronising attitude towards them, he gave him steady support in his despatches, which cemented the bonds between the two men and they were further strengthened when, a few days later, Moorehead dismissed talk of rifts between Montgomery and Eisenhower. The rumours of bickering generals would soon be brushed aside by the great onslaught on Germany that was about to be unleashed, which Moorehead described as "the greatest and most tragic European spectacle since the collapse of Napoleon".[45] The Allied armies were already into Germany but it was the crossing of the Rhine that would be the moment for the full weight of vengeance to fall.

During the usual lull before a major offensive, Clifford returned to London on leave and, soon afterwards, news reached Moorehead and Buckley that he and Jenny had been married on 22nd February at the Royal Chapel of the Savoy. There had been a party in the River Room of the Savoy Hotel afterwards, they heard, dancing to Jenny's favourite band, and as her father, Robert Graves, had forgotten his tie she had cut a strip of velvet from one of the hotel's curtains and made him a cravat. But they did not hear from Clifford himself for nearly a fortnight. "Against all expectations, I enjoyed being married," he wrote while on honeymoon in North Wales, and explained how they had had to get a special licence authorised by the Archbishop of Canterbury. "In the vestry beforehand I was shown ten obscene little choirboys with angelic faces and asked to address them on my experiences . . . Jenny came on the arm of her ribald old father, who had been explaining to her the more licentious marriage customs of the Ancient Greeks en route. He just had time to hiss a question about the cost of the ceremony, when it started. The service was a sissy modern version with the old rugged stuff about flesh and bodies carefully expunged. I had taken immense trouble with the music against the most formidable opposition and, though it wasn't quite what I wanted, it passed; at least there was no Wagner, Mendelssohn or Elgar in it. The choirboys sang like angels in the intervals of picking their noses and each others' pockets."[46] At the reception, they cut the wedding cake with an SS dagger which Clifford thought was one that he had looted from a train in Nijmegen.

Moorehead's hopes of a new career as an author had been encouraged by a letter from Hamish Hamilton:

What a thrilling time you must be having, with a front row seat (and by no means a safe one) at one of the greatest spectacles in the world's history. Your despatches have been magnificent, everyone is agreed you are head and shoulders above the rest.

It is very exciting news that you prefer book writing to the large salaries of Fleet Street after the war and I commend your wisdom and far-sightedness. Many fine writers have ruined themselves by sticking to journalism and becoming household words as reporters . . . I am quite sure that something satisfactory can be worked out.[47]

He had asked that the proposed book about the closing stages of the war and the biography of Montgomery should each run to 150,000 words and asked for a third book with which he could excite the American publishers, Harpers, who were interested in his work.

In Fleet Street, Christiansen was aware of such ambitions and that the time for their possible implementation was drawing near. Recognising Moorehead's need for praise and reassurance, he now wrote to him:

Ever since the beginning of the war I have been telling our fellows that you are the only man who can see copy in a flower growing by the wayside. I know they pulled your leg about my praise but it is the whole secret of journalism. Today there is one thing in your beautiful despatch which stands out as the hallmark of your craftsmanship. You have a phrase saying that you could stand watching a bulldozer for hours. Now the man who writes that homely little touch has my money every time as England's greatest reporter – and I have always thought English reporters, on the whole, were better than the American.[48]

Early in March Clifford returned and The Trio were in Germany awaiting the assault across the Rhine and the advance beyond. They were shocked by what they saw. "If you wanted to see the German people utterly beaten, reduced to the state of herded animals, then here it is," reported Moorehead. "In the big industrial towns like Gladbach and Krefeld, the war is over. It has ended in the ruin of nearly every normal thing in life."[49] Like the chaos in the ruined cities, the great offensive was not the orderly operation they expected. On 7th March the American vanguard near Bonn discovered that the bridge across the river at Remagen had not been blown and rushed across. Then, on the 22nd, Patton's troops "bounced" a surprise assault over the river between Mainz and Mannheim. The grand attack was launched the following night.

Again Moorehead was writing with the adrenalin flowing, his eye shifting focus from the close-up detail to the grand panorama:

It takes just three and a half minutes to cross the Rhine. The water is not very cold and it is pleasant to feel the spray on your face after facing the fine yellow dust which is now beginning to roll over the battlefield . . . The first person I noticed on the German bank was a large woman in a blue dress hanging out something to dry in the back yard of what was left of her house.

Then he continued, "The Germans suffer from shock and surprise. The British attack was a monstrous thing, a fantastic affair of swimming tanks and massed artillery, a large and destructive thing that goes over towns and railways and forests like a bulldozer."[50]

Across the river, twenty Allied divisions and fifteen hundred tanks burst into the heart of Germany. One after another the great cities that had become so familiar in name since the rise of the Nazis fell. Nowhere did the Germans attempt the desperate defence that had been expected. "The countryside is lovely," wrote Clifford in a letter home at the beginning of April. "The farms are very rich in eggs and chickens . . . We are finding nice places to live and I have picked up a displaced Italian as a servant. There is good Rhine wine to be had and plenty to write about."[51] The Trio, David Woodward and other old friends from the Mediterranean travelled in a caravan that excited envy and resentment (the Italian servant was said to be a chef they had brought with them from Naples) and set up a succession of comfortable billets in commandeered inns and villas. Clifford was writing a fortnight later:

We are all old campaigners and usually do pretty well. I, of course, am in charge of the catering and cooking and I dare not serve a meal consisting entirely of rations. My reputation would be gone. We seem to have a dinner party every night because everyone invites their friends freely – we have a kind of mobile salon. Our cellar, of course, is magnificent. By good luck we have acquired a better selection of French wines than any of us will ever drink again. We rescued them from a mob of Russians and Poles who were looting and smashing them.[52]

There was an unexpected shock on 12th April when it was announced that President Roosevelt had died suddenly but other shocks followed fast as the Allies began to discover the horrors of the concentration camps. Next day, Moorehead reported that the headlong advance of the British 2nd Army might have to be delayed or diverted because German officers had arrived with a white flag of truce to tell the British that "typhus had broken out among some 60,000 political and criminal prisoners in a concentration camp just ahead of our position in the village of Belsen".[53]

Moorehead did not visit Belsen for several days after the first British troops entered, and he did so after Sidney Bernstein, now an officer with a psychological warfare unit, called at his billet to say that it was a sight he had to see. The horrors of the place were almost impossible to accept or describe but he later wrote a long and detailed account of this and of the nightmare world the Nazis had created. "What we were seeing was something from the dark ages, the breaking up of a medieval slave state . . . And yet, in early April, we had only begun to glimpse the extent and depth of the Nazi terror system but already one sensed the utter disregard of human life in Germany."[54] Other concentration camps were being found, amongst them Dachau and Buchenwald, but the fighting was by no means over. In a brilliantly successful deception the Germans had convinced the Allies that they would make a final stand in the Bavarian and Austrian Alps and on 22nd April Moorehead wrote emphatically, "Well over 100 German divisions are now known to be concentrated in the Nazis' Southern Redoubt."[55]

That proved a mirage as the armies and the cities surrendered. The Russians were already fighting in Berlin and, as they approached the Chancellery, it was announced that Hitler was dead; killed by his own hand two days after his partner, Mussolini, had been executed by partisans on the banks of Lake Como. The final end was now a matter of formalities. The Germans surrendered on the Italian front on 1st May; next day, Berlin at last surrendered. Two days later, the German armies facing the 21st Army Group were surrendered to Montgomery at his headquarters on Luneburg Heath. The Trio were there and afterwards Moorehead typed one of his last despatches in the usual lower-case lettering for transmission. He began:

> daily express from moorehead montgomery field headquarters may
> fourth take one stop here on a wild stretch of heath just south of
> luneburg at precisely six twenty five pm today montgomery signed
> peace with germany stop five german officers walked into the tent
> and stood behind their chairs at a table over which a grey army
> blanket had been thrown stop presently montgomery arrived and
> as he took his place at the end of the table the five germans saluted
> and in silence they sat down together stop montgomery took out his
> spectacles and in a slow careful voice dash his voice is never strong
> at any time undash read out the following terms of surrender stop.[56]

The other correspondents then asked Moorehead to write a letter of
gratitude to Montgomery on their behalf. He did so, offering "our
heartiest congratulations on the brilliant end of your long journey
from the desert" and ending, "We have all tried tonight to do justice
to the story we have waited so long to write, the best story probably
of our lives."[57]

The final surrenders were still to come: to General Eisenhower at
Rheims on the 7th and to Marshal Zhukov at Berlin next day. On the
day the Germans capitulated on Luneburg Heath, Moorehead wrote
a long summing up:

> Adolf Hitler wanted Germany to go down with him in utter ruin,
> a colossal sacrifice to a colossal vanity. He has done it – thus today
> we attended the funeral of Germany . . . All around us are things
> too monstrous to grasp. Starvation. Fifty great cities in ruins. Ten,
> twenty, perhaps thirty million people roaming helplessly through
> the countryside without homes, their relations lost and all normal
> hope gone out of their lives. For the next year, the prospects are
> the starvation of anything up to five million people, the spread of
> disease, the collapse of most of the things of modern civilisation
> as it was up to the spring of 1945.[58]

There was to be a final ironic twist to the long narrative of The
Trio's journeys across the battlefields. "If you wanted the war to
end in pure fantasy, here it is," he reported. The German garrisons
of Denmark and Norway had not been involved in the final battles
and the liberation of those countries was the one unfulfilled task. For
the last time, The Trio – again accompanied by David Woodward –

set out together on an assignment. It was the day after the surrender on Luneburg Heath when they joined a company of the 1st Airborne Division boarding Dakota transports to fly under fighter escort to Copenhagen. There they received an ecstatic welcome from crowds lining the streets. As they arrived at the Hotel Angleterre, which was to be the temporary British headquarters, David Woodward remarked that it was in the restaurant there that he had been told by the head waiter of the German invasion of Poland nearly six years before. Again he entered the dining-room which was dark and empty, and sat down at a table, hopefully awaiting service. As he sat there, the head waiter appeared in the gloom and announced that he had just heard that Germany had surrendered.

Then, as Moorehead reported in the *Daily Express* in his last despatch of the war, "A dozen of us jumped into a Dakota aircraft in Denmark this morning and flew to Norway, entered the capital and accepted the surrender of 250,000 Germans."[59] They spent one dreamlike day in Oslo, being greeted at the airfield by a German colonel who had received no orders to surrender and had not fired on their approaching Dakota simply because he did not know who they were. He was bemused to find himself being photographed from all angles while Clifford spoke to him in German and relayed the requests from two British photographers to face the sun as he talked. Finally he was persuaded that this was indeed the vanguard of the British Army and provided transport into the capital where another delirious welcome awaited them. When they flew back to Copenhagen that evening they passed two white-painted flying-boats carrying the official British delegation on its way to accept the formal surrender of Norway.

Back at Luneburg in the familiar surroundings of a press camp, that, too, seemed oddly dreamlike. All the same correspondents and Public Relations officers were there, the jeeps and staff cars parked outside, but now there seemed no purpose. There would be no more briefings about the next day's operations, there were no more targets for the bombers and the guns were silent. There would be plenty of news to report – the hunt for the fugitive Nazi leader Himmler; the closing-down of the German provisional government under Admiral Doenitz at Flensburg; the clearing of the concentration camps; the millions of "displaced persons" roaming the countryside; relations with the Russians; finally the formal entry into Berlin by the British and the Americans.

But although this was the sort of news that The Trio had dreamed of reporting and commenting upon when the war was over, they could not bring themselves to do so. It was partly that after the five years of travelling with the battlefront they were tired. They had often felt stale and exhausted before but never as deeply. And there was no reason why they should stay with the armies any longer now that they had fulfilled their purpose. They wanted to see their families, their friends and taste the pleasures of peace. They wanted to start the lives they had been planning for five years: Moorehead to become a famous author; Clifford to find fame as a commentator of international affairs; Buckley to write about the post-war world before entering the cloisters of an Oxford college. There would be plaudits to receive – quite possibly the knighthoods they expected – and laurels to be rested upon for a while. As they thought about such a future, the dismal surroundings of defeated Germany seemed intolerably claustrophobic and depressing.

So, for the last time, they loaded their baggage and bedrolls into a car and that May morning drove westwards with Moorehead at the wheel. Their journey across Germany, through the Ruhr and across the Rhine into Belgium and then over the plains of France to Paris was a strange reversal of their travels. Towns and rivers that had been so important a few weeks or months ago were just names on signposts now. When they drove into Paris, crowds were still celebrating the end of the war but, thought Moorehead, such scenes "had no pattern with everything that had gone before". On the journey they talked about the war and the thoughts it inspired in them.

"Five years of watching war have made me personally hate and loathe war," Moorehead wrote soon afterwards. "But this thing – the brief ennoblement inside himself of the otherwise dreary and materialistic man – kept recurring again and again up to the very end and it refreshed and lighted the whole heroic and sordid story."[60]

At last The Trio were back in London, and there they found that the pattern and structure of events and the disciplines that had formed their characters, their lives and their relations with one another had fallen away.

Chapter Eleven

"In love with life"

Their rendezvous during the summer of 1945 was the Savoy Hotel, which they liked to call "our London club".[1] American journalists had tended to stay there during the war in Europe and it still had the air of an opulent correspondents' mess within walking distance of Fleet Street and a short taxi-ride from Broadcasting House and the Ministry of Information in Bloomsbury. To their initial surprise, The Trio realised that they could no longer charge the cost of subsistence to their expense accounts, but they had all been saving their salaries and could afford to live extravagantly.

Here the six of them would meet to plan an exciting future: Moorehead and Lucy, who had taken a flat in Belgravia; Clifford and Jenny, who were planning to live abroad; and Buckley and Cecilia Brown, whom he was hoping to marry when her divorce had been arranged. She was a tall, poised young woman whose wit and kindliness showed in her eyes and, although she and Buckley had known each other for more than a decade and he had long been in love with her, it was only now that, with her impending divorce, a future together seemed possible. His delight was enhanced by the fact that she had three children and, as a former schoolmaster, Buckley loved their company.

Cecilia had been introduced to his friends at a small party in the flat he had rented in London on his return from Germany. At first she felt over-awed by Lucy, who was beautifully dressed and wore a smart hat, while she herself wore, because of clothes-rationing,

"a home-made frock, probably curtain material". Jenny she thought
"frightfully gushing" but stimulating for her shy, charming husband,
whom she immediately found sympathetic. She was most intrigued
to meet Moorehead, of whom she had heard so much, finding his
conversation lively and original. The party had a sense of occasion
because it marked a drastic change of life for all of them. "It seemed
rather like the end of their last term at a school where they had been
happy," Cecilia thought afterwards. "Undoubtedly they had enjoyed
the war very much." She could be as challenging as Moorehead and
told him what she thought, adding that men knew nothing of war,
unlike their women who waited in agony and tried to protect their
children. Later she thought that the edge of bitterness that had
prompted this was brought about by the relief at seeing the lighted
windows of London again; to look at them, she and Moorehead stood
on the balcony of the flat while they talked.

To Cecilia's surprise, Moorehead began to flirt with her, because,
as she discovered subsequently, "he was always a bit amorous when he
talked to a woman." She was amused, and, as a tall woman, reflected
that "he was so much shorter than me and that makes a chap look a
bit of an ass in that situation".[2] It was nothing serious for he would
hardly have attempted to subvert the girl loved by his friend; but it
was the recurrence of a habit. From adolescence, flirtation had been
an enjoyment and a skill that had reflected a strong and restless
libido, the insecurity arising from his small stature and, when he
first arrived in Europe, his apprehensions of a bewildering social
structure. At first, he had flirted in the hope of seduction; then
in courting Lucy. Now, although his devotion to her was absolute,
he had again been exercising his skill at flirtation as an entertaining
sport that sharpened the wit and perception, with a tingle of sexual
excitement that did not involve the emotions.

With the end of the war in Europe, there was a lack of other
excitement. Clifford hoped to live in Paris or Italy and write about
the post-war development of Europe. Buckley planned a visit to the
continuing war in the Far East before trying to combine political
commentary in newspapers with writing military history and detective
stories and eventually finding an academic haven at Oxford; but, for
the moment, all this was eclipsed by his happiness because, soon after
the party in London, he finally asked Cecilia to marry him when she
was free and was accepted.

Moorehead had decided against offering to report the war in
the Far East and was, in any case, dissatisfied with journalism. But

Christiansen persuaded him to accept another assignment with the promise of a leisurely tour of the Continent, accompanied by Lucy and lasting more than a month. They set out in mid-July – she wearing for the first and only time a correspondent's khaki uniform – and visited France, Belgium, Italy, Switzerland and Germany, which, he reported, "lies quiet as a mouse, scarcely breathing".[3] He sent several collections of vignettes to the *Daily Express* that were entertaining but lacked the power and poignance that his readers had come to expect from his war reports.

During the tour, they twice heard major news. First, on 26th July, came the triumph of the Labour Party in the General Election when the British rejected not only the Conservatives but their war leader, Churchill, and his national coalition. Then, on 6th August, the atomic bomb was dropped on Hiroshima; three days later, another exploded over Nagasaki; then, on the 14th, Japan surrendered. Moorehead was heartened by the news from Britain, for he remained a radical at heart; and the news from the Far East meant that, for him, the option of remaining the most famous of war correspondents was finally removed so that, whatever he chose to do, it would have to be something different.

He was writing a final book about the war, taking the narrative from Taormina to Oslo, and would then start writing the biography of Montgomery. That might set him on the way to new distinction as an author.

Alone of The Trio, Buckley had gone to the Far East to report the war against Japan. It had ended soon after he arrived and he was back in London at the end of the summer with a combination of new theories on future strategy in the light of nuclear weapons and schoolmasterish flippancies. Paul Holt, formerly a senior war correspondent for the *Daily Express*, wrote to David Woodward:

Christopher has returned from Burma. He says that the three dominant impressions he brings back are: 1) That the campaign has been grossly over-publicised. 2) That the Chinese have opened up to him gastronomic avenues he never dreamed existed. 3) That the japanese (small j is mine) have good manners and a perfect talent for flower table-decoration.

Correspondents were returning to find their newspapers still suffering from newsprint rationing and the consequent shortage of space. Holt continued, "The paper situation in Fleet Street gets no better.

Every day more gentlemen full of strange oaths come back from the war and sit around the office with nothing much to do."[4]

Moorehead himself yearned for the freedom that a newspaper career denied. Soon after the final ending of the war with Japan, he called on Christiansen and told him, once again, of his hopes, confirming them in a letter written on 25th August:

> To recapitulate our conversation. I feel my usefulness to the paper on the present basis is ended. After eight years of travel and continued absence from my family, I know I cannot go on in pursuit of the news with the necessary energy and enthusiasm. I very much want to turn to magazine and book writing, where there is less nervous strain and much less rapid moving about. And so I have felt that I should leave the paper.

He did not suggest a complete break for it seemed doubtful whether he could earn the minimum of about £5,000 a year produced by his salary and expense account to maintain his family's standard of living. So he suggested as a compromise a freelance contract based upon his writing thirty articles a year on agreed subjects for the *Daily Express*:

> The kind of assignment I envisage would be, for example, a two months' visit to the USA to thoroughly investigate the atomic bomb experiments. During this winter I plan a sea trip along the Empire route to Australia, returning next spring via Japan and America . . .
>
> I must say again how grateful I am for the generosity with which I have always been treated by the *Express*. But I must ask you to believe me when I say I simply do not have the heart to go on in the old way rushing from one news event to another. I do sincerely feel I can do much more authoritative and better writing if given the time.[5]

So it was agreed once again that a decision on his future with the *Express* would be postponed, this time until he returned from Australia in the spring or summer of 1946. Meanwhile he finished his last narrative book about the war, *Eclipse*, which was to be published in the autumn, and began work on the biography of Montgomery. He knew much about the Field Marshal already, of course, but now he questioned at length two of his senior Intelligence officers, Brigadier Williams and Colonel Ewart, and had interviews with Montgomery himself. He worried a little about the ethics of biography, particularly after Williams had pointed out the inhibiting limits set by personal tact and military reticence, saying to him over lunch at The Ivy, "One can, at this stage, only write a five-shilling shocker; or a definitive biography which includes all the battles – and you can do neither!" To this Moorehead added, "No one in the end can reach the truth." Later he wrote to Williams, explaining the problems facing an intending biographer of Montgomery:

> His own view of himself was hopelessly coloured – and yet that unconscious colouring was part of his character. How honest can anyone be? It's not so much that we have an idealised view of ourselves: I think we set ourselves certain artificial standards, prejudiced standards, which are the result of our environment and we try to live up to them . . . The personal view and the attempt at the objective view are equally false. Somehow the biographer has to slip in between the two: but then he, too, is affected by his own prejudices and his reader is affected by his persuasiveness (or failure to persuade). Where then is the biographer? I feel one can only present a mass of prejudices and the best one can do (either now or in a hundred years) is to be sincere, to gather all the information that is humanly possible and, while enthusiasm lasts, set it down.[6]

By early autumn, Moorehead had completed his research and decided that much of the book could be written on board ship to Australia and completed while there. Lucy and the children together with Olive Wood, who had been nanny to the Lancasters' children and had come to the Mooreheads two years before, were still living at the cottage in Jevington. It was arranged that Moorehead should sail for Australia after the publication of *Eclipse* and Lucy would follow him two months later, when he should have written most of the biography.

On October 25th, he wrote in his diary:

> *Eclipse* comes out tomorrow: the fourth and, please God, the last of my war books. Hamilton insists it is good and is printing 30,000. He says he would go to another 30,000 if he had the paper. How anyone can bear to read a book about the war at this moment is entirely beyond me: I never read them even while the war was on. Jealousy over other writers? Some of that perhaps but

mostly boredom, or wanting to put every experience aside once I had done with it myself. Tomorrow, I suppose, the reviews: H. says *The Spectator* is good. Jack Priestley, too, is kind. Here they come – all the old feelings one has when a book is out: anxiety, smug satisfaction, embarrassment at what people say and, above all, a sense of relief and release.[7]

Next day, he added, *"Eclipse* seems to be selling briskly."[8] The reviews were even better than expected and the book was declared a triumph. So, glowing with gratification, Moorehead sailed for Australia, returning to Melbourne after nearly a decade not only as a famous reporter but as a successful author. After happy reunions with his parents, his sister Phyllis and her young family and the circle of relations and friends who had been watching his mounting success on the other side of the world, he left for Queensland to stay at a cousin's house and write in peace. Early in 1946, he was joined by Lucy and proudly introduced her to his family and friends. She charmed most but not quite all; Beth Thwaites, herself now married, felt that her own robust attitudes were not appreciated by this cool English beauty and remarked later that "Lucy took a scunner to me."[9] In this she was probably wrong because Lucy loved Australian vitality and enjoyed hearing and using their slang.

The Mooreheads sailed from Melbourne for Europe at the end of April. The visit had been a success – a mixture of intense social activity and solitary writing – but he still felt that his future and all prospects of continuing success lay in Europe. Yet he had made new friends with those who had, like him, been away at the war and found their conversation stimulating and lacking in the element of challenge that he sensed or imagined in Europe. Among these was a doctor, Roderick Andrew, who was a fellow-passenger on the liner bound for England where he was to take up a Nuffield travelling fellowship. He had been a contemporary at Melbourne University, but medical students had tended to keep apart from the rest; he had been a lieutenant-colonel with the Australians in the Middle East but they had not met there either. On board the liner the two men talked and, with their wives, played bridge every evening and took to each other. Moorehead liked men who carried their learning lightly – Dr Andrew was well known as a gastro-enterologist in Australia – and Rod Andrew enjoyed Moorehead's vitality and enquiring mind. "Alan is not an intellectual but he is always curious," he decided. "He is in love with life; always reaching for the stars."[10]

On his return to London, one of the first letters that Moorehead received was an official notification from Colonel Cross of the War Office, which ran, "The King has been graciously pleased to appoint you to be an Officer of the Most Excellent Order of the British Empire (Civil Division) for distinguished services as a War Correspondent."[11] Similar letters had also been received by Clifford and Buckley and by many more, including David Woodward, Desmond Tighe, Chester Wilmot, Evelyn Montague and others they had known on the way from the Nile to the Elbe. There were to be no knighthoods for The Trio after all. When none of them had been included in the New Year Honours List, as had been expected, Christiansen had led a deputation of editors to Downing Street to ask why the wartime achievements of their correspondents had not been recognised. It emerged that the Labour Government had decided not to give them high honours partly because the three who were, all agreed, the most deserving were employed by the leading Conservative newspapers, the *Express*, *Mail* and *Telegraph*. So the belated award of a relatively modest decoration would be the same for twenty-one of the more senior war correspondents. The Trio maintained a dignified silence and accepted their honours with grace when they were announced in June, though others showed anger on their behalf, amongst them Howard Marshall, a senior BBC correspondent, who wrote to Moorehead, "It should have been a K – the OBE is an insult!"[12]

Already Moorehead was aiming at new goals and recognition that would come to him alone. He decided that he would finally sever all links with the *Daily Express* and told Christiansen so. He was invited to name his terms and favoured assignment. Remembering his former hopes of being sent to Moscow, the editor now offered this. He was urged to accept by his friend, Ronald Matthews:

I hope you haven't yet turned that offer to go to Moscow down. You should go. The years we are living in are one of the critical points of history, as much so and more as the 16th century, the age of the Reformation. England today, and tomorrow the world, has to choose between two views of human life separated more profoundly by far than were the philosophies of 16th century Protestantism and Catholicism. It has to choose, and probably has very little time to make the choice, between totalitarian communism on one hand and democratic socialism on the other.

You know, from more than one experience, what democratic socialism means; you may find it boring but you can't say it's intolerable. Can you as a journalist – and if you say you are leaving journalism tomorrow – can you as an intelligent man of the world miss the chance to acquaint yourself, as fully as anyone can, with both sides of the terrible dilemma that faces the world today?

I think you realise yourself that most of your objections are sheer laziness and weariness of travel. You say you don't speak Russian . . . Now really, if Mr Wells were to turn up this moment with his Time Machine and offer to take you back to 1st century Palestine to listen to the Sermon on the Mount and watch the Resurrection, would you genuinely object that it would be a waste of time because you couldn't speak Jesus's language?[13]

Finally, there came an invitation to spend a weekend as Lord Beaverbrook's guest at Cherkley Court in Surrey in the hope of persuading him to stay with the *Express*. Later Moorehead told an Australian friend how he had been "received royally – food, drink, talk, flattery" but had refused to change his mind. Beaverbrook accepted defeat but Moorehead added, "From that moment he decided that I did not exist."[14] He had half-expected a "golden handshake" from the *Daily Express* in recognition of his services when he left; there was nothing but Christiansen's disappointment to see him go and the resentment and hostility of Lord Beaverbrook.

Now that he was back in London and *Montgomery* was completed, he looked about, undecided when it came to making precise plans rather than cherishing vague ambitions. As Paul Holt wrote to David Woodward, "Alan has no clear design for living."[15] However, as a start they gave up the cottage in Sussex and took a house on the slopes of Primrose Hill in London, 3 Wells Rise, a semi-detached Art Deco house built in a short street at right angles to Prince Albert Road that runs along the north side of Regent's Park. This was to be where the family would live and from which he could set out on the travels he had in mind.

The success of *Eclipse* had set the seal upon his brilliance as a war correspondent. Harold Nicolson had described him as an historian rather than a reporter and he was lionised by literary London as a successful author and a man of action and taken up by the busiest hostesses, Lady Sybil Colefax and Lady Rothermere, the intelligent wife of the proprietor of the *Daily Mail*. There were constant invitations to dine and meet prominent people from politics, the theatre and finance as well as journalism and publishing. One entry

21 The freedom of Australia: Alan Moorehead amongst the terns of an
island off the coast of Queensland during his triumphant return in 1952.

22 A beginning and an end: Alan Moorehead, silenced by the stroke, with Lucy and John after Caroline's wedding to Jeremy Swift (right) in the garden of the Villa Moorehead at Porto Ercole in 1967.

in his diary ran, "Colefax at Dorchester Hotel introduced fat man who said he had just burst into tears over the ending of *Eclipse*."[16]

Constantly asked what he was planning to write next, he was undecided. There was always fiction and, since his adolescence, he had wanted to write like Ernest Hemingway. So a novel it would be. The story he would tell would be topical, dealing with attitudes in the immediate post-war world. A returned soldier (cynical and materialistic), an academic (cynical and pessimistic) and an artist (cynical and artistic) desire the same girl because of the different aspects of the future she symbolises to each. The novel would be called *It Is Later Than You Think* and he began to write, setting himself a strict daily schedule and shutting himself into his little study at Wells Rise each morning.

On 25th November, 1946, *Montgomery* was published to critical acclaim. The Field Marshal himself was delighted with it, forecasting that it would have "a tremendous sale", although quick to point out that it was far from his whole story. He wrote to his friend Sir Edward Crowe, "Few people will ever know what I went through in the war . . . the whole truth is in my diaries, of course; but they can never be disclosed. We do not want another war!!"[17] The book was serialised in the *Sunday Express* under a profitable contract that had been arranged before Moorehead had decided to leave Beaverbrook Newspapers. It became a talking-point because of its apparently intimate portrait of the great soldier amongst those who did not know him and so did not realise how much of his difficult and egocentric character had been undisclosed.

If Moorehead's future was undecided, his two friends began 1947 with confidence in happy and successful years stretching ahead. Clifford and Jenny had been living in Paris, where he had been writing his political testament which was to be published as a low-key and thoughtful assessment of post-war Europe entitled *Enter Citizens* the following year. He was planning a wide-ranging future as a travelling commentator and needed a comfortable and secluded base. He refused to live in London, where she enjoyed the social activities, because of a dread of what he saw as the ingrained mediocrity there, summed up, for him, by the sight of the lacklustre shopping street in the West End, the Edgware Road. Now he found a haven in Portofino, the pretty fishing village on the shore of a hilly, wooded peninsula on the west coast of Italy south of Genoa.

During the summer of 1947 they had motored south through Italy with the Mooreheads, hoping to find something to equal the house and vineyard on Capri that Clifford had once hoped to buy. They had reached Portofino and walked through its narrow streets, along its waterfront and climbed the crags of the headland that sheltered its tiny harbour, and there they found the ruins of the Castelletto. This had been a watch-tower at the time of raids by the Barbary corsairs and during the recent war had been converted into a gun-emplacement by the Germans. There were several rooms with lovely views of the sea and the whole could be converted into a comfortable house without delay and too much expense, since labour in Italy was cheap. The Cliffords bought it and conversion began.

It was not long before they could stay at their almost-completed home and, on a final visit to their flat in Paris, from which he had been working for the *Daily Mail*, he wrote to Moorehead in London, "Yes, Portofino was a dream. The village square is the most heavenly place . . . I am certain you will all be mad about it. We got so brown and sleek and complacent after three days . . . Jenny, of course, has broadcast thousands of vague invitations . . ."[18]

Life was blissful for Christopher Buckley, too. In August, he married Cecilia and they settled down at Tunbridge Wells, planning journalistic assignments to the Continent on which she could accompany him. He had been commissioned to write histories of the subsidiary campaigns of what was now called the Second World War and was amusing himself by writing detective novels. Above all, he told Moorehead in a letter, "I am gradually shaping in my head something in the nature of a 'spiritual autobiography', which is the really big thing I want to tackle. And there is a book of essays and another novel in the background. I feel that all this is the harvest of the last seven years of experience ready to be gathered . . . I feel I have about four years' writing inside me."[19] He knew that his knowledge of warfare would put him back into a war correspondent's uniform if any major conflict broke out while he was still a journalist, but he announced, "I would give up the rest of my life for ten years of peace to spend with my wife."[20]

The Mooreheads planned to stay with both couples. At Tunbridge Wells, Lucy and Cecilia became close friends, drawn together by their intelligence and humour, but the latter did not become so fond of Moorehead. "He could turn on the charm like nobody else," she decided, "but in his approach to everything in Europe, he was like a small boy with his face pressed up against a sweet-shop window."[21] She was also dismayed by her husband's accounts of Moorehead's flirtations, which on occasion, since the middle years of the war, had become philandering, although it was obvious that he and Lucy were devoted to one another.

Moorehead had finished his novel, was awaiting news of its acceptance by a publisher and was again undecided as to future writing. He eagerly welcomed an assignment from the *Observer*, the Sunday newspaper with suitable gravitas and a liberal outlook to match his own. His destination was to be the newly-divided sub-continent of India, which had been granted independence from British rule on 15th August, 1947, though divided into the Hindu state of India and the Muslim state of Pakistan. He was to tour the countries and the disputed territory of Kashmir, interviewing the leading British participants in the transfer of power – including the last Viceroy, Lord Mountbatten, who had now become Governor-General of the two new dominions – and Indian and Pakistani politicians, reporting both news and comment.

First, however, he and Lucy were to stay with the Cliffords at Portofino after which she would return to London and he would board a British Overseas Airways flying-boat in the Mediterranean, bound for Karachi. The Cliffords' house above the sea was dramatic and comfortable but Alex's apprehensions were well founded, for he had written to Moorehead, "Far more people than one can believe appear to be taking the most casual invitations seriously. I don't mind meeting people in the Piazza for a drink but if they are going to stay in the house it is going to be most distasteful."[22] It would be different with the Mooreheads as guests and they spent a happy September there, hankering after a house in Italy themselves. As a trial experience, they planned to stay with Freya Stark, the writer and traveller whom they had met in Cairo, at Asolo north of Venice, which would be less of a social stage than Portofino. When Lucy left for London, wet weather began as the summer season ended and Moorehead, waiting to leave for Marseilles where he would join the flying-boat, wrote to her, "Portofino would never do as a place to live because it's really a country club arranged for a party and it's forlorn when there are no guests." He was, once again, missing her and wrote, "Dear puss, I abandon you to so much alone . . . I always warm to you enormously when you have just gone . . . This grey, wet Portofino puts me in the way of sad sentiment and I have been thinking of you and the children."[23]

When he arrived in Karachi in Pakistan ten days later – early in October, 1947 – he was still glowing with affection and next day wrote, "Every time I leave you I have this rush of warmth towards you, such a feeling of certainty that there is no one like you and that there is nobody else I could possibly be with or want or think about or touch or remember or confide in." The certainty helped him to relax and enjoy the prospect of travel, hard work and even a little danger, for the deep divisions between the Hindu and Muslim populations in both countries had resulted in inter-communal fighting, massacres and stampedes of fugitives. "The ambience is unrest, crowding and atrocities," he wrote to her. "I am having an expensive and superb Palm Beach suit made. The rush of servants to do the laundry and the food eclipses even Portofino in some ways. I had forgotten the mad luxury of being a white in India."

Also in Karachi was a *Daily Express* reporter, James Cameron, "who is charming",[24] bound on a similar mission. He had been a sub-editor with a flair for feature-writing and had been chosen to report the first post-war atomic bomb tests at Bikini Atoll. His despatches had been brilliant and Christiansen, with characteristic verve, had promoted him to the status Moorehead had so quickly acquired in Cairo six years before. He was a slim, dark young man with sensitivity, a streak of ruthlessness and political views to the left of Moorehead's. Both amusing and sombre, he was good company and they planned to travel together when they could. A few days later, on arrival in New Delhi, both attended one of Gandhi's prayer meetings and Moorehead was able to recount his earlier impressions.

Moorehead was staying with his old friend Field Marshal Sir Claude Auchinleck, who had been Commander-in-Chief of the Indian Army and was now appointed Supreme Commander to supervise its division but without operational responsibilities. He spent a week in New Delhi being briefed on the problems following the transfer of power. Already there was conflict in the northern state of Kashmir, where the ruler was Hindu but the majority of the population Muslim. As this seemed a microcosm of the whole problem, Moorehead flew to the capital Srinagar beside a beautiful lake below the wall of the Himalayas. On the flight he read E.M. Forster's novel *A Passage to India*, which inspired him with a fresh urge to write fiction. "I have been finally overpowered by *A Passage to India* and this morning I wrote to Forster, which may not amuse him," he wrote to Lucy on arrival. "The book is a fantastic echo of India. It needs, he says, kindness and more kindness. You would feel that with me if you were here."

In Srinagar, he met a *Daily Express* correspondent, Sidney Smith, who explained the current dangers of Muslim tribesmen coming down from the mountains to raid the villages in the foothills and even the capital and that there was talk of Europeans having to be evacuated. "Here I am 7,000 feet up at Srinagar, very near to Russia and China and it is a comic little Venice of tumbledown wooden shanties and boatmen," he wrote to Lucy. "Everything is wild and excessive, very Central Asian and I am drawn towards China powerfully. This remoteness: it beckons and acts like a drug, urging one on."

He was already missing Lucy as achingly as at any time during the war and, now as then, his thoughts turned to the possibility of having another child:

Yes, another baby – I am all in favour. We must see if we can time it right. This may be difficult as I rather planned that you should be spending most of your time in bed from the moment I get home. I rarely think of you in any other way now. All your brains, charm, patience, kindness, breeding, knowledge and honesty are really in the end nothing at all compared to the moment of your making love to me. I am being a little pompous about this but I have a rush of blood to the head in thinking now of how it would be if you were here and of how I would feel myself in love with you as I always am, completely, every time, without any reserve and a sort of recklessness and brutality and – I don't know – a kind of utter generosity. Yes, darling, I know, this is bad writing. But if I had you here . . .[25]

The attacks by the hill tribes became more violent but Moorehead was unperturbed, living on a houseboat on the lake at Srinagar and soothed by its peacefulness. He wrote again to Lucy five days later:

I sit in a houseboat with frozen mountains all around and a stove burning. Sidney Smith and his wife are in the next houseboat . . . I have been this afternoon to the Gardens of Shalimar in a boat with three paddlers while I lay on embroidered cushions in the prow . . . I have been asked to go bear-hunting on the mountain opposite and also, tonight, there is the climax of my bearer's wedding which has been raging in different houseboats for three days and nights. One night we sat for two hours and watched a boy dancing for the guests and he never moved more than two yards. Then tonight boatmen came up to the lake and said we could not leave tomorrow to go down to the plains – the tribesmen from the North-West Frontier had crossed the road. It

seems to be a small invasion and may last a day or two. And so
for the moment we are cut off. I do not mind very much yet. The
tribesmen loot and kill and there is holy bloody murder wherever
they go like a typhoon. And then it passes. So we shall get down
to India from the Himalayas somehow I expect.[26]

They did but the danger threatened by the feared, unseen tribesmen
to the evacuation gave Moorehead the setting of a novel that would
combine pace of action and the evocation of India and he began to
sketch the plot and his characters. He continued his tour and, on
reaching New Delhi at the end of the first week of November,
discovered that the adventure in Kashmir had not been without
real danger. Sidney Smith had not been with Moorehead's party
and he was reported to have been killed. But next day Moorehead
wrote to Lucy, "Sidney Smith, having been reported dead, turned up
dramatically in Rawalpindi last night having been ten days a prisoner
of the tribesmen."[27] He was able to break the news to Smith's wife,
who had reached New Delhi, and with James Cameron took her out
to dinner.

While staying with Auchinleck Moorehead visited Indian politicians, dipping into the beguiling and alien society that enticed
as well as excluded him. Then he would return to the world of
"ADCs, servants, bowls on the lawn (where jackals pass back and
forth from the jungle), swimming, tennis and the rest",[28] as he put
it.

Finally he was received by the Governor-General, who had been
warned by his aides that it might be a difficult interview because
Moorehead had long realised that more immediate and trenchant
responses were prompted by aggressive and critical questioning. He
wrote to Lucy:

Was exhausted by the Mountbattens yesterday, male and female.
They had been told, I think, that I was anti their policy. She
attacked me tooth and nail. Then he (sitting up having his shoulder
massaged by a fat nurse) had at me for two hours and never once
drew breath. A tour de force. He has a marvellous memory and a
complete grip on this fantastically complicated set-up. His energy
is beyond belief.

There were more interviews – with General Ismay, the Chief of Staff,
and Pandit Nehru, the Prime Minister of India, amongst them – but

all seemed trivial compared with the overwhelming presence of India.
He wrote to Lucy:

> I have a sudden pain for India sometimes. A lizard watches
> me in my bath with bright black eyes. At night in the garden
> the dew is so heavy the bowls skid on the lawn and mad birds
> wail and wail. The garden billows with bright flowers, too big, too
> rich, so much bigger than the normal austerity in everything. One
> of the house laundresses returning from the Punjab was sitting in
> the train when a Sikh came in and lopped off her foot. She died
> tonight.
>
> For the moment the troubles are over. But they will recur.
> I can't describe this deep-breathing, insect-calling air, the awful,
> terrible pathos. When I pass along the corridor, white jacket,
> black tie, silk handkerchief, past the emblems of the wars and
> the paintings of the Viceroys, the servants get up from the floor,
> place their hands together in the motion of prayer and bow. I
> wish I could tell you more. A sort of sweet hunger in the very
> swell of the ground. It's heart-breaking. One exposes oneself too
> much. And yet sometimes, modestly, one feels like God in being
> a human being here. You must live this sometime. With me.[30]

He longed for Lucy but not for London. "Yes, I realise the London
house has something. And yet something drags me here – abroad,
I mean. Even in this hothouse atmosphere I feel more at ease. It's
simpler somehow; there seems more reason for living."

In his reports to the *Observer* he wrote in his old, sharp-eyed,
conversational style commenting after his tour:

> There is a general retreat into fatalism. Wherever I have been in
> Northern India, one notices very few clocks and those that exist
> are often broken or unwound. This is presumably because not
> many people are interested in the right time anyway . . . Then
> suddenly, as though people wanted to make up for lost time,
> there are these outbursts of mad violence. All the pent-up, petty
> irritations erupt en masse. And, in a moment, wild excess balances
> the long apathy . . . The British find themselves in a special case.
> Nobody really attacks them now; they are the new Untouchables
> – for the moment . . . The mood is one of persistent tension, of
> nervous ennui: an uneasy feeling that anything can happen now
> that the British Raj has gone.[31]

His tour ended where it began, in Karachi, and at the end of the first week of December he began the four-day journey by flying-boat to Poole Harbour in Dorset. Much of this time he devoted to planning the novel about the adventure in Kashmir: the sudden threat of massacre and the drawing-together of the oddly-assorted Europeans hoping for rescue. His return to Primrose Hill was not what he had expected. A letter from his literary agent, Laurence Pollinger, awaited him quoting a letter from an American publisher about the manuscript of his first attempt to write fiction, *It Is Later Than You Think*. He had written:

> I am terribly sorry, the Moorehead novel just is no good. It has some brilliant spots, but they are purely journalistic and, as a novel, it just stinks. It would really do his reputation a lot of harm if this were published . . . We should get together and see if we could not decide on a non-fiction book. We can make a go of Moorehead over here if we can get the right subject. This novel will be the Kiss of Death.[32]

He was shocked but reacted aggressively. He abandoned the first novel and at once began to write a second so that Hamish Hamilton could have the typescript early in 1948 and it could be published by Christmas. It would be called *The Rage of the Vulture* and would be written with an eye to a film treatment that would excite Hollywood. This one was accepted and he again felt a flutter of optimism that he might become an established novelist. Yet now no important ideas gripped his imagination. He toyed with plots for another novel, for films and plays, but none matched in scope his books inspired by the war. Both of his post-war books had sold well, despite the shortage of paper limiting their print-orders: *Eclipse* had sold nearly 37,000 copies and *Montgomery* 53,000.

Early in 1948, the Mooreheads took a more simple decision and another child was conceived. He began to plan and write another novel set in an Italian resort like Portofino and was encouraged to receive an unexpected letter from a successful novelist he had met briefly during the war, Nevil Shute, also an Australian, inviting him to join him on a six-month journey from North Africa, across Asia to Australia. "A novelist is apt to go sour unless he gets around and sees new places and meets new people," wrote Shute. "I wonder if this is in your line? I do not think our writing interests would conflict at all, since mine are purely fiction; I have no desire to write a travel book."[33] Moorehead, flattered at the invitation, accepted in principle, but, still thinking of himself as a novelist, asked if the project could be reconsidered at a later date.

Instead he decided to fly to New York in the hope of making contacts among publishers that would promote him as a writer for an American readership. The visit was not particularly encouraging, but his friend from undergraduate days, Alwyn Lee, and his wife Essie were living in New York. Lee had been a war correspondent in the Pacific and was now a freelance journalist specialising in the arts and writing for the *New York Times* and the *New Yorker* and introduced Moorehead to the editor of the latter, Harold Ross, who invited him to contribute to the magazine, suggesting an article about Venice as a start. In the United States, Lee explained later, freelance journalists could command far higher fees than in Europe and earn a handsome living.

On his return, Moorehead set out for Italy with a series of long articles for the *New Yorker* in mind. His travels took him to Tuscany and, while in Florence, he received another unexpected and gratifying invitation. This came from Bernard Berenson, the American historian of Renaissance art and adviser to galleries and picture-dealers, who lived nearby at Settignano. He had survived the war unmolested, despite his Jewish ancestry, because, it was said, of his friendship with Count Ciano, Mussolini's son-in-law and foreign minister. He had read and admired one of Moorehead's war books and invited him to stay. When he arrived at I Tatti, the house where Berenson had lived so long surrounded by Renaissance works of art, the two men took to each other at once and a friendship began. "There was a current flowing between us, an instinctive liking," wrote Moorehead later, "and, as a result, he became the foster-father I so badly needed."[34] Both seemed very different: Berenson more than twice Moorehead's age, frail and intellectual; Moorehead, robust, inquisitive and restless. Yet both were expatriates in love with their European surroundings; both were small in stature and that was still a factor in Moorehead's self-awareness. When he first visited the solemn house filled with paintings, *objets d'art* and fine furniture and dined with his host, he felt "tense as a cat among the dishes and Venetian finger-bowls".[35] But Berenson charmed him, talking with vivacity, erudition and wit. This old man, his guest decided, had discovered and was enjoying something of what he himself sought.

Although he did not visit Venice on this journey, Moorehead collected material for articles about Portofino and Siena for the *New*

Yorker and returned to London to write them. At the end of August came a blow. His mother had been ill and now a cable arrived from Phyllis to say that she had died. It was only a dozen years since he had left the last of the succession of happy, busy homes she had created in Melbourne, yet they now seemed infinitely remote.

He was excited to hear from the *New Yorker* that his first contribution had been accepted – "We were delighted, though not at all surprised, that you hit the mark exactly with your first piece"[36] – but still the mood of aimless striving continued. The other two members of The Trio seemed to have found their way ahead. Buckley was doing what Ronald Matthews had urged Moorehead to do and was writing about the ideological – and military – crisis in Europe. He had written while on an assignment for the *Daily Telegraph* in Warsaw, "Either one feels it to be intensely important as the essential showdown in Eastern Europe between two ways of government and two ways of life, or it's something completely irrelevant. In my own case, though I hated leaving Cecilia and was absorbed with my war history, it was something I *had* to do." He feared the communist threat of "the omnipotent police and the glance over the shoulder covering all the world", and concluded, "If your evidence can turn the scale, isn't it your duty to be a witness, even though your hate for travel may make you into the Greek for witness, a martyr?"[37]

Clifford, based on Portofino, was travelling widely for the *Daily Mail*, and had visited Moscow, reporting on the intensification of what Churchill had recently named "the Cold War". Yet Moorehead felt no urge to emulate them, only a twinge of guilt that he was not doing so. He told himself that he was destined for great things as a writer, although exactly what was impossible to define. His destiny must lie somewhere between Clifford's way of life of alternating travel and languor at Portofino and Berenson's life of contemplation and quiet enjoyment of good company in the hills of Tuscany. He himself inclined towards the latter, telling himself that he had yet to recover from the strain of the war years and was in need of peace in the fullest sense in which to consider the future and await inspiration.

It so happened that an opportunity for just such a rest now presented itself. Ever since the war, Moorehead had discussed possibilities of living in one of the beautiful or exciting places they had visited. There had been talk of Paris and St.-Jean-de-Luz, Portofino and Asolo, Rome and other places beside or near the Mediterranean. Now they heard of a villa at Fiesole in the hills outside Florence, which belonged to a rich American living in California, who wanted to rent, or possibly sell it fully furnished. It was called the Villa Diana. The Mooreheads went to see it and found a still, calm old house of seventeen rooms standing in a formal garden of clipped box hedges and surrounded by vineyards. It lay in a fold of the hills looking down upon Florence. Five centuries before, the house had been the home of Angelo Poliziano, a poet, a friend of Lorenzo the Magnificent and tutor to his son. At once Moorehead identified with these men of the Renaissance, who, like himself, were men of letters and men of action. To live in Poliziano's house would be appropriate and inspiring. There would be problems over educating the children in Italy, perhaps, and in dealing with publishers in London and New York, but he was unable to resist the temptation of the house. Lucy was thankful that they could settle at last, for as Moorehead wrote to his sister, she was "getting a little punch-drunk with moving and says, 'Okay, just give me the address will you?' "[38] They took a short lease on the old house at Fiesole, and on the last day of August, 1948, went to live there.

Two days later, Moorehead opened the journal that he had kept occasionally during and since the war, wrote what he had once called a dateline and began:

We have been two days in the Villa Diana now: it gives a strange sensation of quietude, the sense of being in the right place. The coal and wood have arrived for the winter. The wine is ordered, we have moved a great deal of furniture from place to place and we have brought car-loads of household things up from Florence. This is the first time I have enjoyed shopping . . .

They had decided that John, who was now aged eight, should be educated at the local school and were delighted when, having told the priest in charge that they were not Catholics, he had smiled and answered, "We make no difference."[39] Although they themselves were not religious, they took pleasure in the proximity of their church and its processions and rituals. When a friend tried to convert Moorehead to Roman Catholicism, he wrote to his sister:

Like my friend Clifford, I can't make up my mind between Christianity and Marxism. Clifford, at least, is taking practical steps. He is building a small shrine on the front drive of his house at Portofino and at the touch of an electric button, it turns from a statue of the Virgin Mary into a bust of Lenin. This is not as blasphemous as it seems because the Communists are on top one moment in the village and the Christian Democrats at the next moment . . .[40]

There were no such conflicts in Fiesole and they quickly felt accepted. Three days later he was writing:

I am almost happy here. For two days I have scarcely been out of the house and the beauty of each room will still take a long time to explore. Tonight we sat on a seat near the monastery of S. Francesco overlooking Florence – it's a guidebook view but nonetheless as complete as any stale phrase could describe it. The evening sun struck a coil of the Arno in the west as in a Bellini. The children are nervous and uneasy with it all – but then John goes to school tomorrow and Caroline will settle.[41]

Next day he wrote the first chapter of his new novel with great satisfaction. It was to be a study of ambitions and loyalties amongst expatriates set in an Italian seaside resort village like Portofino and was to be called *Celine* after a principal character. "I have never worked in such excellent conditions," he wrote in his journal. "Complete isolation from 8.20 until 1.30, a long table, a dark room with two small bright windows." This must have been how Renaissance men of intellect and action had worked. Like them he would make use of the peace he had found to read and write and converse. Like them, he would enjoy the company of scholars, for Bernard Berenson would be his neighbour. He had been a man of action and now, whatever turbulence raged in the world beyond the Tuscan hills, he could turn to becoming a man of letters. After a week at the Villa Diana, he was writing, "There have been violent storms outside – once lightning was continuous for an hour. This distresses Lucy and the children; stimulates me."[42]

Chapter Twelve

"What are the ingredients of my happiness?"

"Count Bernadotte has been assassinated. Hyderabad has capitulated. The Western representatives went again to the Kremlin. The importance of all this? That it will leave me in peace."[1]

Writing this in his diary at the end of his first month at the Villa Diana – and brushing aside the news of the murder of the United Nations' mediator in the Middle East, the agonies of freeing India from the Empire and the mounting hostility of the Russians – Moorehead did not admit to himself that he was again running away. Even in the privacy of his journal he did not wonder whether he was escaping the pressures of newspaper work and the social challenges of London into the shadows of the Renaissance. He saw himself as a writer in the progress of evolving, sloughing off the hard skin of the newspaper correspondent and allowing his sensitivity and style to grow.

He was writing a novel and was pleased with its progress but was more absorbed in creating an atmosphere in which his talent could flourish. He was constructing a private world which he did not want to share with anybody beyond his immediate family and the servants and their families who thronged the kitchen and the garden; it would be pleasant to receive visitors but he did not want to show them the secret and silent rooms of his house. He even decided against having a telephone installed. This would be the setting of his own renaissance. He was certain that this would follow; for he would tell friends, "You can do anything you really want in life; you only have to make the effort." In his own case, it would be a combination of effort, ambience and inspiration:

What are the ingredients of my happiness? The first essential is to be building something, making some work go forward. Today I completed the love scene in Chapter 3, clipped the box hedges in the second garden, got Il Vecchio [the gardener] to spread the gravel at last in front of the garage, climbed the tree outside our bedroom window and lopped off two branches so that we shall have a clear view of the mountains . . .

Then good food and wine. The red and the white, both, improve in the cellar every day and it is hard not to take four glasses with each meal. For lunch, Enrichetta boned a rabbit and stuffed it with herbs and boiled eggs. The figs are at their best.

The weather. This was a perfect autumn day, a steady sun, no wind.

To be loved, of course, and in the end this is first. John is always very close to me. I saw him as he is, a little boy, as he waved goodbye to me on his way to school this morning, his satchel over his shoulder. He waited for Caroline to come down the steps and they set off together as she wanted to go with him as far as the front gate . . .

Then the myriad minor things – a new razor blade, a look on someone's face, a good book (Strachey's *Books and Characters*), cigarettes and not too many, the things Lucy brought back from shopping, one's good health, one's clothes, the pleasure of moving around a beautiful house and garden.

It seems madness that anyone could willingly not live like this.

Absence of jealousy, suspense, antagonism, ambition, ennui.

How long will it last?[2]

It lasted in this pure essence of pleasure for less than two months. There had been good news from London, where *The Rage of the Vulture* had been published in October with 8,000 copies already ordered and friendly reviews. He had been invited, as a literary figure, to join the British delegation to the UNESCO conference in Beirut at the end of the year, which was gratifying. He had written 50,000 words of *Celine* and had an idea for a play about Voltaire. The Cliffords had been to stay. Then, late in October, Lucy, who was pregnant, left for London to see her gynaecologist. Moorehead returned from the railway station to the Villa Diana in a thunderstorm, joined his children and servants in the old house and confided in his journal:

> Now we are alone and the house seems dark and forlorn. Caroline is rather pathetic, John writes letters as though he would anchor himself to England or some other place than this: and I roam about wondering what on earth I am doing here. The novel seems pointless and all energy useless. I will, if I can, write myself into another mood but it is impossible not to remember that there are lives to be lived in which one has friends and stimulus and not this crashing back upon oneself one finds in the rain in the country alone. There are times when I seem deliberately to have turned my back on all the normal amusements of life and other people: the theatre, sports, cards, parties, dinners and, above all, work in the society of other people instead of here, alone, in the most distant rooms of a large house.[3]

Even the arrival of more visitors – Freya Stark and Warren Chetham Strode, the playwright – did not lift the cloud of depression. He decided that *Celine* was "forced and artificial"[4] but tried to become enthusiastic about the idea of writing his autobiography, although much of it would, inevitably, be the sort of war book against which he had set his face. He had been reading André Gide and Georges Simenon in French and, in comparison, brooding upon his own writing:

> I think I know myself as a writer now. Description of scenes, places, action: excellent. Readableness, continuity, tempo, construction: first class. Writing: often first class, sometimes better or worse. Dialogue: natural and fluent but without wit or any particular subtlety or inspiration. Characters: very bad with the exception of occasional flukes drawn from life. Plots: hopeless. Ability to state a meaning, a philosophy: hopeless.[5]

His visit to Beirut for the UNESCO conference was not stimulating since he had no inclination towards or talent for public speaking. At the end of the year, the prospects for 1949 were limited to invitations to write articles for the *Observer* and the *New Yorker* and another from General Airey, the British officer commanding the disputed city of Trieste for the United Nations, to visit him at his headquarters in a castle at Duino. Yet no possibility matched the hopes with which he had arrived in Tuscany. He confided in his journal:

Into another abyss today from which I can see no escape. What shall I do? Write an autobiography? Re-write *Celine*? Turn it into a play? Attempt Berenson's biography? Go to Duino in search of a *New Yorker* story? Do a lecture tour for the British Council? Go to London? Cease writing altogether and get a job? I turn these things over and over in my head and always end in the same vacuum, the same lack of concentration. Poor Lucy is beset by my nervelessness. It is a bad time of year for everything to decline and fail.[6]

His hopes of inspiration would be renewed by visits to Berenson at I Tatti. The old man – fragile as porcelain, immaculately dressed; his white beard perfectly trimmed – was not only a charming host but seemed an ambassador of a lost literary and artistic world, who could not only quote from the literature of his youth in the last century but repeat stories told him by Oscar Wilde. Sometimes a fellow-guest would be Sir Harold Acton, the doyen of the expatriates, whose ancestors had lived in Italy for two centuries; one of them as chief minister to the Bourbons of Naples in Nelson's time. The company, of which Moorehead felt a natural, component part, seemed as erudite, courtly and entertaining as that which he assumed must exist in England but which he had not yet attempted to join.

It was his private meetings at I Tatti that were most comforting. He recorded in his journal at the beginning of 1949:

I went to see Berenson yesterday, and found him in the garden in white gloves, trouser cuffs neatly turned up against the mud, a felt hat, immaculate. I felt him looking askance at my misshapen corduroy trousers and sports coat. That house and garden never fails to soothe me and in the centre of it all, like a spider in a web, that brisk, disenchanted old man, crackling and sparkling . . . He urged me gently not to despair when one cannot write since one is taking in during this time and again pressed the idea that I should write military biography. I said, "The generals are so dull," and he replied, "All generals are myths. You must turn them into myths." There's maybe something in it if I could arrange my biography round an expedition like Garibaldi and the Thousand. Who among the contemporaries?

Gott? No, too small. Wingate? Don't know him and it's been done . . .[7]

Next day, he wrote:

Now, of all things, Berenson suggests I write a biography of Wellington, whom he regards as a great man, never sufficiently revealed . . . (same thing, too, with Cromwell, whom he offers as an alternative). I should, he thinks, take four or five years on the work and the result, he believes, might secure me as a writer . . .

As always one comes away from the old man full of the things he says. He declared yesterday that no people feels secure until it has begun to persecute somebody. Thus the puritans went to America so that in their turn, they could start persecuting people there . . . Among the rest of B.'s obiter dicta: it is insane to destroy the balance of power either in politics or in a family. As soon as it is lost and one man emerges at the top, war and anarchy supervene.[8]

He was about to make a pilgrimage to another literary figure whom he had admired longer and more extravagantly than Berenson. Lucy had continued to keep in touch with Mary Welsh, Noel Monks's former wife, since she had married Ernest Hemingway and now they were invited to stay with the Hemingways at Cortina in the Dolomites. Once, Moorehead had considered his host's early book, *A Farewell to Arms*, the finest writing he knew and had tried to model his own upon it. Hemingway had briefly been a war correspondent in a haphazard and self-indulgent manner in both Spain and North-west Europe and, as Moorehead was more than his equal in that field, he was confident of a stimulating exchange of views.

The welcome at Cortina was not quite what they had expected. Their egocentric host liked to entertain guests of his own choice and was piqued that his wife should invite her own friends. He was out duck-shooting when they arrived. Moorehead later remembered:

When he came in at last he was a walking myth of himself. Cartridge belts and strings of teal and mallard hung in festoons from his shoulders, powdered snow clung to his beard and woolly cap and when his gun was laid aside in the corner, he had to be helped off with his clothes – layer after layer of sweaters, leather jerkins and a coloured shirt. At the end of it all, he fished a cable out of his pocket and held it out to me. It read: "Nothing could be better than a piece on Venice by you but it so happens we have got someone called Alan Moorehead who may be doing it one day so I am sorry . . ." It was signed Harold Ross.*[9]

Hemingway was not welcoming and told them: "When I heard at first you were coming, I thought I'd move out so as to give you a bit more room around the place with Mary." He, too, was having difficulty in writing and he radiated discontent. Yet this was eased when he discovered that the younger man was an admirer and ready to be impressed. Hemingway had led an exciting life but was unable to resist making it more so with wildly exaggerated stories of his adventures. One of his favourite fantasies was based upon his cruises in the Caribbean during the war in his own yacht, the *Pilar*, ostensibly in search of German submarines, but since they had only twice sighted surfaced U-boats in the far distance, these trips had been largely devoted to fishing, drinking and playing the part of rip-roaring seafarers.

So, on his second day at Cortina, Moorehead recorded:

> Talked for five hours with H. yesterday. On the way he sailed his 42 ft. boat without flag and without official backing (though, of course, sponsored and armed by the US Navy) as a U-boat chaser. U-boats surfaced and called them alongside (steel always calls to wood at sea apparently). Once alongside, below the trajectory of the U-boat's 88 mm. gun (sometimes they were touching) H. opened fire from concealed guns, which were shot up on to deck through the hatches at the last moment, and ran for it. In addition they carried depth charges. Crew of nine, including cypher officer, radio operators, three navigators, depth-charge expert; none of them in uniform. H., who holds a master's certificate for all tonnages in all seas, was captain.[10]

When Hemingway could be the centre of the household's attention, all was well. He was particularly pleased at being able to stop a fight between two big dogs in the village street by flinging his coat over one of them and hurling it over a wall. But he did not like the idea of Mary ski-ing with the Mooreheads, when he could not participate and his younger guest would be able to demonstrate his prowess. In a fit of pique he forecast that she would only break her leg, and it

* The editor of the *New Yorker*.

then fell to Moorehead to telephone Hemingway with the news that his wife was in hospital with a broken bone in her ankle and would be incapacitated for a month. Their host was furious, and when his obscenities had ceased, the Mooreheads felt that they were now so unwelcome that they should leave. However, they could hardly abandon Mary, so they stayed and, over bottles of red wine, Hemingway calmed and again began to talk about himself, confident that he had an attentive listener. "We have talked endlessly now over red wine and martinis," Moorehead wrote in his journal, "on Paris in the war, on books and God knows what else. I must say the fishing and boating around Cuba sounds wonderful and I may go there sometime."[11]

Hemingway told him that he began to develop his terse, much-imitated style of prose when a young reporter in American police courts and editing the words spoken by simple people in the dock and witness box down to their essentials. He could not resist some apparent exaggeration when he heard how extravagantly Moorehead had admired *A Farewell to Arms*:

H. said that he had written forty different endings to *A Farewell to Arms* and he asserted that he never knew in any book what was going to follow from one page to the next. His technique seems (or seemed) to be a matter of squeezing out the essence of what you feel with the least rhetoric and decoration possible; the plot and eventually the pattern and style of the book takes care of itself.[12]

As it happened, Moorehead was to meet within a month another literary figure of the eminence to which he himself aspired: George Bernard Shaw. After staying with General Airey and touring Trieste, he had returned to Florence to find a congratulatory cable from the *New Yorker* thanking him for his latest article and another from Paul Holt asking him to write a film script about the Russian blockade of West Berlin and the Allied airlift which was keeping the city supplied. It was arranged that he report on Berlin for the *Observer* but, as he prepared to leave the Villa Diana, he found that the life of contemplation and frustration had left him surprisingly timid. "I am delighted to do all this," he noted, "but I shall clearly be exasperated and lonely at times and the sanity of our life in Florence will become more apparent."[13] He travelled first to London and during the fortnight spent making arrangements for the assignment in Berlin met Lady Astor, the forceful and eccentric American who had been the first woman Member of Parliament, and, when talking about literature, she had offered to introduce him to Shaw.

One Sunday afternoon late in February, they called at his house, "Shaw's Corner" at Ayot St. Lawrence in Hertfordshire. When they arrived, Moorehead recorded:

> Shaw was asleep in his chair, his mouth wide open. We went to see the canvas and wooden hut where he works, screened by a clump of trees at the bottom of the garden, but when we came back to the house he was already outside in a darned, grey Norfolk suit. When asked if he was well, he answered; "At my age I am either well or dead." He is 92, his white head is more stooped in his shoulders than one would have thought from his photographs but his hearing is good, although he moves slowly and unsteadily and complains of his weak legs, he does not give the appearance of great fragility and his blue eyes are entirely clear. He is a clean old man – clean white head and clear complexion. He has a way of hanging his head when he talks as though it were too heavy for him and he speaks with a distinct Irish brogue.

Lady Astor and he were old friends and exchanged hearty banter:

> They had a good deal of this kind of chatter – of how Gertrude Lawrence came and kissed him last week and his irresistible attraction to women. He protested that she knew nothing about love – there was no such thing as falling in love since every case was different. He himself knew all about it since he had twice in his life fallen in love.

When the badinage finally petered out, he talked to Moorehead about writing plays:

> Probably, if he were starting again, he would write for the cinema since it gave wider scope. But his peculiar genius was such that his plays turned easily into pictures. He began by writing five large novels which nobody would publish because the public had turned to the romantic cloak and sword writing of *Treasure Island*, etc. His novels were above popular taste so he turned to plays.

He then gave his guest some practical advice:

In writing dialogue it's no use turning out fine poetical speeches: the absolute rule was this – the dialogue had to be interesting and it had to *provoke the next speech*. One had to study production: the four main characters, the heavy, the comic and so on, had to have four different tones of voice – basso, baritone, soprano, etc. This, perhaps, was not so important in the cinema. Still one had to study voice-production.

Plots – he never invented them. He never knew what was going to develop from one page to the next as he wrote. But you had to have the art of story-telling . . .

On the book slump and the falling off in the relative number of people who read: the young writer, such as myself, had to break in since a purchaser would never buy one of my books if he could get one of his (Shaw's) . . .

Then the talk broadened to writers Shaw had known and Moorehead concluded his account of the day:

We had a good deal of talk of the Webbs, Wells and so on but it was rambling. Then, at the end of an hour and a half, he reverted to the same heavy badinage with Lady A., or rather she with him. He refused violently to have her stay in the house in the summer or to go to her. He urged her not to come back sooner than she felt she must . . .

He trudged slowly out into the crossroads to make sure no cars were coming and then waved us away. That was the last view we had of him, standing there without a hat on his white hair in the roadway, peering dimly about him, gently making a gesture of goodbye . . . I came away with a peaceful feeling that always follows from being with an iconoclastic old man, who has somehow kept his wit and his brilliance, above all his gaiety. It is his *extreme* niceness that affects the most.[14]

Moorehead flew to Germany, spending nearly a month in the British and American zones of occupation and flying in and out of West Berlin with the aircraft carrying supplies. It was something like his wartime reporting assignments but without the stimulus of danger beyond that inherent in flying through bad weather and the distant threat of Russian intervention. It was odd to be in Berlin, which he could not wait to enter with the triumphant Allies four years before, and see devastation such as he remembered from the entry into Hamburg in the spring of 1945. On his return to Florence, he wrote his articles for the *Observer* but, when he was ready to begin the script, was told that the film would not now be made because the airlift had succeeded and the Russians had lifted their blockade.

He had been working at the Villa Diana and it should have been a contented time because Lucy's baby was due in a few weeks and the countryside was at its loveliest in April, May and early June. However, the sirocco was blowing from Africa, disturbing the tranquillity, and he kept taking the manuscript of *Celine* from its drawer and trying to finish it, or convert it into a play or short story and then deciding, once again, to abandon it. It was while attempting to turn the plot of the novel inside out one day that he was called urgently to Lucy, who had started a miscarriage.

She came close to death from loss of blood, the agonising scene in that dark old house heightened by a thunderstorm and, when it cleared, a religious procession passing below her window. As her husband wrote in his journal later that day, when he and a doctor had managed to get her to hospital in Florence, "She had turned quite grey, her hands and arms hung flaccidly, her head sank upon the pillow; she was sweating and the bleeding had now gone so far that no towels would cope with it. She said suddenly that she believed she might die and there were many things she wanted to say. It seemed possible that she might die." She recovered a little on hearing that the doctor was on his way and, Moorehead wrote:

I read to her, at her request, a little Browning and Wordsworth's *Intimations of Immortality*. The hail and thunder now abruptly ceased and the sun poured down. The procession, belated, was a thin little affair as it came down the hill. Many of the children in their white Communion costumes had not turned up because of the storm. But the band was a fine affair and they burst with merry tunes as the men with the Host picked their way through the muddy puddles where the flowers had been laid out an hour or two before. I saw the priest glance up to see if we were on the balcony and we were there . . .[15]

When Lucy was fully recovered they spent a week at Portofino and another at Antibes. But, back at the Villa Diana, he felt "the usual sense of guilt and waste".[16] He set aside the crippled novel for a while and tried to write a play but when Martha Gellhorn – Hemingway's former wife, whose opinion he respected – came to stay and read it, he recorded her opinion: "It is no good, never can be any good and ought to be abandoned. She is the last of many to urge me to abandon fiction and now, after a struggle of two years, I am inclined to think that she is right."[17]

Instead, he planned a biography of Angelo Poliziano, in whose house they were living. Berenson was not wholly dismissive of this idea, conceding that "He was an interesting chap but with no real intellect. You might dip him into what I call the sauce of the epoch but then the little shrimp would disappear."[18] Berenson was cautious with encouragement because he knew that scholarly history was no more suited to Moorehead than fiction. On another occasion, when told that he had been asked to write a biography of the Florentine sculptor and goldsmith Benvenuto Cellini, he was more blunt. "You must not do it," he commanded. "You are not, I think, quite scholar enough for that."[19] Moorehead persevered with the Poliziano, although modifying his scale from a book to a long article about him for the *New Yorker*.

He had been bewitched by Poliziano's house. "We have never had this tranquillity of mind before," he wrote in his journal. "The servants have grown into our lives and we into theirs. And we love the house more than ever." Yet, "at the Villa Diana I am lulled into quiet thoughts and a mental apathy descends."[20] The only successful writing that had come from those long hours in that dim Renaissance room had been articles about his journeys away from Tuscany and these were occupying half of his time. It was a life of comfort and ease and yet, he knew, he could not afford it. During the first year there he estimated to have spent about £3,000 and, although his income had just balanced this, half of it had been from publishers' advances on work not yet completed. The second year was better, with earnings just exceeding expenditure, enabling John to be educated at a preparatory school in England.

The prospects for 1950 were quite encouraging, with commissions for another series of articles for the *New Yorker*, book reviews and five articles about the defence of Western Europe for the *Observer*. His travels during the year should take him around Europe and to the Middle East. But still there was no book, or writing of any kind, that came near to matching the hopes with which he had first sat at the table in the Villa Diana, pen in hand. Taking Berenson's advice, his reading was wide and eclectic: Chekhov, the Sitwells, Greville, Lytton Strachey, T.S. Eliot, Mérimée and, of course, Berenson. "Finished the Maupassant this morning," he wrote early in 1950. "What is it that kills writers so young?" Then he added pessimistically, "Somehow then it is necessary to find a philosophy, to accept the downgrade. To read, to be content with smaller work, to develop habits and hobbies."[21]

This mood followed a long-dreaded decision. They would have to leave the Villa Diana. He summed up the reasons in his journal:

> In these two years I have lost faith in myself. I tried to write every day when often I had nothing to say. The only enthusiasms I had were for Poliziano, which was a sidepath, and the *New Yorker* articles, which became stylised and forced. I can only write well from personal observation and experience – not from books, or imagination or reflection. Here, I was too comfortable and I saw too little. I don't think these two years have been a dead loss. God knows I ought to be rested. I ought to be ready to undergo new experiences which will make me write again.[22]

The immediate necessity was to earn a substantial and regular income. He could always find work on the staff of a London newspaper but he had put that behind him. Indeed, he had shocked a visitor to the Villa Diana, Edward Pickering, who had been a sub-editor on the *Daily Express* before the war, then become a lieutenant-colonel on General Eisenhower's staff and was now managing editor of the *Daily Mail*, by the contempt with which he had spoken of popular newspapers. Pickering sharply reminded him that popular newspapers had created him as a famous journalist and that Fleet Street needed men of his quality to improve them. He found Moorehead "completely changed, sophisticated, confident and worldly",[23] but then he had found Clifford altered, too, and had had much the same conversation with him, trying vainly to persuade him to move to his newspaper's London office to help change it to appeal to more intelligent readers. Clifford had, however, been less vehement than Moorehead and had not repeated to Pickering the comments he had made in a letter that the *Daily Mail* was "as trashy as ever and Fleet Street just as allergic to foreign news".[24]

Moorehead went to London to enquire into other possibilities. There he was stung when, at a chance encounter, Arthur Christiansen asked him pointedly, "Well, how much are you earning *now*, Alan?"[25] His old friend from the Tunisian campaign, Philip Jordan, whose liberal views matched his own, was now press secretary to Clement

Attlee, the Prime Minister, at 10 Downing Street and suggested something in his own field. Another influential friend, Lord Montgomery – as the Field Marshal now was – might help as Chief of the Imperial General Staff. Finally, largely through Jordan's efforts, Moorehead was offered a job as a senior public relations officer at the Ministry of Defence. He would be responsible for briefing journalists and visiting politicians on the Labour Government's defence policy as it was adapted to meet the needs of new strategy and weaponry, notably nuclear weapons and inter-continental missiles. He accepted and agreed to take up the appointment in the autumn at what would be the unusually high salary for the Civil Service grade of £2,000 a year with freedom to continue writing when he could.

There was no alternative, it seemed, to what amounted to the abdication of his ambitions, even though he might tell himself that this was temporary. Now, for the first time, he would no longer be the pre-eminent member of The Trio. Both Alexander Clifford and Christopher Buckley were quietly making their ways towards their goals. The latter had been travelling, accompanied by Cecilia, and reporting the mounting dangers of the Cold War and this had taken him to Malaya, where Chinese communist guerrillas were in rebellion. He was writing books of quiet distinction and there was irony that he, too, should hanker after writing fiction. "I very much want to settle down intensely to a new novel which shall be *serious*," he had written to Moorehead as the latter was abandoning his own attempts to write fiction. "I want to move on to something profound and write about Elemental Passion and Fundamentals, etc., etc." Meanwhile he felt it his duty to continue as a witness to events:

> Grannie *Telegraph* treats me very well on the whole. I seem to have become a sort of Elder Statesman of Cabinet rank but without a portfolio, a sort of Lord Privy Seal or Chancellor of the Duchy of Lancaster. I would dearly like to edit a weekly. That would be an entirely fascinating occupation. I even toyed with the idea of a political career recently but as I am a natural cross-bencher and, as the only party I could attach myself to, if really compelled to declare myself, would be the Liberals, there does not seem much future in that.[26]

Relations between the Mooreheads and the Cliffords were not happy because the former were finding Jenny temperamental and too assertive. Indeed something of a rift had developed since the summer of

1948, just before the move to the Villa Diana. Then they had regularly stayed at Portofino and had occasionally been lent the Castelletto in its owners' absence. Lucy did not enjoy Jenny's company, writing to her husband that a mutual friend had told her that she "now has marmalade-coloured hair but is immensely full of herself and successful. I must get my strength up before I see her."[27] For her part, Jenny was indignant that Moorehead had written about Portofino in the *New Yorker* for she regarded it as her own domain. One of their guests, Lady Rothermere, wrote to her lover, Ian Fleming, the author of the James Bond books, that she had shown the Cliffords one of Moorehead's articles:

> Jenny glanced at it, put her head in her hands and burst into tears, occasionally uttering imprecations and curses against Alan Moorehead, while Alex sat scarlet and shamefaced. Apparently they lent this house to the Mooreheads, forgoing a large rent from rich Italians, and Jenny, before leaving them in possession, had confided that she was writing a book on Portofino and was foolish enough to read them her manuscript, most of which is embodied in the offending article. It cast a great shadow over the day and whenever we passed a post office Jenny sent abusive telegrams to Alan while Alex was dumb and miserable but unable to save the Clifford–Moorehead axis from becoming an Italian vendetta.[28]

That trouble had passed and the Mooreheads resumed their visits to Portofino, Moorehead enjoying the company of the celebrities who clustered around the Castelletto. Both he and his host had become accustomed to such circles and of one gathering Clifford wrote to his brother in England:

> We had the Mooreheads and Osbert Lancaster staying and Evelyn Waugh was with the Herberts; an American columnist friend of ours, Joe Allsop, was staying in the village and a terrible American writer called Truman Capote, who we had met somewhere, turned up with six kerry blues, whatever they are, dogs, I think. When we all had dinner together with the local eccentrics, like Francis Toye, at the Nazionale, the place really looked like Capri. I took Osbert and Evelyn over to tea with Max Beerbohm, and Osbert has drawn us a splendid cartoon of the occasion.[29]

Now two years later there were fresh worries about Clifford. Other friends wondered whether his marriage was entirely happy, or whether the contrast between his retiring nature and Jenny's social aspirations was proving a strain. This was indeed the case. Although Clifford loved his wife he told her that she must make more effort to understand the differences in their characters. While some of their friends saw her as hospitable, generous and stimulating, others found her socially ambitious, extravagant and domineering; they found him either shy and prudent or remote and mean with money. "What is the matter with Alex?" Buckley had written to Moorehead. "We both found him quite curiously cold and distant and he almost pointedly avoids us when he is in London. Why?"[30]

One reason and possibly *the* reason became apparent early in 1950 when Clifford wrote to Moorehead to tell him, "They say that I have an incurable disease and I have to go back to London to see about it." He had not been well and it was while he and Jenny were staying in Frankfurt with Brian Connell, the *Daily Mail* correspondent in West Germany whom they had first met in Normandy that he discovered a swelling in his armpit. They consulted the Connells' doctor, a German woman, and she feared that it might be a form of cancer. The Cliffords returned to London for a second opinion and there they met Moorehead, who was arranging details of his new job. Clifford, he thought, did not seem to have changed but he announced, "It's a thing called Hodgkin's Disease. You have two years to live."[31]

The news soon reached Buckley in Tunbridge Wells and he wrote to Moorehead at the end of March:

> What a terrible thing. I only heard, and in very vague and improbable terms, about Alex the day before yesterday and then it seemed so unexpected that I thought it had probably got exaggerated. I am told that it is one of those things which is quite hopeless if you get it when you are under twenty but that if it develops after you have passed the age of thirty-five it is not necessarily hopeless and with luck you can go on for a good many years.[32]

The news was particularly poignant because everything was evolving so happily for Buckley. His marriage was blissful and now one of his hopes seemed about to be fulfilled as Lady Rhondda, the proprietor of the gentle political and literary weekly review *Time and Tide*, had offered him the editorship. This seemed the right moment to leave daily journalism for he felt that his five years of reporting the post-war world had borne fruit, both establishing his reputation as a commentator rather than a war correspondent and, he liked to think, helping to sound the alarms that brought massive American aid to the West. Indeed, he told his wife, "I think I helped the Marshall Plan come into being."[33]

Now, just as the initial turmoil of the First World War had frozen into the trench-system of the Western Front, so post-war Europe had been fossilised by what Churchill had called "the Iron Curtain" dividing the eastern Russian-controlled countries from the West. Buckley saw that the open conflict between the ideologies would move to the Far East and he was right. On 25th June, 1950, what amounted to civil war broke out in Korea, which had been divided in half under the 1945 peace settlement, when the communist north invaded the capitalist south. Taking advantage of a Russian boycott of the Security Council, the United States persuaded the United Nations to intervene on the side of South Korea and a large American expeditionary force was sent there under the United Nations flag, followed by a British contingent.

The invasion of South Korea was launched on a Sunday and that evening the telephone rang in the quiet house at Tunbridge Wells. It was the foreign editor of the *Daily Telegraph*. He told Buckley the news from Korea and asked him to go there as a war correspondent. He needed time to think and told Cecilia what had been said. It seemed, she thought, like the beginning of the Third World War and it was obvious that he was torn between all his hopes for happiness and what he saw as his duty as a witness. Finally, he said, "I'm not going. I can't leave you." She replied, "If you do go, I'm coming too." And so it was decided that they would both go to the Far East, she acquiring the necessary accreditations as the correspondent of *Time and Tide*, which he hoped to edit on his return from this last assignment. Her company made the decision easier and the journey enjoyable. They laughed when at London Airport, where she happened to be carrying her husband's portable typewriter, an official asked him, "Do you often travel with your wife on her assignments?"[34]

When they reached Tokyo, the news from Korea was bad – the North Koreans had thrust far south and were almost within striking distance of the vital port of Pusan. Buckley therefore left Cecilia in Tokyo and flew to the battlefields alone. For six weeks he reported with his old flair and there were references not only to Tolstoy's *War and Peace* in his despatches but also a quotation from Wordsworth. He missed the companionship of Moorehead and Clifford but made friends with Ian Morrison, the correspondent of *The Times*, and the two would travel forward each day to see the fighting in the old familiar way. On Sunday, 13th August, seven weeks after answering the telephone at Tunbridge Wells, Buckley and Morrison, accompanied by an Indian Army colonel attached to the United Nations as an observer and guided by a South Korean lieutenant, made another journey to the scene of action. From the South Korean divisional headquarters to the forward battalions they had to negotiate six belts of mines, the one weapon that Buckley had feared during the campaigns in Africa and Europe. Some time after they had left, another party, following the same track, came upon the wreckage of their jeep, blown to pieces in the sixth and final minefield. Morrison, the colonel and the lieutenant had been killed instantly but Buckley was severely wounded and unconscious. He was taken to the American field hospital at Taegu at 7.15 that evening; soon after his arrival, he died. He was aged forty-five.

Moorehead heard the news on the island of Ischia, where he had been spending a long summer holiday and hobnobbing with celebrities such as Ingrid Bergman, the film star, and her lover Roberto Rossellini, the film director, the actress Ruth Draper and William Walton, the composer. He at once wrote to Clifford who was recovering from his radiation treatment at Lake Bled in Yugoslavia and received an immediate reply:

Yes, Christopher was something of a shock I must say. Perhaps an appropriate end but so horrible that there should be an end. And if either you or I had been with him, we should have been in that jeep with him and it would have been our end too.

I really don't think I could take another war – at least, not as a war correspondent. I have tried to write to Cecilia but how can one say anything that can help her? It's a very absurd convention for it forces her to write back which is even more difficult. I contemplated writing him some form of obit. for some publication but don't really like doing that and, like you, the news took some time to reach me.[35]

Moorehead, too, was out of touch with Fleet Street and so could not write about his friend. But he felt the need to ease his grief by writing something, somewhere, and so entered in his journal an idiosyncratic note worthy of his friend:

239

Christopher Buckley was the only man I ever knew who bought a sedan chair for himself. It was a genuine article dating back to the Regency days when gallants in flowered coats and tricorne hats were carried through the muddy streets of London with a link boy out in front to light the way. Buckley bought it out of sheer ebullience and a love of the eighteenth century. There never was a chance that he would ride in it and indeed I remember that at the time he bought it we were over in France having lately arrived in an invasion barge and there was a war on. A friend had come over from England and reported that he had seen the chair in Harrods store in the Brompton Road. Buckley paid a hundred guineas for it on the spot and for some time after that it lingered in his wife's home at Tunbridge Wells. It got crowded out at last by Buckley's books and the weird bric-à-brac he used to bring back from his travels to the Far East, but he was determined that it should never fall into the hands of the debased night club owners in London who used to think it chic to buy up sedan chairs and turn them into telephone booths. He sent it to the Tunbridge Wells museum and there it is, I fancy, to this day. Buckley had several other passions – perhaps manias is a better word – besides the eighteenth century. One was the game of cricket. Another was the art of war.*[36]

A month after Christopher Buckley was killed, the Mooreheads were making their farewells to Tuscany. Lucy and the children left the Villa Diana and before Moorehead departed on Saturday, 16th September, he called on Berenson and noted his "last obiter dicta". These included his thoughts on Korea, where the Americans had outflanked the North Korean invaders two days before by landing behind their lines at the port of Inchon. "It now remains to see what the Chinese will do," he said prophetically. "The day will come when we will be appealing for help for the poor Russians to save them from the Chinese."[37]

It was the war in Korea that was dominating thought in Whitehall when Moorehead reported for work at the Ministry of Defence buildings at Storey's Gate at the end of the year. First he was introduced to the Minister of Defence, Emmanuel Shinwell, a Labour Party politician and trade union activist who had been a conscientious

* Christopher Buckley's published books were: *Road to Rome* (1945); *Rain Before Seven* (1947); *Royal Chase* (1949); *Norway. The Commandos. Dieppe* (1951); published posthumously: *Greece and Crete* (1952); *Five Ventures* (1954).

objector during the First World War. To everybody's surprise, Shinwell had shown enthusiasm and aptitude for the job and had struck up a friendship with Field Marshal Montgomery, the Chief of the Imperial General Staff and in most respects his opposite. Korea apart, the Ministry of Defence – the policy-making department that tried to coordinate the policies of the Admiralty, War Office and Air Ministry – was preoccupied with the development of nuclear weapons and strategy, the formation of the North Atlantic Alliance between most of Western Europe and the United States and the development and production of new weapons and equipment, notably new generations of jet-powered fighters and bombers. It was interesting, but for Moorehead, as with most former journalists, there was the sense of guilt in becoming a public relations officer, which was a poacher-turned-gamekeeper transformation and implied failure as a writer.

When the Mooreheads returned to London, the Cliffords were already there, living in Albany, and they met again. Clifford looked much as he had before the dreadful diagnosis, talked calmly about the treatment he was undergoing and the prospects of a cure being discovered. Lord Rothermere, the proprietor of the *Daily Mail*, had given him a comfortable office with a carpet on the floor and an open fire down the passage from his own and he was going there from time to time.* When his course of radiation was complete, he said, they would return to Portofino and he would carry on with his work as before. The Mooreheads consulted their own doctor who told them that there was no hope of a cure.

Meanwhile they resumed their social life in London. Osbert Lancaster provided a link with smart literary society, and other friends, the artist John Piper and the landowner and writer Peter Fleming and his wife Celia Johnson, the actress, were links with the upper classes amongst whom Lucy moved effortlessly and whom Moorehead envied, sometimes admired and was tempted to emulate. Yet he was still living on his reputation as a war correspondent and writer of war histories. His one current success was that the film rights of *The Rage of the Vulture* had been sold and there was talk of the popular actor Alan Ladd playing the leading part. Otherwise there was a failed novel and several attempts at play-writing and that was all.

*When the author met Clifford in this room and remarked on its comfort, the latter replied, "Yes, I can't think why they have given it to me."

During the winter and in the spring of 1951, Moorehead was a civil servant, carrying a briefcase embossed with the royal cypher and attending meetings in conference rooms. His move to Whitehall had aroused criticism, the Institute of Professional Civil Servants objecting to his appointment over the heads of their members, and some of the once-familiar carping amongst journalists had begun again. Indeed, Brigadier Nigel Dugdale, the Director of Army Public Relations, who had once run the 8th Army's press camps with such style, took to telling them, "Don't crab Alan, he's doing a good job."[38] From time to time Moorehead travelled abroad, mostly with Shinwell, visiting Washington, Brussels and Paris. When away from home he found some entertainment in escorting pretty women, who had caught his eye but were no threat to his devotion to his wife. He had stopped writing his journal except for a single paragraph in which he noted, "On the whole, less ennui than in Florence but a much less healthy life and a pointless one",[39] but always at the back of his mind were the hopes of success and his imagination roamed in search of ideas that would bring that about.

A collection of his articles about Italy – including his sketch of Poliziano's life – which had appeared in the *New Yorker*, were published as a book called *The Villa Diana*, illustrated by Osbert Lancaster. Now work in Whitehall allowed him some time to write and he was suddenly struck with the idea for a new book: a biography of Augustus John, the painter, whom he had met when writing the life of Montgomery, whose portrait the artist had painted with such lack of success. John was now in his seventies and with a reputation as a bohemian and a seducer of women to match his standing as a painter. When they met again, Moorehead was captivated by the old man, whom Osbert Lancaster had described as "a Rasputin-Jehovah". Moorehead found "a pantherish quality" about him and "an air of wild but absolute authority". As they talked about the proposed book, John's "snowy beard fairly bristled, the piercing blue eyes bored through one like a cat's and these effects were embellished with a flowing scarlet tie and a huge, sombrero-like hat".[40]

Moorehead had been warned that John, despite his public flamboyance, was a private, indeed secretive, man and that his biographer would run into trouble. However all seemed well and, although John declared that he had no memory for dates and soon showed that to be true, he gave his blessing to the research which Moorehead began by visiting Somerset House to check on dates in various wills and interviewing friends of his subject. He also met John for more talks in Chelsea and at his home at Fordingbridge in Hampshire. Finally, by the end of the year, he had enough material to write an article of 15,000 words, which could be extended into a full-length book or published in a magazine as it stood. He sent this to John for his approval at the beginning of 1952.

In March he received a reply which left him "appalled and humiliated" and which he was to consider "the worst setback I have ever received in my attempts to write". John had written, "I dislike the way you have thought fit to perpetuate a lot of foolish gossip . . . *All your statements of fact are wrong.* I prefer the truth. Your own observations I find incredibly out of place. I must refuse to authorize this effort at biography."

Soon afterwards the two men met. Moorehead was determined to have the matter out with John and there was a confrontation. John demanded to know why he had been "spying" by getting a copy of his father's will at Somerset House and wanted to know where he had heard "the gossip" about his early life. Moorehead realised, as he put it later, that when he had written "about the money and the drinkings and the escapades, it was tearing down a facade he had built up and he hated it with an old man's rage". When they parted, Moorehead wrote to say how sorry he was at the outcome and received the reply, "I don't suppose you could be more distressed than I have been. By all means let us *both* forget it and remain good friends."[41]

This episode wasted several months of thinking, research and writing, but now another idea for a book occurred and it was prompted by Moorehead's new proximity to the secret world of espionage and counter-espionage. Both the British and United States governments had been surprised and shocked by the discovery of Russian spies at the heart of their secret defence establishments. These had been the nuclear scientists Alan Nunn May, Bruno Pontecorvo and, most importantly, the German-born Klaus Fuchs. The story of their treason and eventual capture was significant, and Moorehead's superiors agreed that he could be given access to secret documents in order to write a book about it, which would suit their purpose better than the emergence of the stories through newspaper investigations and scandals damaging to Whitehall and Westminster. The book would be called *The Traitors*. The idea of writing again made him feel even more unsuited to public relations; then his mentor, Philip Jordan, died; and after only eight months at the Ministry of Defence, he resigned.

There was another reason for optimism. Lucy had become pregnant again at the beginning of 1951 and on 11th October, their second son was born and named Richard after Moorehead's father. The Cliffords sent flowers to Lucy and Alex wrote a bravely jocular note on the card, "Let us know when we can bring round some champagne and have a coming-out party for him."[42]

It was a happy household on Primrose Hill; Olive Wood was still helping with the children and John was now aged eleven and destined for Eton in two years' time. The Mooreheads entertained old wartime friends – amongst them Edward Ward, who had recently succeeded his father as Viscount Bangor and married his fourth wife, Marjorie Banks, a BBC radio producer – and a growing number of new ones in publishing and the arts, although they had now lost touch with most of their former colleagues in Fleet Street. Amongst his new literary friends Moorehead was lionised as their man of action, and was regarded by his publishers as a demanding and professional author but possessed of "total charm". But over all hung the knowledge of the tragedy of Alexander Clifford.

As the illness progressed, Clifford found that he could no longer climb the steep steps from the harbour at Portofino to the Castelletto and they moved to Rome, where he continued to write his commentaries for the *Daily Mail*, although they were less trenchant than hitherto, while Jenny wrote freelance articles for magazines. In his letters he would mention clinical details of his medical treatment in a detached, matter-of-fact way, almost as if he were describing efforts to repair his car, but he did invite old friends to a series of lunch parties, which they realised were occasions for unspoken farewells. Early in January, Clifford wrote to Lucy:

> I am enjoying Rome in a mild way. Jenny is working too hard for *Picture Post* to be able to take much of the social whirl which gives me an excuse for staying out of it, too. I find it quite easy to write a trifling column every two or three days and they seem to publish them gladly enough. I am at the moment bombarded with demands for short stories because one I wrote the other day (the only one I've ever written) has won a prize in a competition in the *Observer*. But I don't think there is much future in writing any more.[43]

It seemed that the progress of his illness had been arrested and, on the spur of the moment, the Mooreheads suggested that the Cliffords join them for a ski-ing holiday in Austria. They met in Kitzbuhel in January, 1952; the weather was perfect and Clifford seemed strong enough to ski. For a few days it was idyllic and a reminder of the strenuous travels the two men had once shared. They would picnic on the mountain-tops and ski down in the sunshine to the village for tea, followed by hot baths, dinner and cards. Then Clifford had a relapse with pain and fever. An Austrian doctor prescribed drugs and he seemed to rally. All four attended a fancy dress dance and Clifford seemed so much stronger that Moorehead suggested the two of them try the highest ski-run, eight miles long, next morning.

"It was a raw morning and even when we reached the heights the sun had not really broken through," wrote Moorehead later. "I baulked a little at the ice and the steepness of the descent. But Alex, wrapped in a black jacket, his head in a bright woollen cap, spread his wings and flew. He skimmed away into the milky space like some great black bird on the wing and, when I rejoined him after several headlong falls at the bottom of the first run, he was grinning." But in the train back from the end of the run to Kitzbuhel, Moorehead noticed that his friend's face had "gone a ghastly shade of whitish green",[44] there was a little foam on his lips and his eyes were glazed and dull. That night he had another relapse and they all returned to London two days later.

On arrival, Clifford was taken straight to St. Mary's Hospital at Paddington to be given treatments that had not hitherto been tried, one involving chemicals used in the manufacture of mustard gas. Again he seemed to rally. When Moorehead visited him after one bout of such treatment on 13th March, he had a bright, feverish light in his eyes but, as for some days past, showed for the moment no sign of recognition. He was struggling to speak and finally said in a low excited voice, "I see it all now. There are two sides, two levels. On one level I am vulgar . . . disgusting . . . But on the other level . . . clear . . . beautiful."[45] Moorehead could see in his friend's eyes that now he was recognised but his voice trailed away and his breathing became laboured. Just then Jenny and Lucy came into the room and gradually his breathing ceased. Alexander Clifford, aged forty-two, was dead.

Moorehead made the arrangements for the funeral and suffered a *frisson* on discovering that the undertaker's address was in the Edgware Road, the street that had once symbolised for Clifford all that he found unworthy in his own country. On their return from the funeral, Moorehead wrote to his sister Phyllis about his friend, "He, Lucy and I were inseparable and I find it odd continuing without him. We were with him when he died and, although there was something else he had to say, he could not speak."[46]

Robert Graves, his father-in-law, paid tribute to Clifford's "staggering talent" in *The Times*, concluding the obituary:

> He expected courage, restraint and common sense from everyone. When he was warned two years ago that he was suffering from an incurable disease, he accepted the news apologetically, rather than with despair, regarding sympathy as irrelevant, and gave everyone as little trouble as possible . . . and politely assumed that his friends would not allow themselves to be any more emotionally involved in his death than he was himself. In this, for once, he was wrong.[47]

Later there was a memorial service at St. James's church in Piccadilly and then talk of an annual award for journalism bearing his name and sponsored by Moorehead, Edward Ward, Chester Wilmot, Malcolm Muggeridge, Brian Connell, Alastair Forbes (formerly of the *Daily Express*) and James Cameron, though it came to nothing.*

Now only Moorehead survived of The Trio and it still seemed that, while he had once been the predominant partner, his two friends had been more successful in fulfilling their ambitions; from both he had received what he described as "a late education". By chance some distraction was at hand because, at the end of 1951, he had been invited to visit Australia by Sir Keith Murdoch, the newspaper magnate, to write his impressions as a returning exile. He would combine this with a visit to New York and would be away for four months. It was an escape from grief and failure for, as Lucy said when telling Marjorie Bangor of Clifford's death, "It's the end of an era."[48] She did not usually employ clichés but just then there was nothing else to say.

* Alexander Clifford's published books were: *Crusader* (1942); *Three Against Rommel* (1943); *The Sickle and the Stars* (with Jenny Nicholson; 1948); *Enter Citizens* (1950).

Chapter Thirteen

"There is so much I want to explore"

The voyage to Australia was an interval for rest and reflection. Moorehead sailed in the P&O liner *Himalaya* at the beginning of April, 1952, knowing none of the four hundred first-class passengers and feeling no inclination to do so. As the days passed and the weather grew warmer and the sea more blue, he fell into a routine of eating and sleeping, reading and taking gentle exercise on deck. Eventually he fell in with a group of Indians with whom he played bridge.

It was after they passed the Suez Canal that he at last felt detached from Europe and a long way from Lucy, to whom he was writing long letters to be posted at their ports of call: Port Said, Aden, Bombay and Colombo. The limbo in which he lived cleared his mind and he felt with relief that he was bound for a country where he had belonged and where he would be writing newspaper articles, instead of books, something of which he knew himself to be a master. Twelve days out and in passage down the Red Sea, he wrote to Lucy:

Europe, now, seems like a book or a play, filled with the most splendid and glamorous things, richer than anything in colonial life. This is the reality here: over *there* is the mirage, the dream-city and the escape. Here one is down to earth and does the washing-up. The time is now – there is no past in the colonies. Over *there* the time is past and, seen from this boarding-house, it is full of Napoleons and Tintorettos.

What the colonial does not realise is that the washing-up still has to be done in Europe, one still has to live in the present there. It is much easier to cope with these material things in the colonies. In other words, it is easier to live in New Zealand but there is less point in living . . . These things seem to be coming into my mind as a result of this trip: I am less agitated and I begin to feel that I know what I know and can speak confidently. There are too many critics in Europe; one has to watch one's step too much and pretend to know too much.

He wondered whether Berenson and Hemingway had been right to urge him to read and learn and stock his mind. Away from Europe – and particularly in Australia – he would be open to fresh and immediate experience which he could transmit through his writing as few others could. "I think Alex, too, would have been less confused and happier if he had left Europe for a while. His mind was a museum and he did not know what to do with his collection. He was full to the gills with knowledge and it was choking him. Ah, what a pity he is not with me now."[1]

He was writing a memoir of his friendship with Clifford and it occupied the hours and deferred the moment when he would have to decide what to write next. Since he had finished the last of his four books arising from the war he had sought inspiration and failed to find it, although he sometimes thought that he had. He wrote to Lucy from the ship:

I'm *never* happy until I get a moment of inspiration. All the brightly-polished technical work like *The Traitors* doesn't really do any good. But then, where in hell is the inspiration? Alex didn't have it. Nor Christopher (though he knew more about it than Alex). Will I, one day, turn some wonderful corner and there it will all be, acres and acres of inspiration staring me in the face? Or do I take a nose-dive into suburbia? The one thing I can't do is stand off and be a vagabond: I'm too weak a character, too prim at heart and too serious. I'm only good and strong when I'm working, really working, and God knows how long it is since I have done that.[2]

Wrapped in introspection, he had led a solitary existence on board the *Himalaya*, only striking up acquaintance with an elderly Australian woman, with whom he shared a table in the dining saloon, and the Indians with whom he played bridge. Then one evening in

the tropics he was suddenly forced to join the social activities of the
other passengers. He explained the reason for this in a letter he wrote
to Lucy next day:

It is the result of a sudden outburst by a Calcutta widow in
the moonlight last night. She said that while she, personally, was
fascinated by me, it was perfectly obvious that I despised everyone
on board. I was conceited, ruthless, superior and good-looking. It
might be true that there was no one in the ship of my intellectual
gifts but that did not mean that these others did not live lives that
were just as important as mine. She added further that I had great
charm. I don't think you would like this Calcutta widow very
much.[3]

Her words with their sharp point of perception had echoed those of
others who had met Moorehead in the past dozen years. For all his
looks, charm, intelligence and lively conversation there were other
elements that were not so attractive. The woman in the ship had
identified them but did not understand that the apparent ruthlessness
was the outward sign of aspirations driven by determination, and the
air of superiority a cloak to hide real or imagined inadequacies. But
her aim had been accurate and the point had penetrated. In response,
Moorehead lowered his guard, relaxed and enjoyed the undemanding
company of the others, although he met no one he wished to meet
again. Soon after, as the liner steamed across the Indian Ocean, his
imaginings of Europe seemed to dip below the horizon astern and he
wrote, "I begin to feel Australia reaching out to me."[4]

The *Himalaya* docked at Port Melbourne at the end of April
and Moorehead was accorded a rousing welcome both as a celebrity
and as the son of a local family. The headline over an interview with
him in his old newspaper, the *Herald*, proclaimed "FAMED AUTHOR
REVISITS AUSTRALIA" and, over a large photograph of him, laughing,
"WON FAME ABROAD".[5] And then he was back in the once-familiar surroundings, albeit a different house; this one owned by his father and
called "Moondai" in the suburb of Croydon. Much else had changed.
After his mother's death, his father had married a school-teacher
much younger than himself. The old man had contracted Parkinson's
Disease and there was worry in his family lest the new wife collect the
bulk of his modest estate when he died. Moorehead's sister Phyllis he
found was "still incredibly good-looking and active"[6] and his niece was
now a medical student. His friend Rod Andrew, the doctor met on

his first post-war visit to Australia, was there to welcome him with a formal dinner at the Melbourne Club. "Certainly no English club could keep pace with it," he wrote with surprise. "Waiters all in full livery, drinks laid out in decanters from which you help yourself, barrels of oysters and millionaires in spats and English voices. The furniture is Buckingham Palace."[7] He lunched there with Nevil Shute, the novelist, and suggested that instead of making the journey across Asia together as Shute had suggested, they make a joint expedition to the centre and north of Australia, visiting Alice Springs and Darwin.

"My first view of Australia does not make me think we would live here," he wrote to Lucy on the day after he arrived, "but it's got something nevertheless, an absence of strain. People here are much more vigorous and healthy than in London, more direct. One and all, those who have been to London loathe it and at the same time yearn for it. All that culture. It is the women particularly who feel isolated here."

He tried to find old friends and wrote, "Beth is buried somewhere in the country. Erl Gray is a sub-editor on the *Herald*. Very little unexpected happens except a slow progression to a known end and they sweeten the process with golf, drinks and bridge. But Australians are much more worldly than they were."[8]

Gradually he began to feel at home and, a few days later, was writing to Lucy:

I am sitting on the verandah where, do you remember, I wrote bits of *Montgomery*? White trunk of the gum tree on the left, kookaburras, bell birds and the clear squawk of the magpies. An amber light on the hills. The lemon orchard is a tangle but the garden is bright and full of autumn leaves. There is one kind of peace here washed down by cups of tea: a sort of steadiness. It seems as unchallenged and inevitable as a boiled egg or a baby . . . Some of all of this would be good for you but far from all . . . but with the advantage of fresh cream and possums on the roof.

It all rushes on top of me and I have been here only six – no, five days. The light is going and the sky on Dandenong is pink. I must go inside to the fire.

He had expected to meet Sir Keith Murdoch, at whose invitation he had come, not only because it would be intriguing to meet his former employer on revised terms but because both had been war correspondents – albeit in different world wars – and had a hankering after the arts. But Murdoch was ill in hospital and, although Moorehead met his intelligent and energetic wife Elizabeth, he had to meet the directors of the *Herald* at a luncheon they gave for him instead. For him there was, of course, none of "the treatment" that had been accorded Noel Monks and Sam White after they had won reputations reporting wars in Europe and had been "cut down to size" by being given the most menial assignments on their return. But, wrote Moorehead to Lucy, "All the old chums sniffed about me like dogs looking over an imported champ and reserving the right to bite later on."[9]

He was to meet Nevil Shute at Alice Springs and began his own travels with a visit to Adelaide, where he stayed at Government House as guest of the Governor-General of South Australia, Lieutenant-General Sir Willoughby Norrie, whom he had known in the desert war. Then he took the train to Alice Springs, where Shute was waiting. He wrote with his old relish:

It was just growing dark with indigo and orange light on the hills. Altogether I like this oasis very much indeed – for thousands of miles there is nothing but deserted plains and we here in the middle . . . A marvellous warm sun pours down all day and at night it nearly freezes. Very like Tucson, Arizona. Dry air, bare ground, lights in the hills, modern gadgets in the houses, drugstores but no advertisements, silence, no wind, vast drunken drinking in the hotel last night . . .[10]

From Alice Springs they drove for three days to Darwin, from which they were to visit a uranium mine called Rum Jungle, which was to be the subject of one of his articles. "Lovely day chasing wild buffalo today," he wrote to Lucy soon after they arrived. "There was one lagoon full of wild duck, pelicans, cockatoos and many other birds. Wallabies kept getting up under the car. No crocodiles as yet though Nevil was playing with four baby ones this morning."[11] From Darwin they flew to Townsville in Queensland for an expedition to the Great Barrier Reef and already he had written eight of his planned fifteen articles. "I feel so well here," he told Lucy, "I cannot imagine why everyone does not live in the bush; some place like Alice Springs. But I suppose it is hell if you remain: to travel through it, as we have, seeing the blackfellows and the cattle and the birds and kangaroos – it's heaven at times."[12]

Nevil Shute left Moorehead at Townsville to explore the Reef and he was as fascinated as he had expected to be: "In the middle of the ocean you sail into a calm lagoon with the breakers falling on the coral to your right and here below the calm water, through the glass bottom boat, enormous sea slugs, fish like confetti, gardens of coral and clams the size of a man with great jaws . . . You gaze and gaze." Back ashore, a sad letter from a bored Lucy awaited him and he wrote back sympathising and admitting again, "I spend my life running away." But now there was a new element in his self-analysis and it was almost as if he was not having to run away any more:

Something is happening to me I do not quite understand. Outside me is a delight in most of the things I find here. I love it. I feel so well. I feel alive physically. All day long one wants, and can do, so many exciting things. The material side of oneself travels here over distances impossible in Europe – tomorrow shall we drive 500 miles and see a crocodile, or sign a contract for a new house, or sell a horse or buy a farm? The mind lags behind, dumb and muttering. I don't know. I have moments of saying let's all come here – John to Geelong Grammar, Caroline to Toorak College, a house at Frankston, start a farm, a boat on the bay, trips up to Java and Singapore and then on to New York and London every other year and what have we in Europe anyway now that Alex is dead and Christopher and Philip and that long harassed battle over money? It could be done and very well.[13]

Five days later, he wrote again:

I must warn you that I am constantly thinking of the possibility of our all coming to Australia . . . I keep thinking of this. There is so much I want to explore on this side of the world and we could do it so much better from a base near Melbourne. I definitely want to go back to the Northern Territory. I want to go to Bali, Hong Kong and Bangkok. And to New Guinea. These places are just one day away from here. Also I am turning over in my mind this book called *Rum Jungle*, which would be about uranium and the history of the road across Australia from Adelaide to Darwin.[14]

This enthusiasm did not dim as his tour continued to Hayman Island for more underwater exploration, Brisbane, Canberra and finally Sydney from where he would fly to the United States. The

Australian tour had been a success although, as he had expected, the Australian editors had rejected his first two articles; but he took this philosophically and noted that after this token rejection of him, they had published the rest. He had taken a liking to his new step-mother and persuaded the family to agree to sharing the future inheritance with her. Most of all he felt a longing for a return to the wild places of Australia, where there would be no need to run away from anything, for there he felt he belonged. In that mood he left Sydney to arrive in New York by 22nd July, his forty-second birthday.

Manhattan was always stimulating, especially in the company of his old friends Alwyn and Essie Lee and with the entrée into literary society provided by the editors of the *New Yorker*. They wanted articles about Australia as did *Holiday* magazine, which paid lavishly. He was gratified to hear from London that *The Traitors* was selling well and he set about assembling assorted articles from his Australian tour for publication as a book.

Soon after his return to London he heard that Sir Keith Murdoch had died. Although they had not met in Melbourne, his host had implanted two ideas in Moorehead's mind. One was a hankering after the country of his birth. The other was the germ of an idea for a book; even an inspiration such as he had been seeking. During his stay in Australia, Sir Keith had often cropped up in conversation, and certain similarities between his career and Moorehead's had been discussed. Murdoch had made his name by his instigation of a crisis over the conduct of the campaign in the Dardanelles during the First World War. He had, as a young newspaper reporter, gone ashore on the Gallipoli peninsula, ostensibly to enquire into postal arrangements for the Australian troops there. But he had become involved in criticism of the generalship which seemed heading for disaster and later in London and Australia had helped bring this to a head.

In Australian mythology, Murdoch had completed the heroic legend of Gallipoli. There was an epic quality about the tragedy of the young Australians and New Zealanders, raised in the sunlight, security and freedom of their remote countries, coming to the aid of the mother-country to capture Constantinople, the capital of another empire. Their courage seemed to have been betrayed by the stupidity of the old generals of the motherland they had come to save, and the fact that this should be revealed by the initiative of a young compatriot created a potent tradition founded upon truth.

It was, Moorehead recognised, the event which more than any

other had given his country a sense of nationhood. Murdoch had begun the companion-myth of the journalist as a lone, fearless crusader and Moorehead, who liked to see himself as the journalist-turned-man-of-letters, felt a bond with him. Hitherto, Moorehead had never felt any urge to write about this catalytic Australian experience. "All my life I was brought up in Australia surrounded by my elders talking about this campaign, having their parades, and they bored me and bored me and bored me," he said. "It was part of Australia which had simply irritated me."[15] He did not, however, decide at this time to complete Murdoch's work by writing a history of the campaign, but the seed of such an idea was planted in fertile ground.

That had to lie in the future, for, on his return to London at the end of the summer, his sister Phyllis arrived from Melbourne for a holiday and, with Lucy, they set out on a tour in France, Switzerland and Italy. They visited Bernard Berenson at I Tatti and the old man urged him to keep reading and trying to "improve himself" because "a man's reach should exceed his grasp". They returned to London in November but inspiration had faded yet again and Moorehead confided in his journal, "I feel empty and lazy not because I have no job but because I will not commit myself to anything."[16]

He was invited to expand the articles he had written for the *New Yorker* on his last visit to Australia into a short book to be published in 1953 under the title *Rum Jungle*. "Almost writing with the same ease I had five or ten years ago," he noted. "These are scenes I have seen and know. Particular pleasure in writing about birds and animals."[17] While engaged in this agreeable but undemanding work, he called at the London Library and happened upon an account of the Ajanta Caves in India, illustrated with colour photographs of the exotic, and often erotic, paintings and carvings there. He wrote in his journal:

> The whole effect is provocative, voluptuous and, somehow, protective. And behind this, presiding, the meditative figure of the Buddha. He is detached but he knows it all and does not disapprove. There is no suggestion of the struggle between the male and the female as in the West: it is, instead, a feeling of complement and fulfilment: the man and the woman . . . and, through it all, a feeling of harmony and natural pleasure.[18]

He decided that the Ajanta Caves should be an objective in travels he was planning in Asia for the spring. He would be accompanied by Lucy and their friends, Sidney and Zoë Bernstein, and after India they would continue to Thailand and Cambodia – to visit Angkor Wat – and finally Singapore and Hong Kong. On his return, he had been asked to write a biography of John Derry, a test pilot who had been killed in front of the crowds at the Farnborough air display, and that would again postpone any serious work on a book about Gallipoli.

An air disaster now claimed the life of a friend. In Australia, Chester Wilmot had never been a close friend but Moorehead had come to admire him as a war correspondent for the BBC and, although he thought his magisterial book about the rivalry between the Allies towards the end of the Second World War, *The Struggle for Europe*, too dry for his own taste, he recognised his fellow-Australian as an important historian. Wilmot had been in the Far East for the BBC and was flying home in the new Comet jet-powered airliner, which Moorehead had admired at Farnborough. When it stopped at Rome airport to refuel, Wilmot had met their old friends Noel Monks and Geoffrey Keating, who were on their way home from the Middle East, where they had been visiting an oil refinery with a party of journalists led by Keating, who was now a public relations officer with British Petroleum. Monks tried to persuade Wilmot to fly home with them in their piston-engined aircraft but he refused because his family would be waiting to see him arrive in the Comet, which would touch down before his friends, although they would leave Rome first. An hour or so later, airborne over the Mediterranean, Monks sent a jocular message by radio to the Comet asking Wilmot to arrange a car to meet them at Heathrow Airport. Wilmot replied, Monks sent another message but the wireless operator said, "That's funny. I can't raise them." He tried to contact Rome and then came back to tell Monks, "I think the Comet's had it."[19] The airliner, its structure weakened by many fast ascents to high altitude, had exploded over the sea and all on board had been killed.

Chester Wilmot was the latest in a post-war casualty list of Moorehead's friends. The loss of Clifford and Buckley had hurt most, of course, but both Evelyn Montague and Philip Jordan had also died young. As a survivor, Moorehead began to feel he was becoming unique.

In August, a cable from Melbourne told him that his father had died, the news setting a final seal on his own past youth. Later he was told that, although the old man had been unable to feed himself for months, "his brain remained clear, furious, protesting." According to his wife, his last words had been, "I won't stand it another minute," then, "Damn."[20]

These tragedies added to the depression he felt in London. Although he described it as "the finest library in the world"[21] and the most important centre for research, he disliked the climate and was nagged by the knowledge that this was a social citadel he had yet to conquer. Nevertheless he regarded the city as a refuge, writing to a friend:

Am not really surprised that you are thinking of returning to London. Nearly everyone does in my experience. It's the door-mouse in us. There's a sort of winter in one's life and London is a safe place in which to go to ground. I shall die in London. We'll all die there, firmly believing to the end that there's been a mistake made somewhere, this isn't us, we ought to be in Bermuda with a floosie on our knee. God knows.[22]

Again he felt the need to get away, complaining, "We meet no one of interest, we don't go out, the expense is staggering and it's not very good for the children,"[23] and, when he tried to concentrate on writing, he had begun to suffer severe headaches. The Asian tour would only produce more magazine articles but it would offer the hot sun he loved and, once again, an escape. On their return he wrote the articles including a long one about the Ajanta Caves for the *New Yorker*, then again revised his novel *Celine*, this time with success for it was finally accepted by Hamish Hamilton, renamed *A Summer Night* and scheduled for publication in 1954, more than six years after he had begun to write it.

The final urge to write a book about Gallipoli came, ironically, on meeting an Englishman who had fought there. He talked about the campaign, produced his diaries kept in the trenches and Moorehead suddenly saw the familiar story through fresh and excited eyes. Yes, he would follow Murdoch as the war correspondent-turned-writer who could understand what had happened there. So he began by reading military histories and interviewing more survivors, the youngest of whom were now in their sixties, and finally would visit Turkey, where the historical section of the General Staff of the Turkish Army offered him a guide to take him to the rocky hills of the deserted battlefields. He again felt inspired and satisfied.

"Now, more than at any time since the ending of the war, I am settled," he wrote in the journal, "at any rate as far as work is concerned and probably for the next eighteen months or two years."[24] At last he would be able to use his abilities to describe places and dramatic events and his understanding of warfare, and tap the Australian ethos which had been sublimated in him for so long. His visit to the Anzac beach-head on Gallipoli would be for him, as for any Australian, a pilgrimage, and he wrote, "I should preface the Gallipoli book with an account of how I grew up with the legend in Australia (which could also include a reference to the demi-god status of the Australians at Anzac)." His enthusiasm even overcame a setback when Sir Winston Churchill, who had then been First Lord of the Admiralty and the principal strategist of the campaign and was now Prime Minister again, would not find time to see him.

He worked on research throughout 1954 and, from time to time, still suffered relapses into depression. "I do not know what to do with myself, except smoke endless cigarettes,"[25] he wrote in July and, in October, he added that only by writing what he wanted to write and *"feeling* again" could he "defeat this aimlessness: the awful, hysterical emptiness and ennui".[26] In one such depression he even wrote to the Prime Minister of Australia, Robert Menzies, to ask if there was any diplomatic post in the Department of External Affairs that would suit him, and was dashed to be told politely that there was not. Yet as the year ended he began to realise that it had been successful. His writing – mostly magazine articles – had earned more than £7,000, their modest holding of shares was doing well on the Stock Exchange and John was happy and successful at Eton, where he would be followed by Richard. In the spring, they would go to Greece, where, after visiting Turkey, he would write the book about Gallipoli. When that was done he planned a biography of Churchill and a book of his collected travel articles.

During the first three months of 1955 he finished his research, visited Turkey, then spent the summer and early autumn on the Greek island of Spetses, writing the first draft of the book. The house they rented was crowded with a succession of guests from the smart literary set – Cyril Connolly, Patrick Leigh-Fermor and his wife, Maurice Bowra and Osbert Lancaster among them – and the ubiquitous Geoffrey Keating disembarked from the American millionairess Elsa Maxwell's yacht to call. Another visitor to arrive by yacht was George Millar, who had also abandoned journalism to write books.*

---

* After Millar had met Moorehead and Clifford at Gibraltar early in 1944, he

In October, back in London, he had talks with Harold Nicolson about the diplomatic background to the events of 1915 and with the military historian Basil Liddell Hart about the strategy and tactics of the campaign itself. Finally he revised the text and began to collect maps and photographs to illustrate it. Although the year ended happily, with frustration banished by activity, he realised that it was the first for three decades when he had earned no money at all.

While awaiting the publication of *Gallipoli* at the end of April, 1956, he set off on more travels to the Middle East, this time heading south to Kenya, Uganda, Tanganyika, the Congo and South Africa to write more magazine articles. While he toured the Middle East, Lucy stayed in London putting the final touches to the proofs of *Gallipoli* but would join him in East Africa. In January, he arrived in Cyprus – staying at Government House with General Harding, the Governor, who was beset by Greek Cypriot terrorism – and from there flew to Iraq, Syria, Lebanon, Egypt and Israel, which he described as being "like a Fabian camp run by Butlin's".[27] The Middle East bored him as "all the same, all, more or less, as one expects or remembers".[28] But Africa in the company of Lucy was as stimulating as he had expected and after two months they returned to London at the beginning of April in time for the publication of *Gallipoli*.

At first it did not seem as successful as he had hoped. No American publisher wanted to buy it and, although Hamish Hamilton ordered a first printing of 35,000 copies, sales were slow. Yet Hamilton was confident that it would be a success and might win awards and, with this optimistic reassurance, Moorehead set sail for the United States, where he was to write a series of travel articles and see publishers about future books.

He sailed in the Cunard liner *Mauretania* and found that the novelist C.S. Forester, the author of the successful Hornblower historical novels, and his wife were fellow-passengers and proved to be, as he wrote to Lucy, "extremely nice, he just as you would imagine, practical, modest, twinkling kind of bird . . . so unassuming, so honest, so English". He was particularly cheered to learn that Forester was so relaxed about his own writing: "He works *two hours* a day and only for three months of the year. For three months, he isolates

had returned to London to find his marriage at an end, volunteered for the Special Operations Executive and been parachuted into France. His service with the Resistance, for which he was awarded the Distinguished Service Order, became the subject of three books. Later, he was to write about sailing in the Mediterranean with his second wife, Isobel.

himself, producing 1,000 words a day – 90 days = 90,000 words = a book." Moreover, Forester regarded Moorehead as an equal and, as he told Lucy, "astonished me – and pleased me – by treating *me* as a distinguished operator".[29]

He was in need of such reassurance particularly after the long series of disappointments that had preceded the writing of *Gallipoli* and even that was not a certain success, although the first reviews were enthusiastic. It was sometimes provided by the admiration of attractive women, and flirting with them to this end had become part of his nature. When at parties without Lucy he enjoyed using his charm and good looks – particularly his large, clear blue eyes – to attract them, much as a fly-fisherman tempts a trout. "Alan was a naughty boy," recalled one woman journalist of such occasions, remembering how he had discovered a newly-patented electric implement for massaging muscles in his hostess's bathroom, declared that it was designed to arouse the erotic instincts and began to apply it to the necks and shoulders of the younger women present, asking them to describe their sensations. Even when encounters went further – and they sometimes did – he shied away from emotional involvement and had, in any case, warned her two decades before that he would inevitably be unfaithful. However, when Lucy, who was now a charming, mature woman in her mid-forties, was invited out by a man during her husband's absences, he became jealous.

On occasion he would be surprised and excited by the power of his own sexual attraction and he told Lucy about an incident on board the *Mauretania* when he wrote to her from New York:

There was one charming girl from Chicago, a child of twenty, beautifully brought up and intelligent and to my stupefaction last night when I was talking to her, she burst into tears. She was struggling quite helplessly with an intense emotion of love: not love for me physically but at some skein of feelings I happened to release, a storm of hero-worship. I suppose this sounds awful. At all events I got her to go to her cabin instead of pacing the foggy deck all night and there she was this morning, calm, sophisticated, meeting her family, even though I am pretty sure she stayed awake in her cabin most of the night. She came up to say goodbye, retracting nothing and not apologising but very friendly: it was an admirable performance.[30]

In Manhattan, he was at once caught up in a swirl of entertaining with invitations from Cass Canfield, the publisher, the novelist John Steinbeck, the journalist and broadcaster Alistair Cooke and William Shawn, who had become editor of the *New Yorker* in 1952 on the sudden death of Harold Ross. He was to tour the country from coast to coast but first he had to accept an irresistible invitation to stay in Cuba with the Hemingways, whom he had cabled in the hope that they might meet in Florida. His host now behaved as if Moorehead was a fellow-writer rather than just an admirer and the three days at their house outside Havana thrilled him. He described it to Lucy:

> . . . the house exotic beyond belief with flowering trees, swimming pool among the palm trees, nine servants, books, Cuban characters, stuffed animals everywhere. The bibulous sea captain was in residence and we sang a great deal. In the intervals when we weren't bowling down to the docks in a red Cadillac convertible, drinking iced daiquiris on the way, we were out in the Gulf Stream fishing and I got a monster known as a Horse-eyed Jack. Really it was quite marvellous. Why have we never had small home-grown peaches and mangoes with champagne poured over them? We talked and talked, a good deal about Africa, of course, and Ernest pressed me to send his love to you . . . They have become very good friends.[31]

This way of life appealed as much as Berenson's: the one rumbustious the other cloistered; but both of them stimulating. The house on its little hill, the Finca Vigia, had been chosen for Hemingway by his last wife, their friend Martha Gellhorn, and it set Moorehead a new goal: one day, when he himself was rich and famous, he would live in a house that combined the attractions of I Tatti and the Finca Vigia.

From Cuba he flew to Miami and thence to Dallas and Los Angeles where he made friends with the film director George Stevens, who claimed to have met him in Normandy, before going to stay with C.S. Forester at Berkeley. From California, he travelled by train to Chicago where he stayed with the columnist Lucius Beebe – "a lush character, very rich, who has his own railway carriage complete with marble dining table and built-in cherubs over the chimneypiece, the only really original thing I have seen in the USA"[32] – and then to Philadelphia. Finally he returned to New York for more entertainment and talk of further articles and books, including a study of the Russian Revolution to be published on its fortieth anniversary in the following year.

This headlong travelling stimulated, bored, inspired and exhausted him but he felt driven to continue it and explained his motives to Lucy when she wrote sad letters from London wondering why he constantly felt impelled to leave her and their home in this way. He wrote from the United States:

I hate you to be forlorn like this. It makes me feel that there is something madly wrong, almost inhuman, about me. I love you better than anyone else in the world and I run away and leave you in misery. These awful departures. Stay, don't pack, don't follow. But it isn't like that. You know that in your heart. I go away only to come home, for how long now, 17 years? Isn't the coming home good? Better perhaps than had I stayed and nagged miserably. I have to work things out alone, I don't know why: and so I go away and get a sort of balance again . . . I have a brief illusion of escape when I am travelling – as in Africa – and that is the only reason I travel. And when – as on the return from Africa – I cannot (I think through sheer weakness) immediately sink myself in work, then all the frustrations and doubt rushes back at me. You feel you ought to be able to help me demolish this foul monster and so you could with any normal, non-weak character. And so it's not home, not you that makes me so impossible, but myself.[33]

In Philadelphia, he heard the shocking news that his old friend from the Paris office of the *Daily Express*, Mara Scherbatoff, had been killed in a road accident when, as head of the *Paris-Match* bureau in New York, she had been on her way to Marilyn Monroe's wedding to the playwright Arthur Miller. He wrote to Lucy:

Oh God, about Mara being killed chasing Marilyn Monroe on her marriage day. I never called her when I was in New York. How we all deserted her. How much all our lives were bound up with hers . . . The papers said she was forty-seven. Yet, I suppose she had done most of those things she had set out to do . . . Yet to die in those circumstances, swallowed up by the little nameless Monroe. It's the lack of dignity in this rat-race one minds.[34]

Back in New York – with visits to Long Island and New England – he was again caught up by entertaining and more famous names appeared in his letters home: P.G. Wodehouse, the novelist John O'Hara, and Charles Addams, the cartoonist, amongst them. His social life had, he confessed, "a whiff of the Scott Fitzgerald world"[35] about it. There were interesting men for conversation and beautiful women for flirting and conversation and it was with one of these that, for the first time outside his marriage, his emotions became involved. She was elegant, intelligent and artistic, married to a successful writer and at home in all the interlocking social circles in which he had been entertained in America. This relationship developed despite his love for Lucy, which was mutual, deep and, beneath the surface of domesticity, passionate. One reason for this was, in the view of a sympathetic woman friend of them both, that he needed the admiration that he felt she might no longer hold for him as she once had, knowing his weaknesses, particularly for the casual involvements with other women. Another was that Lucy, often alone when he was abroad, had recently accepted invitations from an admirer and had, Moorehead felt, been less than candid about this to him, even though her reticence might have been to avoid his needless jealousy. But he was jealous and, becoming hurt rather than angry, considered himself free of another bond of fidelity. When he sailed from New York for Plymouth at the end of July, he was, for once, unable to consign all the experiences of the journeying that was ending to his memory.

On his return to London, he discovered that, in his absence, he had become an important literary figure. It was not so much the reviewers' praise or the satisfactory sales figures of *Gallipoli* that had achieved this but the talk of the literary world. Bernard Berenson had written to him from Tuscany to say that he had had the book read aloud to him: "I listened with all my ears, was fascinated, delighted. You have achieved a masterpiece of historical writing. I certainly have read nothing as good among histories of my time."[36] His view was seconded by the successful writer and traveller Colonel Peter Fleming, who was combining his life as an Oxfordshire landowner with writing quietly witty "fourth leaders" for *The Times*; in congratulating Moorehead, he urged him to concentrate on writing military history. The political *grande dame*, Lady Violet Bonham Carter, who had known Rupert Brooke, one of the first to die in the Gallipoli campaign, and had advised Moorehead in his research, wrote to say that his account of the poet's attitude to the war "*exactly* expressed his state of mind and feeling"[37] and that she had recommended the book to Winston Churchill.

A few charges of inaccuracy were to come, but it was welcomed as a vivid and perceptive account of a tragedy that haunted the memories of middle-aged and elderly people in Britain, as well as in Australia, and in France where it was soon translated. It also brought a response amongst those of all ages concerned about present events in the Middle East, where Britain and France were again allies in a military expedition that evoked uneasy parallels. They had invaded Egypt at the beginning of November in an abortive attempt to capture the Suez Canal, which had been nationalised by the Egyptians. So, although sales of the book had been slow at first, they were now steady and continuing.

As a result of the success of *Gallipoli*, Moorehead was elected a member of the Society of Literature on the recommendation of Peter Fleming and John Betjeman. It was chosen as Book of the Year by the *Sunday Times* with a prize of £1,000 and won the newly-endowed Duff Cooper Memorial Prize, which was awarded at a formal presentation by Sir Winston Churchill.

The success established Moorehead as a serious author and the book's steady sales and offers of commissions and advances for more secured his finances. In the year that followed, his income amounted to £31,750, of which only £2,500 came from investments and letting the house in London.

Both older children had been aware of money having been a problem – although Richard, now aged five, would grow up in the family's prosperity – but this had not affected their sense of well-being. Caroline, now twelve, would recall "the great sunniness" of her childhood in a family that seemed "so uniquely happy, gifted and charmed that it must have been chosen". She adored her mother as the kind, wise controller of their lives and found her father an exciting person, travelling to distant places and returning to concentrate on his children: reading aloud before supper from *The Jungle Book*, perhaps, and, later, stories by "Saki" and Chekhov. He was a great games-player: bridge, canasta, Scrabble or backgammon indoors, or tennis and badminton out of doors. He could be funny and imaginative, telling her when she was little that specks of dust in sunbeams were microscopic wild animals like those he had seen in Africa, and ordering her not to eat the holes in the Gruyère cheese. He never lost his temper but could be stern, once writing to her on hearing that she was unhappy at school and wanted to leave that "if you throw this in, I would not think much of you".[38] Now she became conscious that he was also famous and successful.

John, who was sixteen and at Eton, shared his sister's love for their mother as the central figure in their happy family. But he was slightly in awe of his father, whom he found rather formal though direct and fair. He was orderly, too, liking to make plans and writing them down on a ruled pad even if they were to be changed. John also found him an exciting father, active and generous, but behind the jollity was the sense that he was the guardian of the codes of behaviour within which they led such happy lives.

The blow to this contentment was not only unexpected but fell when success seemed to have set the seal upon it. The chance discovery of an opened letter to Moorehead from New York revealed the extent of his emotional involvement there to his family. The structure of their lives and the standards that governed it seemed to have been betrayed and ruptured. Worst of all for the children was the fact that their mother, so loyal and loving, had been wronged by the father to whom they had all looked for moral guidance.

The anguish was sublimated and a visitor to the house on Primrose Hill might not have noticed that anything was amiss. Lucy was aware that her husband's involvement in New York was more than the casual peccadilloes that she had come to accept as probably necessary for his strong drives. Yet in the past the knowledge of these had contributed to her own depression when he left on his travels and now worsened when he returned to New York to discuss the book, the articles for *Life* magazine about the Russian Revolution and more articles about Africa which he was planning to write. This, she knew, was not his only reason for wanting to go there.

Moorehead was on the move for the first half of 1957. He was briefly in New York at the beginning of the year, then spent six weeks in Africa before returning to New York for a month. When he crossed the Atlantic the second time that year, there did seem a chance that, on his return, family life might return to normal. They had decided, after renting a cottage in Surrey for what proved to be a spell of cold, wet weather, to return to Italy and were planning to stay in a villa near Rome while they looked for a house to buy. Even Moorehead, caught up in the usual round of entertaining in Manhattan, looked forward to it, writing to Lucy at the end of April, "Of course I am going out too much and already am longing to be in Italy and for the first sight of the villa. Once there, the thing will be to lead a sensible life. The drink is the bad thing. In New York one is besieged by it – and people. People one really likes very much – but one should only see them once in a long while."[39] Yet he could not resist the excitement of Manhattan, even in a spring heat-wave. "It is over-stimulating," he told Lucy, "and nothing seems real."[40]

He returned to London in May and at the beginning of June they arrived at the villa in the Alban Hills, where he was to complete his

book on the Russian Revolution. The house had once been rented by
the actress Audrey Hepburn, when she had been filming in Rome, and
was of a style suited to a famous author. Indeed, Lucy had chosen it
after Martha Gellhorn, who understood her husband's susceptibilities,
advised, "Get a glamour house for him."[41] There the family lived until
November when Moorehead, leaving Lucy in Rome, again flew to
New York with his completed typescript. The book was an efficient
exercise in journalistic history but neither journalism – as he had not
experienced the events himself – nor true history, since he had not had
time for original research. But now there were hopes of work suited to
his talents, notably further expeditions to Africa for books and articles
about its past and present; its little-known history and remote places.

His letters from Manhattan were full of plans for such projects
and commiseration with Lucy, who was lonely and troubled. He
knew he was living dangerously, risking the love and stability his
family gave him and, from time to time, would promise her that he
would ensure that all would be well; that, if need be, he could now
afford to buy happiness. He wrote in December:

> I guarantee that I will make things far, far better. Don't worry
> about the expense . . . I am making money here. *So don't worry
> over the money*. We never had so much as we have now. As soon
> as I get back I am going to throw myself into the business of making
> life more bearable. We will get a small country place – Sardinia
> can be tried first, then if necessary another look at Tuscany . . .
> I am enjoying it here but I will love coming back and everything
> is going to be much, much better.[42]

It was not money and the expense of the villa outside Rome that
she was worrying about, however, and while he would make such
resolutions, she knew he drifted back into the company of his lover
and her circle of clever and amusing friends. He recognised the crisis
he was creating but could not quite shake himself free of it. "Poor
Puss," he wrote to Lucy just before returning to her. "At the bottom
of a well. Who threw her in? I did."[43]

He did not stay long at the cold and draughty villa in the Alban
Hills for a succession of journeys had been planned. He could now
choose where he went and when. Not only was *The Russian Revolution* to be Book of the Month in the United States but it was to
be serialised in the *Sunday Times* as well as *Life*. There were to be
short visits to Florence and to Greece, which would produce travel

articles for magazines, and then a major expedition to Africa, which might produce more than one important book.

A short visit to Africa in February was followed by three weeks in Uganda, Kenya and the Sudan. The first book that he had decided to write was to be about wild animals and the threat to their existence from poaching and encroaching development. A second was to be the exploration of the basin of the White Nile and the search for its source in the last century. Both would also be written as articles for serialisation and would give him good reason to make repeated journeys into a remote and challenging part of the world that increasingly attracted him, recalling the enchantment of the Outback in Australia, where he had felt at ease. Also, he would admit, it was a refuge from the complexities and worries of life in the over-civilised worlds in Europe and the United States. It was, as he would put it, another case of running away from himself.

His visits to African game parks over the past three years had given him the material for the first book, but the writing of it was difficult because everything he had to say about wild animals had been described so often before. After writing several drafts and tearing them up, he had appealed to William Shawn, while on a visit to New York. "Take no notice," Shawn had said, "of the fact that the hippopotamus, the elephant and the other animals have been described so often before. Say what *you* think, say what *you* felt, write whatever you yourself found."[44] This simple advice cleared the block and, as Moorehead said, "the work took wings." He wrote most of it on his return to the villa near Rome, where they were still living, in the spring and early summer of 1958.

In September, he set out for Africa again to gather material for the book about the White Nile. This time he took a companion, Dick Waller, to whom he had been introduced by Freya Stark and who had visited them at the Villa Diana. Waller had been in the Indian Army, flown as a fighter pilot with the RAF and, as a result of an Oxford degree in geography and agriculture, had joined the Food and Agriculture Organisation of the United Nations for a time. He had visited Moorehead at their villa and found him immersed in books about African exploration from the London Library. The two had got talking about the characters of the explorers and the extraordinary problems they had faced and decided to mount a joint expedition themselves, each paying his own way. In September, they sailed from Venice for Dar-es-Salaam, where Moorehead knew the Governor, Sir Richard Turnbull, and had an invitation to stay at Government House.

The expedition into the interior was an echo of the war-reporting years. They travelled daily, driving their Land Rover across country and by rough tracks, usually sleeping under a roof at the house of a district officer but occasionally beneath the stars. They became healthy, hungry and energetic, curious for the next experience. Their particular aim was to follow the track of the expedition in search of the source of the Nile by Burton and Speke in 1857 but the others – notably Livingstone and Stanley – also haunted their imaginations. "We must try to get into the minds of the old explorers," Moorehead would say. Travelling by compass between points identified in the explorers' own accounts of their journeys, they would seek and sometimes find in the villages descendants of those who had met the strange white travellers a century before. Sometimes Moorehead would stop, gaze at a view and say, "This is exactly what Burton and Speke would have seen."

The personalities of the explorers interested them, too: the rivalry between Burton and Speke; the contrast between Dr Livingstone, the Christian gentleman, and Henry Stanley, the pushy, sometimes bullying, American journalist. Sometimes it almost seemed that the characters of the latter pair were reflected by Waller and Moorehead: the former, gentle and reflective and something of a mystic; the latter, assertive, vigorous and with no time for anything like mysticism. As in Moorehead's friendships with Clifford and Buckley, the contrast was mutually attractive. Waller found Moorehead as active in mind as in body with a quick and methodical brain. He was as unsparing of himself as of others, and he showed little sympathy for those who became tired or unwell.

Occasionally there was an edge of danger to their travels. Once when walking on the shore of Lake Victoria with Dr Edna Lind, a botanist at Makere University, they were charged by a hippopotamus, ran for their lives into the bush and, when the danger had passed, found that they had lost their bearings and sense of direction. Then Dr Lind began to examine the plants, saying, "Those are water-loving; those are not,"[45] and so eventually led them back to the lake.

All the while, Moorehead was making notes, marking maps, and reconstructing the Victorian expeditions in his imagination. This was a task for which he was supremely fitted, he could feel confident, for few historians would have the stamina to undertake such journeys and few, if any, had the ability to describe places and people and choose the telling detail that he had acquired as a journalist.

His publisher and then his readers thought likewise. First, his book about the wild animals of Africa and their conservation, *No Room in the Ark*, was published in May, 1959, to universal acclaim. It was chosen as Book of the Month in the United States and serialised in the *New Yorker*, the *Sunday Times*, the *Liverpool Post* and *Figaro*, was translated into four languages and, during the first six months, sold 30,000 copies in Britain alone. Glowing with gratification at the reviews and constant congratulations, Moorehead returned from Central Africa at the beginning of 1959 and, after a month in London, retired to Freya Stark's house at Asolo to write his study of African exploration, *The White Nile*, for publication the following year.

Although the Mooreheads had decided to use London only for research and occasional bouts of social activity, they had found nowhere to settle since they left the Villa Diana. The house in the Alban Hills had been cold in winter and unsettling in summer; they had not liked Portofino; Paris might prove as chill and claustrophobic as London and St.-Jean–de-Luz, for which Moorehead still hankered after twenty years, was too far from the mainstream of literary and social life. So again they looked at Tuscany and there, at last, they found somewhere to rest. The search had been a regular topic of conversation in Italy and eventually some English friends told them of a stretch of hillside on the Tuscan coast that was to be sold by an Italian landowner. It was on the Argentario peninsula near Porto Ercole, a part of the coast that had not been developed for tourism. It was about two hours by road or rail from either Rome or Pisa and they went there on reconnaissance.

There was no house, just ten acres of scrub-covered hillside from which they could see between the wooded slopes of a valley an empty beach of yellow sand and, beyond and between two hills crowned with ruined castles, the roofs of the fishing village of Porto Ercole. Otherwise there were only olive groves, vineyards and dense woods of oak; it was, in effect, a canvas upon which they could paint their own idyllic *capriccio*. They bought the land and commissioned an Italian architect to design a house to a specification that would suit an industrious and successful writer, his family and their guests.

It was a time of promise and excitement. The house in Wells Rise was sold and a flat in Eccleston Square near Victoria Station taken as a base in London. The planning and the building were a constant pleasure, particularly in the siting of its modest extravagancies: a work-room for him; a swimming-pool for the children. "Listen," wrote Lucy to him during one of his travels, "do you want your little studio – how pathetic that sounds – run up right away? If you wish me to lay it on now – and the swimming pool – you only have to say so. I am now at the point where I could fix the building of a cathedral and several chapter-houses."[46]

They moved into their new house in the spring of 1960 and were delighted with it, not least because it and its surroundings would be entirely their own creation, reflecting only themselves. It was a low, two-storey building with a large living-room opening upon the terrace and its view down the wide valley; most bedrooms were upstairs but with a separate wing leading off the hall with a bedroom, dressing-room and bathroom for the master and mistress of the house. There were staff quarters, kitchen and garages and particular attention had been paid to a small stone building uphill and about a hundred yards from the back of the house. This was the studio where Moorehead would work at a desk facing the wall, which would be covered with maps and photographs concerned with whatever he was writing. The grounds themselves he began to plant with vines, olive trees, cypress, umbrella pine and Australian gum trees. In a deep dell at the end of a hillside path, a swimming-pool was to be built and nearby ground would be flattened for a badminton court. Being new, the house had no name so it became just Villa Moorehead.

That year his second book about the wilds of Africa, *The White Nile*, was published to renewed acclaim and was chosen as Book of the Month in the United States. He was particularly delighted by a letter from Martha Gellhorn, whose opinion he valued as highly as Hemingway's:

I think it is a dream book and a humdinger. You are really a clever boy; I have just realised you are a first class historian, although I have always realised you write like a bird . . . And what a wonderful way of life you've found, it combines derring-do (which we all pine for, or anyhow I do, sicken for want of it), with the pleasures of the mind, your mind at work.[47]

At once he decided to write *The Blue Nile* as a sequel, and that would mean further visits to New York to discuss serialisation and more visits to Africa, including a tour of Egypt with the Lancasters that winter. For Lucy, her husband's visits to New York had become periods of depression for she knew that, despite their own love for one another and for their family, his attachment there continued. Indeed, he made assignations with his lover elsewhere – notably in Paris – and, although he attempted to keep this relationship separate from the rest of his life, it set up conflicts and worry that clouded what would otherwise have been a clear and sunlit prospect of the success he had sought so long.

The theme of *The Blue Nile* was the European expeditionary forces rather than the explorers in Africa: the French in Egypt, the Turks in the Sudan and the British in Ethiopia. It was almost as successful as *The White Nile* had been, selling 40,000 hardback copies in Britain alone in the first year, as against the 60,000 copies of the earlier book. Together the two books would earn their author about £100,000, bringing his capital in shares and property to more than £200,000, and this affluence enabled the family to travel almost at will.

John was at Oxford University and Richard would also go to Eton, while Caroline would follow schooling in Switzerland with university courses in Paris and London. It was recognised that the family was administered by Lucy. She was efficient with money and accounts, ordering the house and the servants, who now included an Italian couple living at the Villa Moorehead, and arranging visits by friends and their own expeditions as well as acting as her husband's editor, secretary and agent.

A daily pattern emerged as the family settled at Porto Ercole. Moorehead himself would rise early, write from about seven in the morning until noon; then, after lunch, he would sleep, swim and perhaps revise his morning's work, or prepare for the next day's writing before it was time for drinks and dinner, which would be accompanied by much conversation and were often followed by card games, Scrabble or canasta. Their friends not only stayed at the house but several bought their own houses in the neighbourhood, including the Alwyn Lees and the Sidney Bernsteins, while the Bangors – the former Edward Ward and his wife – bought a flat, then sold it to Geoffrey Keating. They made friends with others who had made their own way to the Argentario peninsula, notably an English painter, Anthony Fry, who was converting a simple cottage nearby, where Moorehead would sometimes join him, complaining that his own house was too full of guests and he needed an escape. An aptitude for painting, which had been aroused in New York, was encouraged by Fry, and Moorehead began to show promise. They arranged picnics and expeditions to restaurants in the Tuscan hills and Moorehead agreed to share the costs of a yacht with Sidney Bernstein. Sitting, on the deck in the harbour of Porto Ercole, Moorehead observed to a visiting yacht-owner, Irwin Shaw, the American author, that a sure sign that a writer was successful was when he could command his own yacht.

Much of their social success was due to the quiet, self-effacing presence of Lucy. Indeed, some of their guests – such as Martha Gellhorn – accepted their invitations in order to see her rather than him, admiring her warmth, gentle generosity and the intellect that she devoted to his service at the sacrifice of what would have been a successful – possibly brilliant – career of her own. Friends knew that she did not share his hankering after the company of celebrities and smart literary society and that she devoted herself to their children and his ambition. As the years had passed, she matured into middle age with grace, while he remained boyish, highly charged and quick in reacting to praise or slight. Older than her husband, the gap in their ages seemed to widen.

Even the final ascent of the English social strata seemed possible for he had met John Sparrow, the Warden of All Souls – the Oxford college exclusive to the most distinguished graduates – who had suggested that, if he planned to spend much time in England he should apply for a fellowship. It was also gratifying to offer guests wine from their own vines, although he had to admit that it was not yet very good. When they had first drunk it, he had written to his sister, "Yesterday, we tasted for the first time our own wine. Lucy threw hers away. Caroline gave hers to the parrot and only Richard would drink it."[48] Yet it was an amusing talking-point at dinner parties.

Just as he found himself on the uplands of literary success, the restlessness began again and now it was such that it could not be assuaged by another safari in Africa, or even gaiety in New York. He was hankering after Australia. About half of his closest friends were Australian; those from his youth, like Alwyn Lee, and others made more recently like Rod Andrew and the artist Sidney Nolan. Increasingly his thoughts turned to the Australian wilds, where Europeans often felt uneasy but he felt at home. Like Africa, the outback could offer wild animals for him to describe and stories of exploration for him to tell. Australian history now engaged his imagination as the Italian Renaissance once had. When a young Australian, Robert Hughes, who had ambitions to become a writer and whom he had befriended, came to stay at the Villa Moorehead, he advised him to choose a subject from their own history, perhaps the early penal settlements.* So it was that the subject for his next

* Robert Hughes's book about this, *The Fatal Shore*, which was published in 1987, is dedicated to Alan Moorehead.

book was one of Australian exploration: the terrible trans-continental journey of Burke and Wills a century before. He wrote it in 1962 and it was published the following year as *Cooper's Creek* and, with an initial print-run for Hamish Hamilton of 45,000 copies, was another success.

The importance of *Cooper's Creek* was that it established him in Australia as an Australian writer and not just as an Australian who had made a name for himself in Europe. His next book, too, would have an Australian theme, he told Rod Andrew in a letter, and his particular ambition was to bring his whole family back to Australia for the first time.

He returned alone early in 1964 for a triumphal progress as an Australian celebrity. There were invitations from the important, press conferences and interviews in the cities, and they moved comfortably among literary and artistic notables. Nevil Shute was an old friend as was Professor Manning Clark, the leading historian of Australia; Sidney Nolan was another friend and he met Sir Russell Drysdale, the artist who painted the outback and to whom he took an immediate liking. He was invited to make two television programmes about Australian wildlife and Sidney Nolan and he planned a joint expedition to the Antarctic with the United States Navy.

At the beginning of this Australian tour, Moorehead had opened an exhibition of Nolan's painting in Adelaide and had written about the artist and his work. Now Nolan put an original idea into his head: why not write the libretto for an opera? Nolan had designed scenery for the operatic stage – as had Osbert Lancaster – and he inspired his friend to find an Australian subject with the necessary simplicity and power. The idea was greeted not only with enthusiasm by Stefan Haag, the director of the Australian Elizabethan Theatre Trust, but with a commission for Moorehead to write the libretto to music by Peter Sculthorpe and decor by Nolan for a new opera. It was to be called *Mrs Fraser* and tell the tragic story of the sea-captain's wife who survived a shipwreck on the coast of Queensland in 1836 only to be held captive by the Aboriginals. The new form of composition proved stimulating and he looked forward to the excitement of hearing his words sung.

After their visit to the South Pole he and Nolan continued to Tahiti and here a new subject presented itself. After investigating the plight of wild animals in Africa, Moorehead realised that the people of the South Pacific had undergone a somewhat similar experience at the hands of the Europeans. In Australia, the voyages of discovery by Captain Cook had been regarded as the opening up of uninhabited land and the exposure of primitive peoples to civilising influences. Now he saw the process differently. In the wake of Cook and the other explorers came the exploiters to plunder the resources and debauch the simple people, to slaughter the wild animals and destroy patterns of living that had evolved naturally over centuries. He described this process as it had overtaken Tahiti, Australia and Antarctica from their discovery by colonisers and merchant-explorers in the eighteenth century. He entitled his book *The Fatal Impact* and it was an immediate success, serialised in major newspapers and magazines. He now found himself in the vanguard of the new, growing and world-wide movement for conservation.

From time to time, Moorehead attempted to write his autobiography but had only been able to complete those chapters dealing with his friendship with Alexander Clifford. This had been given a sudden immediacy by the unexpected death from a brain tumour of Clifford's widow, Jenny. After Clifford's death she had married Patrick Crosse, a former war correspondent for Reuter in the desert, who had been taken prisoner in the "Crusader" campaign, and reminded some of their friends of his gentle, reflective predecessor, and they had lived happily in Rome. Now most of those friends who had surrounded him two decades before had died – Noel Monks, his trail-blazer, and Ernest Hemingway, his hero, among them – and were fading rapidly into the past. Writing about Clifford helped him hold on to his memory and he composed an elegy for several of them, which he delivered in a lecture at a literary festival in London.

I will be forgiven, I hope, if I make some special mention of a small group of war correspondents, whom I knew very well. They are dead now – they died in the most unpredictable ways soon after the war was over – and there is some danger that they may be overlooked and forgotten. I am thinking particularly of Alexander Clifford, who wrote for the *Daily Mail*, of Christopher Buckley of the *Daily Telegraph*, of Philip Jordan of the *News Chronicle*, of Evelyn Montague of the *Manchester Guardian*, Ian Morrison of *The Times* and Chester Wilmot of the BBC . . .

Nearly all of them were in their forties when they died and on purely literary grounds I think it is a shame that they are dead. They set a standard of reporting and of commenting upon the things they saw which was very high indeed and had they lived they would certainly have gone on and written even better books. Naturally I miss them very much indeed . . . They died at a moment when they were most needed – when mass communications were to burst upon the world, the mass-circulation newspapers and magazines, the movies, radio and television.[49]

In 1965, Moorehead returned to make the television film about Australian wildlife and to complete his libretto for the opera. Meeting Moorehead soon after his arrival, Manning Clark thought that, despite his success, he was "a lonely and unhappy man". He always seemed to be on the move like a fugitive but, as the days passed, Clark noticed that he seemed to relax and appear more confident. "It was as if he didn't have to put on an act any more," he decided, "because he was among his own sort of people."[50]

After spending nearly half the year in Australia, Moorehead was again on his travels: to Mexico and then Hollywood, where *The Rage of the Vulture* had finally been filmed and where he discussed the writing of a film script about Darwin and his voyage of exploration in the *Beagle* for a handsome fee and a share of the eventual profits. There were possibilities of films based on *Cooper's Creek* and both books about the Nile explorations and options for these had already earned him £10,000. He was again in New York, where his attachment persisted, returning to London for the publication of *The Fatal Impact* at the end of January. This, too, was an immediate success and serialised on both sides of the Atlantic.

The principal plan for 1966 was to take his family with him to Australia. It was not just that he himself felt increasingly drawn there, but he was planning to invest in land on the coast of New South Wales and thinking of buying a house there. John would not be able to come because, on coming down from Oxford, he had worked for a while as a journalist on the *Western Mail* in Cardiff and had now moved to the *Evening Standard* in London as a reporter on *The Londoner's Diary* column which was regarded as a nursery for the most promising young journalists. But Moorehead was anxious that Caroline should come with him, Lucy and Richard. After a spell at the Sorbonne in Paris and with the expectation of taking a good degree in psychology at London University, she had come of age in October – when they had given a "coming out" dance for her in Mayfair – and had grown into an intelligent and exceptionally attractive young woman. Naturally enough, she had chosen a favourite suitor, though her father was not sure that he was the right one. Jeremy Swift was a tall, dark, good-looking and clever young man but it seemed to

Moorehead that he lacked self-discipline and a sense of direction. He had been an Oxford undergraduate working on a conservation project in the Camargue when he and Caroline had met in 1962 and now he was working for the United Nations' Food and Agriculture Organisation in Rome, which was all too convenient for visits by fast sports car to Porto Ercole. A long spell apart would be good for them both, Moorehead decided.

For himself travel was an escape from depression, and a search for inspiration was again a necessity. "Nearly everything I have touched in the last twelve months has gone wrong," he wrote in his journal that June. "My libretto has been rejected. The book on Australian natural history that I planned I find I cannot do. The film I made there has not been shown. The Hollywood producer has not bothered to acknowledge the receipt of the Darwin script and will pay only a part of my expenses. I find I cannot write my autobiography. I have nothing to do."[51]

These failures had been compounded by a sudden and unexpected humiliation. The film producer Jack Le Vien had commissioned Moorehead to write the script for a biographical film about General Wingate, the eccentric soldier who had been killed while commanding the Chindit forces behind the Japanese lines in Burma, and he had travelled to Scotland for an interview with his widow. On his return, his son John was surprised to find him early one morning at the flat in Pimlico, having just arrived by the night train, drinking whisky, agitated and angry. He had arrived at the widow's remote house in Scotland to an extraordinary reception: she had, he told John, accused him of being just another journalist trying to make money out of a great man's achievements. He had left for London, hurt and outraged.

Escape was needed. First, there was another short visit to Africa and then the four of them flew to Australia. Again he was treated as a celebrity, with press conferences, newspaper and radio interviews and even a banner strung across a street proclaiming "WELCOME TO MOOREHEAD". On arrival in Melbourne the newspapers accorded him particular attention and one, *The Australian*, reported that:

> . . . as a world-famous author, who has written more successful books than any other Australian, Alan Moorehead is down to earth and, apart from natural pleasure at having achieved what he always set out to do since he was a boy, to write books, he still has a journalist's direct approach and a wit that

has become devastating over the years. He hates talking about himself and shuns publicity. And this clever Australian, who owes everything to his own hard work and determination, can afford to.[52]

He enjoyed Australian life even more on this visit, proudly presenting his children to his family and friends. The influx of European – but not necessarily British – immigrants had, he noticed, improved the quality and variety of the food in restaurants and he delighted in Australian wine, which had not been produced in his youth, comparing it favourably with the wine from his own vines, which, he told interviewers, now filled seven hundred bottles a year, all of which were drunk at the Villa Moorehead. He was asked his views of Australian writers and declared, "Australian letters have never enjoyed greater prestige abroad and I am one who believes that Australian writers have never had it so good." His advice to those hoping to emulate his success might have been given by Berenson or Hemingway: "Your young writer should start reading as much as he can and write incessantly."[53]

His view of Australia's place in the world was changing, particularly now that Australian troops – but not British – were fighting alongside the Americans against the communists in Vietnam:

It seems quite possible that after the Vietnam war is over, Australia will seek a much closer alliance with America, and that, before the end of the century, we shall see a new alignment of power in the Pacific: America and Canada in the north joined to Australia and New Zealand in the south. In other words, a union of English-speaking people in the Pacific, with Britain, the original homeland, acting as its agent in Europe . . . It is an attractive theory . . . while America would obviously be the leader, there would be no poor relations in the union . . . the common language would do away with many of the misunderstandings that bedevil relations between countries . . . Such a union – should one call it the United States of the Pacific? – would clearly not do much to settle the major problems of the world. The Bomb and over-population would still be with us. But it is a viable proposition. It would be a step ahead.[54]

His old employer, the imperialist Lord Beaverbrook, with whom he had often argued and who had died two years before, would have grinned with approval.

In November, he returned to London leaving Lucy to take Caroline on a tour of the Far East and South-east Asia, while Richard had already returned to school in England. There was another spell in the creative doldrums, and this was made more troublesome by a recurrence of the headaches he had suffered a few years before. What next? There was the autobiography still awaiting completion and the hope of writing a major book about the wilds of Australia. It was becoming more difficult to decide upon a subject worthy of his talent and his name. Indeed he startled his friend Dick Waller, the companion of his travels in Africa, by the apparent pride which prompted the rhetorical question, "What is my future? I've done it all. Where can I go?"[55]

Chapter Fourteen

"Everything must come out of my mind"

It was thirty years since Alan Moorehead had first left Australia and now, at the age of fifty-six, he had achieved almost all of the ambitions that had driven him. The first decade of his exile had seen his rise to pre-eminence amongst newspaper journalists and he was still seen as the outstanding war correspondent of the Second World War, certainly amongst those of the British Commonwealth. No other reporter, then or in the past, had brought the sights and sensations of warfare to a mass readership with such immediacy and this achievement was only now being challenged by the daily television reports in colour from the war in Vietnam.

As a writer, his development over the two subsequent decades and the long struggles to find his forte had at last brought him world-wide fame and substantial reward. The combination of his vivid powers of description and eye for detail, his sense of news unfolding into history and his skill as a story-teller had established him as a successful author. As yet, he did not claim to have become a major literary figure with the power of Hemingway or the distinction of Berenson, but such standing now seemed within his grasp.

Towards the end of 1966, he was in one of the familiar troughs between times of inspiration. There was no urgency to write for money because, although his annual expenditure had risen to about £12,000, his income from books and investments was at least twice as much. It was the aspirations that drove him still. The ultimate triumph might yet lie in Australia, where he again felt he belonged and which was now giving him unstinted recognition; he was particularly pleased by the invitation from Monash University in Melbourne, where Rod Andrew was now Dean of the Faculty of Medicine, to become a visiting professor. He might divide his time between Australia and Italy, visiting London for research and to see old friends and New York for the discussion of future writing and a little dalliance. All that was immediately necessary was the inspiration for another book and of this he remained confident, although, as he had once remarked to his sister Phyllis as they walked beneath the Australian gum trees he had planted in his Tuscan garden, "Everything I can do to earn our living must come out of my mind – it's frightening."[1]

When the family assembled at the beginning of December for John's twenty-sixth birthday and then Christmas, there was some concern about Moorehead's health. He had again been suffering from headaches and one day when the postman rang the bell of the flat in Eccleston Square, he had answered through the loudspeaker beside the door and his words were so garbled that it sounded as though he was drunk. These and other symptoms, including occasional numbness or loss of power in a limb, pain in his neck and arm and the stumbling over words, worried Lucy and she persuaded him to see a doctor. A serious cerebral condition was thought a possibility and he was sent to consult a neurologist, who decided that tests of the blood supply to the brain must be carried out immediately. He entered the Westminster Hospital for tests, which would include an X-ray involving the injection of a dye into the arteries to show up any abnormalities. He was cheerful, telling his family that he would describe the experience when it was over.

John had been warned by Caroline that there was a possibility that their father's condition might prove serious, but he was shocked when a convivial lunch in Fleet Street was interrupted by a telephone call from his mother asking him to come to the hospital at once because this had proved to be so. There they were told the diagnosis, that he had been subject to ischaemic attacks resulting from a cerebral vascular condition which had threatened damage to the arteries and that the investigation had brought on a major stroke. It was possible that a remedial operation could be performed but the family's permission was necessary. It was explained that this might effect a complete cure, or he might survive but only as "a vegetable", or he might die. Lucy asked the children for their opinion and it was decided that he should be operated upon.

Moorehead was unconscious for a week afterwards so that his condition was impossible to assess. When he recovered consciousness, it was soon apparent that the operation had been only a limited success. Most of his mental processes seemed to be functioning but there had been brain damage, particularly to the communications nerves, and some paralysis. He could not speak, read or write and hardly move, yet there was optimism that he could still recover. Lucy wrote to Rod Andrew in Melbourne:

It has been a terrible time, but Alan is improving all the time. The trouble is, as you will know so well, that no one can (or will) say how long it will take for him to recover completely; he can't read, which is maddening and gets very frustrated over his speaking. But still he *is* getting better all the time. What a bloody thing it all is, seems so damned unfair to happen to Alan but I suppose everyone feels this . . . He is allowed to drink, thank goodness, but I am determined to keep him off cigarettes. (I myself am now an alcoholic and pickled with smoking, of course.) I have been talked *at* so much by so many doctors, surgeons, neurologists, the lot, during the last few weeks that I break out into a heavy sweat if I see one. This would not apply to you, dear Rod . . .[2]

After a month in hospital, Moorehead returned to their flat while he continued to receive physiotherapy and speech-therapy. Progress was very slow. He had difficulty in moving at all and it had become clear that his right arm and leg were paralysed; he could hardly speak, could not make any of his needs known by voice and, after six weeks, when improvement can become apparent in stroke patients, he seemed no better. So they travelled to Italy for the summer and on warm days he would be taken out in their yacht from Porto Ercole and lowered into the sea to attempt swimming movements. This was producing results when he fell from the boat and cut himself so badly that he had to be admitted to the local hospital at Orbetello, which Lucy described as "something out of the darker pages of Dickens".[3]

Yet some optimism did seem justified and Lucy wrote to Rod Andrew again to say that Moorehead ought to be able to deliver an important address to Monash University the following year. More to the point, he was well enough to give Caroline away in marriage to Jeremy Swift, whom he now regarded as a suitable son-in-law, at a ceremony in the Etruscan town of Tarquinia, mid-way between Porto Ercole and Rome, and to attend the festivities afterwards. Yet, apart from his movements, little progress had been made when, about eighteen months after his stroke, he saw in a magazine a large photograph of the American film actress Patricia Neal and held it up to Lucy, jabbing it with his forefinger. She realised what he meant: Patricia Neal had also suffered a severe stroke two years before and, thanks to the therapy inspired by her husband, the writer Roald Dahl, seemed to be making a remarkable recovery. So, through theatrical friends, they made contact with the Dahls and, in 1968, visited them at their home in Great Missenden, a village in the Chiltern hills of Buckinghamshire not far from London.

Roald Dahl suggested that Moorehead might benefit from meeting their neighbours who had helped his wife by talking and reading to her, trying to enable her to associate words and ideas and to articulate them. The most effective member of this group was Valerie Eaton Griffith, who had worked for Elizabeth Arden, the cosmetics company, and had had no medical training but showed a remarkable flair for conjuring speech from Patricia Neal. So, to be near her and the others, the Mooreheads took a cottage at Great Missenden in the autumn of 1968, planning to try this therapy for a year. Soon Lucy was writing to the Andrews that Patricia Neal and her husband were "most kind and charming . . . Alan works daily with her and a group of her friends, trying desperately to learn to read and write and speak again. He works just as hard as he ever did. My God, if ever anyone earned a recovery, he has."[4]

When Valerie Eaton Griffith met him, she soon realised that he was proud, reluctant to admit the extent of his disabilities and full of frustration and rage. "He was devastated," she said later, "I saw him with tears in his eyes. His brain was active, his memory was clear but he could not communicate. He was imprisoned within himself."[5] First she had to win his confidence in herself and in the therapy used in teaching the meaning of words at infant schools. She would spread out on to a table drawings of simple objects – a fish, a tree, a boat – and, on separate pieces of paper, the words describing them and ask him to match them. She would ask him questions which could be answered by a nod or shake of the head and, remembering how she had captured Patricia Neal's interest by reading to her from a Hollywood gossip column by Louella Parsons, had found that Moorehead was interested in Africa and so produced a map and asked him questions about where he had been and what the country was like. Sometimes she would try to draw information from him by asking questions in the form of a quiz game.

In an attempt to coordinate words and physical movement, she tried to interest him in jigsaw puzzles but at first without success for he clearly regarded this as infantile. Then, sensing from his presence that he was still a man with a strong libido, she made a jigsaw for him from the centrefold of *Playboy* magazine. Piecing together the naked body of a girl concentrated his attention and soon she could interest him in other subjects, and jigsaws became part of his routine, although he was seldom able to add more than three or four pieces a day.

The Mooreheads spent weekends in London, returning to Great Missenden for five days' therapy: two hours a day with Valerie Eaton Griffith and more time at their cottage working on the exercises she had devised and listening to tapes she had recorded. It was also important to give him self-confidence and it was suggested that he might walk the half-mile to Valerie Eaton Griffith's house on his own. At first he would lose his way so she invented a simple paperchase game, pinning scraps of white paper to trees along the road through the outskirts of the village to help him. She agreed with Lucy that he might gain confidence by sometimes visiting a gallery or museum in London on his own, even if he travelled by taxi after showing the driver his destination in writing. He was so reluctant to try this that there seemed to be some reason he would not admit. Eventually this was discovered. As with many who have suffered strokes, he sometimes spoke the wrong word when he was able to say anything at all. On one occasion he had travelled by taxi and, to his embarrassment, had called the driver "darling".

Not only the choice of words was impaired but the inhibiting process, so that instead of saying the polite word he sought, he might produce an obscenity, and loudly, too. He had as much difficulty with names as with nouns, unable to associate a well-remembered person with the appropriate name. He could always call his eldest son "John" but Caroline was usually "that person there" and he sometimes even had difficulty in addressing Lucy by name. After a year, his speech had improved only slightly and, although Valerie Eaton Griffith had some hope of further improvement, others, including the Mooreheads, were convinced that no further recovery of significance could be expected. However, he had gained in self-confidence, seemed less embarrassed by his condition and determined to make an effort to live a more active life.

So, in 1969, he ventured back into the world he had known. He looked as alert, aware and healthy as before but he could not communicate except through some sign-language and a few words, notably "fantastic", "absolutely", "do that thing" and "bloody awful". When asked how he was, he would sometimes say, "Boring." Once, when showing the painter Anthony Fry and his wife that his right arm and leg were still partly paralysed, he looked up at them and asked, "Why? Why?"[6]

He was able to read newspaper headlines but not the smaller type below. Books were useless but, in time, he was able to make his way slowly through books printed in large type for the poorly sighted if, at the same time, he could listen to a tape-recording of the same words. He found television and the theatre difficult to follow but could enjoy the cinema, particularly if the plot and dialogue of the film were slow.

He was unable to write, although he could manage to scrawl his name with his left hand. Certainly as he could neither write nor dictate anything original, his life as a writer was ended and a friend, on learning this, suddenly saw a new and terrible meaning to the verse by John Donne, which Moorehead had loved to recite, about the imprisonment of the spirit.*

Moorehead looked so fit that friends who did not know his true condition assumed that he must have been cured. When visiting the Garrick Club or at a cocktail party, a member of the family or a friend would hover nearby to tactfully join any conversation that might be started by somebody expecting Moorehead to respond.† Some old friends, hearing of what had happened, could not bring themselves to visit him and some of those who did embarrassed him by seeming embarrassed themselves and he remained silent, so helping to perpetuate the myth that he was, indeed, "a vegetable".

---

* *But O alas, so long, so far/Our bodies why do we forebear?*
They're ours, though they're not we, we are/The intelligencies, they the sphere.
So must pure lovers' souls descend/T'affections, and to faculties,/
Which sense may reach and apprehend,/Else a great Prince in prison lies.
                                    John Donne (1571?–1631).

† The author met Alan and Lucy Moorehead at a small party given by Lord and Lady Bangor in London at this time. Seeing Moorehead looking so alert and healthy, he assumed that he had recovered and said, "How good to see you." "Fantastic." "It's years since we met." "Absolutely." "We're late because of the traffic." "Bloody awful." "I lunched with your friend David Woodward yesterday." At this Moorehead looked bewildered and walked across to his wife, who took up his side of the exchange as it was clear that he had almost exhausted his small vocabulary. A three-cornered conversation ensued, with Moorehead throwing in one of those few words occasionally.

But his family and close friends knew that, while he might be confused by rapid cross-talk between a number of visitors, he could understand what was said to him when it was clear and addressed directly. He could even conduct conversations with the few words he could speak and with signs when amongst those with whom he felt at ease. He and Lucy had taken some of the agony out of this by turning difficulties into a quiz game: "Come on," she might say, "is it a difficult one? Is it to do with animals? Or vegetables? Or minerals?"[7] Once he visited the London Library with John but found it impossible to indicate what book he wanted, except that it was to do with art and then with "'Stralia". Eventually, Moorehead laughed and holding his hands beside his head like ears, hopped about the Art Room until John guessed, "Kangaroo!"[8] He led his father to a shelf of books about Australian Aboriginal art and had guessed correctly.

Although he was unable to write or dictate, Lucy completed two books for him, taking none of the credit herself. First she edited the film script about Darwin's expedition and it was published under his name as *Darwin and the Beagle* in 1969, and, a year later, his fragments of autobiography – mostly about his friendship with Alexander Clifford – were published as *A Late Education*. This she had also edited as "a disordered sort of autobiography" but again claimed no credit, even in a letter to a friend in which she wrote, "Alan has a new book coming out in November (written, of course, before he was ill, but now gathered together)."[9] There was other unpublished work amongst his papers – the libretto for *Mrs Fraser* and attempts to write fiction – but she decided that none would add to his stature and sadly came to the conclusion that there would be new editions of his books but no more writing. She herself was as resolute as ever and several friends, who had found her a sad person over recent years, noticed a tranquillity about her as if grateful that, despite the tragedy, the years of roaming had ended.

Yet they continued with the travels that had once been recorded in articles for the *New Yorker*, *Holiday* magazine and the rest. Now they were like repeated showings of familiar films, but silent and in slow motion. They travelled on the Continent between London and the Villa Moorehead and even went to Africa to see the wild animals again. They flew to the West Indies, and once when they were staying with the Bernsteins on Barbados the American playwright Lilian Hellman came to lunch. She talked of her youth to her host's fascination but never drew a word from Moorehead. Next day, he pointed to the chair in which she had sat and said, "Bloody marvellous." Bernstein found that a conversation could be created around Moorehead, involving him but requiring him only to interject one of his available words if he was able. "This man, who wrote and spoke so beautifully, cannot pass on his quality," he said. "It is a Gothic tragedy."[10]

Moorehead remained physically active, walking alone in London but carrying in his pocket a card bearing his name and address since he could say neither. Sometimes he would visit Anthony Fry's studio in St. John's Wood when a model was there to pose and he was wistfully diligent in painting the female nude. Fry found these paintings charming if not always anatomically accurate and his work in oils, gouache and water-colours promising, sensing their importance to Moorehead who found some fulfilment and peace in the studio. He also visited the Mooreheads at their flat and was surprised to find Lucy there with another artist who had influenced her husband: his former lover from New York, whom she had invited to their home in the belief that anything that could give him some happiness must be acceptable. With the energy he had devoted to writing Moorehead painted in his little studio at Porto Ercole, where he produced landscapes of Italy and a variety of *capriccios* based upon Aboriginal and Ancient Egyptian art, and in London, where he covered a wall of his study with a mural of wild animals in the African bush. Sometimes Lucy would accompany him to exhibitions, but this could prove embarrassing: his stroke had damaged his capacity to edit whatever he wanted to say and slight deafness meant that those words he could articulate were often spoken loudly. Thus at one private view of a friend's pictures, he walked round the gallery remarking audibly, "Bloody awful."

More surprisingly, he could play cards and his game of bridge was no better and no worse than before his illness, although he had to place his cards on a wooden rack on the table and had difficulty in bidding with sign-language. At such times – particularly with his family and a few intimate friends – he could relax and laugh. The company of his family gave him joy, particularly as he was now a grandfather: Caroline had had a daughter – named Martha after Martha Gellhorn – while her husband had been granted a fellowship at Sussex University. John, who was now a journalist on the *Daily Mail*, had married and also had a daughter – named Laura – in 1970. Now that there was no more editing of his work for Lucy she had begun to edit the voluminous letters of Freya Stark, who was in her eighties and so full of her own opinions of the work in hand that her editor remarked that "she compares herself with Shakespeare, which makes literary discussion ticklish".[11]

Occasionally he travelled without Lucy, usually with some companion but once or twice alone. He flew to New York to stay with friends on Long Island and to Australia to visit his sister. In Melbourne he would go for long walks through the tree-lined streets he had known as a boy and seemed determined to find little regular services to perform in the house, like laying the table for meals. He enjoyed the company of a few old friends, like Rod Andrew, but sometimes shocked Phyllis's more genteel guests when, instead of saying "absolutely", or "fantastic", he pronounced one of the rougher swear-words. He would become depressed and sit, sunk in gloom, and it would be time for another change of scene, and what he would once have seen as more running away, except that now there was no escaping his imprisonment.

In London, too, he would fall into troughs of depression despite everything that Lucy and his children could do and the one word that he would speak then was, "Bored". Yet, even so, he kept to a routine of painting, walking and appearing for meals. Any fears that he would take to drink were needless for, as part of this discipline, he limited himself to two glasses of sherry before lunch and two glasses of wine with it; two glasses of whisky in the evening, a little wine with dinner and ten cigarettes a day. Yet he became increasingly lonely, feeling that old friends were often too embarrassed to visit him, and those that were not went abroad or died. Since the loss of so many intimates twenty years before, others had gone – Alwyn Lee had died in 1970 – as had his heroes: Berenson in 1959 and Hemingway, by his own hand, in 1961. Now the inner circle of friends was limited to about a score in England and half that number in Australia and the United States. At times he would sit, deep in despair and loneliness.

At such times there were fears that he might attempt suicide. Indeed, he once alarmed Lucy when they were walking near a cliff by indicating that he might throw himself over the edge; but it was only an illustration of his mood. On his walks alone, there were many opportunities for self-destruction which he never took. Those close to him remarked not only on his courage and resolution but his discipline, and that was a continuation of the working routine he had imposed upon himself for so many years.

The conviction that he was forgotten would be temporarily relieved when a new edition of one of his books was published, particularly when illustrated, and, two years after his stroke, there was brief

286

gratification when the OBE, which he had been awarded with the other war correspondents, was advanced to the status of Commander of the Order of the British Empire. Then, after twelve years of incapacity, he heard that he had been awarded the highest honour within the gift of the Australian Government: the Order of Australia. Another recipient in the same Honours List was Rod Andrew, to whom Lucy now wrote: "I must give myself the pleasure of writing O.A. on this envelope . . . Alan refused to take any of it seriously but feels a bit different now that he knows you've got it too. Bloody good show. Pity it isn't Lady Andrew and Lady Moorehead in a way."[12]

Another honour followed but it was also a final farewell to his active life. He and Lucy decided to present his papers – all his notes for books and correspondence except his letters to Lucy and the children and his private journal – to the archives of the National Library of Australia in Canberra. An Australian archivist arrived to inspect them before the packing began and, at the beginning of 1978, Lucy noted in a letter, "Strange but good to see Alan's papers being sorted."[13] Others would now read what he could not.

Lucy herself had not been well. She had had an abdominal operation, her heart was found to be weak and her eyesight was so poor that she had been advised not to drive their car. When at Porto Ercole, they employed an English girl as a help in the house and to drive. In the spring and early summer of 1979, Lucy maintained the usual variety of entertaining, visiting and travel to give variety to their lives. Much of this was devoted to their family. John, whose first marriage had ended in divorce in 1975, was just married again to a charming girl who delighted his parents: Sarah – nicknamed "Boo" – the attractive and intelligent daughter of Sir Hugh Brassey, the Lord Lieutenant of Wiltshire. In June, Osbert Lancaster and his second wife, Anne Scott-James, had been to stay as had Essie, the widow of Alwyn Lee, and now they were alone with Moorehead's sister Phyllis.

Each day had to be planned to include both routine and incident, with Moorehead usually painting in his studio throughout the morning and some small expedition planned for the afternoon. On 16th July, he was more than usually restless and it was decided that, although the girl driver was off-duty, they would motor a little way down the coast for lunch in a restaurant at Ansedonia. So, with Lucy at the wheel, Moorehead beside her and Phyllis at the back, they set out, crossed the causeway between the lagoons to either side of Orbetello and turned south to join the autostrada. As Lucy drove down the slip road on to the motorway, she did not see a lorry, travelling fast and approaching the junction from their rear. It struck the car with tremendous force, flinging Lucy and Phyllis into the road, stunned, but leaving Moorehead strapped to his seat and conscious. They were taken to the hospital at Orbetello, where Lucy died a few hours later. Phyllis, suffering from concussion, recovered and Moorehead was physically unharmed.

When the news reached the children they found it almost impossible to believe. For nearly thirteen years they had been half-expecting the news that their father had suffered another stroke, but their mother had seemed indestructible, the rock upon which their lives were founded. They flew to Italy and tried to discover exactly what had happened. There were conflicting accounts and theories of what had caused the accident, which included the possibility that Lucy had had a heart attack and swerved into the path of the lorry and the probability that she had simply failed to see the lorry which had been travelling very fast indeed. Phyllis had no memory of the impact and Moorehead had remained fully conscious throughout and presumably knew what had happened but was unable to tell them.

Lucy was buried in the little municipal cemetery at Porto Ercole at the foot of the lane that ran uphill to the Villa Moorehead, and the grove of cypress that cast their shade on her grave could be seen from the terrace of the house. Soon after, her family returned to London and Caroline took her father to Mali in Africa, where her husband was working and she had been living, but the memories of travels in happier times were too strong and he returned to London after a few weeks. He and Caroline decided to set up house together – she had moved into their old flat in Eccleston Square when, soon after his stroke, he and Lucy had moved into a block of flats with a lift nearby – and they jointly bought one in Fitzroy Road on the opposite side of Primrose Hill to Wells Rise. This would be near John's house in Egbert Street and Moorehead went to live there until the new house was ready. At the beginning of 1981, he and Caroline and her family – and Olive Wood, who was now looking after her children: Martha, now eleven, and Daniel, three – moved in, with Moorehead occupying the ground floor and joining the others for meals. From here he could set out alone on his walks into Regent's Park, across Primrose Hill and over Hampstead Heath.

Although his three children were determined to give him as active and interesting a life as they could, he had lost his link with the world when Lucy died. There were more and longer spells of despair, he showed increasing irritability with those he loved and there were renewed fears that he might choose suicide. A year after Lucy's death, he spoke the word "Finish" and made a gesture as if swallowing pills. Since he had to take half a Mogadon sedative each night there was concern about the amount available to him. On another occasion, when with John, he pointed towards the Regent's Park Canal and made swimming gestures. "You want to drown yourself?" "That's right." "But it's only three feet deep," said John, "and you swim too well."[14] Moorehead laughed and went into the next room to continue painting. It was apparent that such threats were more of a form of protest with a touch of gallows-humour than a notice of intent.

After his stroke, he and Lucy had visited Australia and he continued to do so, travelling with a companion and, once, on his own. Staying with Phyllis at her house in the Toorak district of Melbourne, he followed the same routine as in England and Italy, giving himself small tasks to perform, going for short walks and pouring a small and set number of drinks before and during meals. He visited the Drysdales' studio and seemed to relax among the familiar surroundings and smells of paint and canvas. Sometimes he saw old friends, who remembered him from the days of his rise to success. They were warned what to expect but all seemed stunned by the tragedy of his state, whether, like Douglas Brass, himself a former war correspondent, who would say "We raw Australians hadn't really appreciated him,"[15] or, like Erl Gray, who had worked with Moorehead on the *Herald* in Melbourne, and now said, "There had always been a sense of destiny about Alan." Now he sat looking at them, and "bursting to say something" and finally being able to say, "Absolutely."[16]

After a few weeks with Phyllis, he would show signs of restlessness and it would be time to leave for London and join his children again. Neither he nor Caroline found it easy to share a house. She found him difficult and demanding while he found a household geared to the needs of a young family irritating since it disrupted the routine of his day. Yet, despite bouts of melancholy and restlessness, his discipline held. However, it was clear that an alternative way of living had to be found, and it was decided that he should move into a flat of his own, close to Caroline and John, and have a resident housekeeper-companion. So, early in 1983, he moved to a flat at the top of a large house, 25 Elsworthy Road, overlooking Primrose Hill, with an Australian girl to look after him, cook his meals, drive his car and take him to a restaurant or a cinema when he wished. He felt relaxed with her familiar accent and enjoyed the company of a young woman. The move was an immediate success. He saw his children frequently and their relationships with him became easier. He enjoyed entertaining and showed a certain grim satisfaction when Osbert Lancaster, his near-contemporary, took longer to climb the stairs than he did.

In the summer, he and his family returned once again to Porto Ercole and he would sit in the shade of the gum trees he had planted looking down the valley. It had changed since he had bought his land: new holiday houses for rich Italians were being built and most of the friends who had followed him here had left: Geoffrey Keating, who had taken a flat overlooking the harbour, had died in London two years before. At the bottom of the hill, the cypress trees showed where Lucy lay. It was not the idyllic place it had once been.

Sometimes clouds blanketed the hills of the Argentario peninsula and on one such day he and John looked from the terrace at a gloomy prospect of dark trees and white mist. Suddenly, Moorehead said, "Finish." "You mean you want to sell the house?" He nodded and spread his hands as if flying. "Australia then?" "Absolutely."[17]

Soon afterwards they returned to London and began plans for further travel, including another journey to Australia. One evening in September he said that he felt unwell, but next morning, the 29th, he seemed better and his housekeeper went out shopping. When she returned, she found him in the bedroom. At the age of seventy-three, Alan Moorehead was dead; a second stroke had ended his life seventeen years after he had last exercised the talents that had taken him so far.

Epilogue

News of Moorehead's death was printed on the news-pages of newspapers as well as in the obituary columns, but the stir was far less than it would have been had not his working life ended so long before. He was buried in Hampstead Cemetery at Fortune Green in London and his plain white headstone was enscribed simply, "Alan Moorehead. Writer."

His children continued to lead lives according to his influence on them: John and Caroline as writers; Richard, who was much like him in looks and temperament, roamed the world for several years – two of them in Australia – before taking his A-levels at the age of twenty-four and reading Economics at the University of East Anglia, then becoming a director of research for the World Wildlife Fund in Africa. The two eldest continued to live in the houses they had shared with their father, and Richard, after his marriage, kept his father's flat in Elsworthy Road as his base in London. In 1988, their aunt Phyllis, who had regularly been playing golf and tennis died suddenly at the age of eighty-three while preparing to go out to dinner.

Several of Moorehead's books remained in print and it was for these that the younger generations remembered him. In Australia, there was a sense of gratitude as well as loss for, as another journalist – his friend Michael Charlton, who had also made his name abroad, but as a correspondent for British television – put it, "He gave Australia back its history."[1] Ironically, the achievements that came nearest to his hopes of greatness are hidden from the vast readership he commanded. His despatches, which brought home the Second World War to millions and were, in the opinion of many, unrivalled eye-witness accounts of that time, remain only on microfilm in the British Library's newspaper archives at Colindale, not far from Fortune Green, and in the reference library of the *Daily Express* a short way from Fleet Street.

Another kind of greatness is preserved in memory by his family and a few friends and that is of the courage with which he faced seventeen years when, as in the allusion by John Donne that he liked to quote, a prince in prison lay.

Source Notes

Abbreviations
MFC   Moorehead Family Collections.
NLA   National Library of Australia.
CP   Clifford Papers.
AM   Alan Moorehead.
LM   Lucy Milner/Moorehead.

   Prologue
1   Tom Driberg in *Leader Magazine*, 11/11/44.
2   *Daily Express*, 7/5/45.

   Chapter I
1   Allan Fleming in interview with the author, 13/11/87.
2   Sam White in an interview with the author, 6/3/87.
3   Mrs Beth McInnes (née Thwaites) in an interview with the author, 18/11/87.
4   Undated letter from AM to Beth Thwaites.
5   Ditto.
6   Mrs Joan McClelland in an interview with the author, 6/11/87.
7   Undated letter from AM to Beth Thwaites.
8   Undated MS, NLA.

   Chapter II
1   *A Late Education*, p. 40.
2   Undated MS, NLA.
3   *A Late Education*, p. 44.

4   AM to Beth Thwaites, 18/8/36.
5   Undated letter to AM from Noel Monks.
6   Phyllis Whitehead (née Moorehead) in an interview with the author, 16/11/87.
7   AM to LM, 7/11/38. MFC.
8   Ditto, 14/11/38. MFC.
9   AM to LM, undated, 1938. MFC.
10 Ditto, undated, 1938. MFC.
11 Chester Wilmot's diary, 13/3/38.
12 AM to LM, 24/11/38. MFC.

Chapter III
1   AM to LM, 10/11/38. MFC.
2   Undated Moorehead notes, NLA.
3   George Millar in an interview with the author, 25/5/88.
4   *A Late Education*, p. 104.
5   AM to LM, 15/12/38. MFC.
6   Ditto, 28/12/38. MFC.
7   Ditto, 11/1/39. MFC.
8   *A Late Education*, p. 116–7.
9   AM to LM, 7/1/39. MFC.
10 *Daily Express*, 12/1/39.
11 AM to LM, 11/1/39. MFC.
12 Ditto, 13/1/39. MFC.
13 Ditto, 8/3/39. MFC.
14 Ditto, 10/3/39. MFC.
15 Ditto, 9/2/39. MFC.
16 *Daily Express*, 13/2/39.
17 AM to LM, 17/2/39. MFC.
18 Ditto, March, 1939. MFC.
19 Ditto, March, 1939. MFC.
20 Ditto, March 1939. MFC.
21 Ditto, 18/3/39. MFC.
22 Ditto, 1/4/39. MFC.
23 Ditto, 13/4/39. MFC.
24 Ditto, 15/4/39. MFC.
25 *Daily Express*, 10/4/39.
26 AM to LM, 24/4/39. MFC.
27 Ditto, undated, 1939. MFC.
28 Ditto, 15/6/39. MFC.
29 Ditto, 7/7/39. MFC.
30 Ditto, 17/6/39. MFC.
31 Ditto, 23/6/39. MFC.
32 Ditto, 16/6/39. MFC.
33 Ditto, undated letter, 1939. MFC.
34 Ditto, undated letter, July, 1939. MFC.

35 Ditto, undated letter, 21/7/39. MFC.
36 AM to LM, 10/7/39. MFC.
37 Ditto, 22/8/39. MFC.

Chapter IV
1 AM to LM, 23/8/39. MFC.
2 Ditto, 24/8/39. MFC.
3 *Daily Express*, 24/8/39.
4 Ditto, 26/8/39.
5 AM to LM, 25/8/39. MFC.
6 Ditto, 31/8/39. MFC.
7 Ditto, 3/9/39. MFC.
8 Ditto, 18/9/39. MFC.
9 Ditto, 28/9/39. MFC.
10 George Millar in an interview with the author, 25/5/88.
11 AM to Mrs. Vincent Milner, 6/10/39. MFC.
12 AM to LM, 1/1/40. MFC.
13 Ditto, 30/12/39. MFC.
14 Ditto, 15/1/40. MFC.
15 Ditto, 17/1/40. MFC.
16 Ditto, 18/1/40. MFC.
17 Ditto, 19/1/40. MFC.
18 Ditto, 26/1/40. MFC.
19 Ditto, 26/1/40. MFC.
20 Ditto, 1/2/40. MFC.
21 Ditto, 3/2/40. MFC.
22 *Daily Express*, 7/2/40.
23 AM to LM, 9/2/40. MFC.
24 *Daily Express*, 13/2/40.
25 AM to LM, 13/2/40. MFC.
26 Ditto, 16/2/40. MFC.
27 Ditto, 16/2/40. MFC.
28 *Daily Express*, 3/5/40.
29 AM to LM, 7/5/40. MFC.
30 Ditto, 18/5/40. MFC.
31 Ditto, undated, May, 1940. MFC.
32 Ditto, 20/5/40. MFC.
33 Ditto, 23/5/40. MFC.
34 *A Late Education*, p. 4.
35 AM to LM, 23/5/40. MFC.
36 Ditto, 26/5/40. MFC.
37 *A Late Education*, p. 34.
38 AM to LM, 27/5/40. MFC.
39 Ditto, 26/5/40. MFC.
40 Ditto, 27/5/40. MFC.
41 Ditto, 24/5/40. MFC.

Chapter V

1   *Mediterranean Front* (*African Trilogy*, p. 19).
2   *Daily Express*, 4/7/40.
3   *A Late Education*, p. 62–3.
4   *Three Against Rommel* by Alexander Clifford, page 143.
5   *A Late Education*, p. 63.
6   *Daily Express*, 9/7/40.
7   *Daily Express*, 26/7/40.
8   *Mediterranean Front* (*African Trilogy*, p. 40).
9   Ditto, p. 42.
10 *Daily Express*, 5/8/40.
11 AM to LM, 10/8/40. MFC.
12 Ditto, 14/8/40. MFC.
13 Clifford to Mrs. Marian Clifford, 29/7/40. CP.
14 AM to LM, 15/8/40. MFC.
15 Ditto, 29/8/40. MFC.
16 *Mediterranean Front* (*African Trilogy*, p. 48).
17 *Daily Express*, 6/9/40.
18 *Mediterranean Front* (*African Trilogy*, p. 52).
19 *A Late Education*, p. 123.
20 Ditto, p. 125.
21 *Daily Express*, 26/10/40.
22 *Mediterranean Front* (*African Trilogy*, p. 65).
23 *Daily Express*, 18/12/40.
24 *Mediterranean Front* (*African Trilogy*, p. 67).
25 *Daily Express*, 21/12/40.
26 *Mediterranean Front* (*African Trilogy*, p. 79).

Chapter VI

1   *Mediterranean Front* (*African Trilogy*, p. 85).
2   *Daily Express*, 7/2/41.
3   Allan Fleming in an interview with the author, 13/11/87.
4   *A Late Education*, p. 127–8.
5   Ditto, p. 129.
6   Allan Fleming in an interview with the author, 13/11/87.
7   AM to Mrs. Edith Wilmot, 13/3/55.
8   *Mediterranean Front* (*African Trilogy*, p. 121).
9   Christiansen to AM, 16/7/41. NLA.
10 Clifford's diary, 13/7/41. CP.
11 Ditto, 6/11/41. CP.
12 Christiansen to AM, 25/8/41. NLA.
13 Ditto, undated, 1941. NLA.
14 *A Year of Battle* (*African Trilogy*, p. 196).
15 *Daily Express*, 5/9/41.
16 *A Year of Battle* (*African Trilogy*, p. 201).

17   Ditto, p. 206.
18   *Daily Express*, 30/6/41.
19   Ditto, 8/7/41.
20   Ditto, 30/10/41.
21   Ditto, 21/11/41.
22   *A Year of Battle* (*African Trilogy*, p. 226–7).
23   *Daily Express*, 27/11/41.
24   *A Year of Battle* (*African Trilogy*, p. 228).
25   *Daily Express*, 5/12/41.
26   *Three Against Rommel* by Alexander Clifford, p. 173.
27   Clifford's diary, 11/12/41. CP.
28   *Crusader* by Alexander Clifford, p. 151.
29   *Three Against Rommel*, p. 20.
30   *A Year of Battle* (*African Trilogy*, p. 246).
31   Foley to AM, 27/10/41. NLA.
32   Ditto, undated, 1941. NLA.
33   Ditto, 14/7/42. NLA.
34   Christiansen to AM, 13/1/42. NLA.
35   Ditto, 3/12/41. NLA.
36   Ditto, 3/12/41.
37   Ditto, 14/1/42.

      Chapter VII
 1   Clifford's diary, 18/1/42. CP.
 2   Clifford in a letter to Mrs. Marian Clifford, 17/2/41. CP.
 3   Clare Hollingworth in an interview with the author, 6/10/87.
 4   *A Late Education*, p. 58.
 5   Charles Foley in a letter to the author, 6/10/87.
 6   Christiansen to AM, 1942. NLA.
 7   Foley in a letter to the author, 6/10/87.
 8   *Daily Express*, 10/2/42.
 9   Ditto, 19/3/42.
10   Clifford's diary, 27/3/42. CP.
11   *A Year of Battle* (*African Trilogy*, p. 264).
12   Ditto, p. 270.
13   Ditto, p. 263.
14   Ditto, p. 272.
15   Ditto, p. 278.
16   *Daily Express*, 6/4/42.
17   *A Year of Battle* (*African Trilogy*, p. 281).
18   Ditto, p. 292.
19   Ditto, p. 294.
20   AM to Christiansen, 27/5/42. NLA.
21   *A Year of Battle* (*African Trilogy*, p. 322).
22   *Daily Express*, 8/6/42.
23   Ditto, 15/6/42.

24 *A Year of Battle* (*African Trilogy*, p. 353).
25 *Daily Express*, 23/6/42.
26 Ditto, 6/7/42.
27 Ditto, 6/7/42.
28 *Daily Express*, 15/7/42.
29 *A Year of Battle* (*African Trilogy*, p. 363).
30 AM to Christiansen, 6/8/42. NLA.
31 Christiansen to AM, 11/8/42. NLA.
32 *Daily Express*, 20/8/42.

Chapter VIII
 1 *Daily Express*, 5/10/42.
 2 Ditto, 12/10/42.
 3 *The End in Africa* (*African Trilogy*, p. 411).
 4 *Daily Express*, 7/1/43.
 5 John Redfern in an interview with the author, 12/9/87.
 6 *The End in Africa* (*African Trilogy*, p. 493).
 7 Ditto, p. 494.
 8 AM to LM, 10/3/43. MFC.
 9 Ditto, 10/3/43. MFC.
10 Ditto, 10/3/43. MFC.
11 Ditto, 10/3/43. MFC.
12 Ditto, 10/3/43. MFC.
13 Ditto, 10/3/43. MFC.
14 Ditto, 10/3/43. MFC.
15 *Daily Express*, 17/12/42.
16 AM to LM, 10/3/43. MFC.
17 Ditto, 11/3/43. MFC.
18 *The End in Africa* (*African Trilogy*, p. 527).
19 Ditto, p. 527–8.
20 Ditto, p. 530.
21 *Three Against Rommel*, p. 384.
22 *The End in Africa* (*African Trilogy*, p. 530).
23 *A Late Education*, p. 135.
24 *Daily Express*, 28/4/43.
25 *The End in Africa* (*African Trilogy*, p. 563).
26 *Daily Express*, 19/5/43.
27 AM to LM, 18/8/43. MFC.

Chapter IX
 1 *Daily Express*, 13/8/43.
 2 *A Late Education*, p. 136.
 3 *Road to Rome* by Christopher Buckley, p. 26.
 4 Ditto, p. 68.
 5 Ditto, p. 69.
 6 Ditto, p. 135.

7   AM to LM, 18/8/43. MFC.
8   *Daily Express*, 17/8/43.
9   General Belchem in an interview with the author, 20/2/58.
10   AM to LM, 18/8/43. MFC.
11   Ditto, 24/8/43. MFC.
12   Ditto, 22/8/43. MFC.
13   Ditto, 30/8/43. MFC.
14   Ditto, 5/9/43. MFC.
15   Ditto, 24/8/43. MFC.
16   *Eclipse*, p. 14.
17   Ditto, p. 15–17.
18   AM to LM, 20/9/43. MFC.
19   Ditto, 27/9/43. MFC.
20   AM to Christiansen, 22/9/43. NLA.
21   AM to LM, 20/9/43. MFC.
22   Ditto, 27/9/43. MFC.
23   Ditto, 18/11/43. MFC.
24   Ditto, 2/10/43. MFC.
25   Ditto, 7/10/43. MFC.
26   Ditto, 17/10/43. MFC.
27   *Eclipse*, p. 65.
28   AM to LM, 25/10/43. MFC.
29   Ditto, 28/10/43. MFC.
30   Ditto, 2/11/43. MFC.
31   Ditto, 25/11/43. MFC.
32   Ditto, 8/11/43. MFC.
33   Ditto, 28/10/43. MFC.
34   Ditto, 8/11/43. MFC.
35   Ditto, 6/12/43. MFC.
36   Ditto, 9/12/43. MFC.
37   Ditto, 14/12/43. MFC.
38   Ditto, 23/12/43. MFC.
39   *The Diary of a War Artist* by Edward Ardizzone, p. 85–9.
40   AM to LM, 26/12/43. MFC.
41   Ditto, 28/12/43. MFC.
42   Ditto, 1/1/44. MFC.
43   Ditto, 11/12/43. MFC.
44   Ditto, 1/1/44. MFC.
45   George Millar in an interview with the author, 24/5/88.
46   AM to LM, 9/1/44. MFC.

Chapter X
1   Hamish Hamilton in an interview with the author, 9/6/87.
2   Cyril Ray in an interview with the author, 3/6/87.
3   *Leader Magazine*, 11/11/44.
4   John Redfern in an interview with the author, 12/9/87.

5   AM to LM, 12/4/44. MFC.
6   *Daily Express*, 4/2/44.
7   Ditto, 11/2/44.
8   Ditto, 3/3/44.
9   Ditto, 17/3/44.
10 AM's journal, 10/2/44. MFC.
11 Ditto, 11/2/44. MFC.
12 Ditto, 9/2/44. MFC.
13 Ditto, 13/2/44. MFC.
14 *Daily Express*, 3/3/44.
15 AM's journal, 4/3/44.
16 *Daily Express*, 29/5/44.
17 Sir Edgar Williams in an interview with the author, 23/9/87.
18 AM's pocket diary, 6/6/44. NLA.
19 *Leader Magazine*, 11/11/44.
20 Doon Campbell in a letter to the author, 23/2/89.
21 Clifford to Mrs. Marian Clifford, 20/7/44. CP.
22 *Daily Express*, 23/6/44.
23 Ditto, 10/7/44.
24 Sir Edgar Williams in an interview with the author, 23/9/89.
25 *Daily Express*, 19/7/44.
26 Ditto, 20/7/44.
27 Ditto, 21/7/44.
28 Ditto, 23/7/44.
29 AM to Christiansen, July, 1944. NLA.
30 Ditto, 31/7/44. NLA.
31 Christiansen to AM, 11/8/44. NLA.
32 AM to Christiansen, 3/9/44. NLA.
33 *Eclipse*, p. 135.
34 *Ernest Hemingway* by Carlos Baker, p. 597.
35 Douglas Brass in an interview with the author, 17/11/87.
36 *Daily Express*, 2/9/44.
37 Christiansen to AM, September, 1944. NLA.
38 Richard McMillan in an interview with the author, 24/1/88.
39 *A Late Education*, p. 142.
40 Clifford to Mrs. Marian Clifford, 28/12/44. CP.
41 *Daily Express*, 12/9/44.
42 Clifford to LM, 2/11/44. MFC.
43 *Daily Express*, 6/1/45.
44 Ditto, 8/1/45.
45 Ditto, 1/2/45.
46 Clifford to AM, 4/3/45. MFC.
47 Hamish Hamilton to AM, 6/9/44. NLA.
48 Christiansen to AM, 3/3/45. NLA.
49 *Daily Express*, 1/3/45.
50 Ditto, 26/3/45.

51 Clifford to Mrs. Marian Clifford, 7/4/45. CP.
52 Ditto, 21/4/45. CP.
53 *Daily Express*, 14/4/45.
54 *Eclipse*, p. 213.
55 *Daily Express*, 23/4/45.
56 AM to *Daily Express*, 4/5/45. NLA.
57 AM to Field Marshal Montgomery, 4/5/45. NLA.
58 *Daily Express*, 7/5/45.
59 Ditto, 11/5/45.
60 *Eclipse*, p. 255.

Chapter XI
1   Mrs. Cecilia Russell-Smith (formerly Buckley) in an interview with the author, 5/9/87.
2   Ditto, 5/9/87.
3   *Daily Express*, 21/8/45.
4   Paul Holt to David Woodward, 20/11/45.
5   AM to Christiansen, 25/8/45. NLA.
6   AM to Brigadier Williams, 15/10/45.
7   AM's journal, 25/10/45. MFC.
8   Ditto, 26/10/45. MFC.
9   Mrs. Beth McInnes in an interview with the author, 18/11/87.
10 Dr. Roderick Andrew in an interview with the author, 15/11/87.
11 Lt. Col. Lionel Cross to AM, 20/6/46. NLA.
12 Howard Marshall to AM, June, 1946. NLA.
13 Ronald Matthews to AM, 2/11/46. NLA.
14 Prof. Manning Clark in an interview with the author, 11/11/87.
15 Paul Holt to David Woodward, 20/11/45.
16 AM's journal, 3/11/46. MFC.
17 FM. Montgomery to Sir Edward Crowe, 21/11/46. NLA.
18 Clifford to AM, 2/6/47. NLA.
19 Buckley to AM, 1946. NLA.
20 Mrs. Russell-Smith in an interview with the author, 5/9/87.
21 Ditto, 5/9/87.
22 Clifford to AM, 18/6/47. NLA.
23 AM to LM, 25/9/47. MFC.
24 Ditto, 6/10/47. MFC.
25 Ditto, 20/10/47. MFC.
26 Ditto, 23/10/47. MFC.
27 Ditto, 8/11/47. MFC.
28 Ditto, 11/10/47. MFC.
29 Ditto, 8/11/47. MFC.
30 Ditto, 11/10/47. MFC.
31 The *Observer*, 2/11/47.
32 Pollinger to AM, 10/12/47. NLA.
33 Shute to AM, 27/12/47. NLA.

34 *A Late Education*, p. 149.
35 Ditto, p. 150.
36 William Shawn to AM, 14/10/48. NLA.
37 Buckley to AM, 12/1/47. NLA.
38 AM to Phyllis Whitehead, 1948. MFC.
39 AM's journal, 2/9/48. MFC.
40 AM to Phyllis Whitehead, 1948. MFC.
41 AM's journal, 5/9/48. MFC.
42 Ditto, 6/9/48. MFC.

Chapter XII
1   AM's journal, 18/9/48. MFC.
2   Ditto, 18/9/48. MFC.
3   Ditto, 26/10/48. MFC.
4   Ditto, 8/11/48. MFC.
5   Ditto, 11/11/48. MFC.
6   Ditto, 28/12/48. MFC.
7   Ditto, 13/1/49. MFC.
8   Ditto, 14/1/49. MFC.
9   *A Late Education*, p. 156.
10 AM's journal, 19/1/49. MFC.
11 Ditto, 23/1/49. MFC.
12 Ditto, 26/1/49. MFC.
13 Ditto, 14/2/49. MFC.
14 Ditto, 27/2/49. MFC.
15 Ditto, 12/6/49. MFC.
16 Ditto, 23/7/49. MFC.
17 Ditto, 1/8/49. MFC.
18 Ditto, 5/11/49. MFC.
19 *A Late Education*, p. 154.
20 AM's journal, 31/7/49. MFC.
21 Ditto, 20/4/50. MFC.
22 Ditto, 14/9/50. MFC.
23 Sir Edward Pickering in an interview with the author, 29/7/87.
24 Clifford to AM, undated letter, 1950. NLA.
25 AM to LM, undated letter, 1950. MFC.
26 Buckley to AM, undated letter, 1950. NLA.
27 LM to AM, 29/4/48. NLA.
28 *The Letters of Ann Fleming*, ed. Mark Amory, p. 72.
29 Clifford to Tony Clifford, April, 1950. CP.
30 Buckley to AM, 22/1/49. NLA.
31 *A Late Education*, p. 165.
32 Buckley to AM, 29/3/50. NLA.
33 Mrs. Russell-Smith in an interview with the author, 5/9/87.
34 Ditto, 5/9/87.
35 Clifford to AM, 30/8/50. NLA.

36 AM's journal, August, 1950. MFC.
37 Ditto, 16/9/50. MFC.
38 Brigadier Nigel Dugdale to the author, 1951.
39 AM's journal, 21/12/51. MFC.
40 Memorandum by AM, 1952. NLA.
41 Ditto, 1952. NLA.
42 Clifford to LM, 11/10/52. MFC.
43 Ditto, 3/1/52. MFC.
44 *A Late Education*, p. 170–1.
45 Ditto, p. 173.
46 AM to Phyllis Whitehead, 18/3/52. MFC.
47 *The Times*, 28/3/52.
48 Lady Bangor in an interview with the author, 1987.

Chapter XIII
1   AM to LM, 10/4/52. MFC.
2   Ditto, 26/4/52. MFC.
3   Ditto, 10/4/52. MFC.
4   Ditto, 22/4/53. MFC.
5   *Melbourne Herald*, 30/4/52.
6   AM to LM, 30/4/52. MFC.
7   Ditto, 3/5/52. MFC.
8   Ditto, 30/4/52. MFC.
9   Ditto, 3/5/52. MFC.
10 Ditto, 1/6/52. MFC.
11 Ditto, 9/6/52. MFC.
12 Ditto, 17/6/52. MFC.
13 Ditto, 22/6/52. MFC.
14 Ditto, 27/6/52. MFC.
15 AM in script of radio talk, 14/3/64.
16 AM's journal, 5/11/52. MFC.
17 Ditto, 8/12/52. MFC.
18 Ditto, 8/11/52. MFC.
19 Noel Monks in an interview, 1954.
20 AM's journal, 5/8/54. MFC.
21 AM to Walter Goetz, c. 1954.
22 AM to Walter Goetz, 6/9/54.
23 AM's journal, 17/1/53. MFC.
24 Ditto, 4/5/54. MFC.
25 Ditto, 22/7/54. MFC.
26 Ditto, 30/10/54. MFC.
27 AM to LM, 13/1/56. MFC.
28 Ditto, 10/1/56. MFC.
29 Ditto, 27/5/56. MFC.
30 Ditto, 2/6/56. MFC.
31 Ditto, 17/6/56. MFC.

32 Ditto, 27/7/56. MFC.
33 Ditto, 2/6/56. MFC.
34 Ditto, 2/7/56. MFC.
35 Ditto, 7/7/56. MFC.
36 Bernard Berenson to AM, 4/7/56. NLA.
37 Lady Violet Bonham-Carter to AM, 20/4/56. NLA.
38 Caroline Moorehead in an interview with the author, 28/1/88.
39 AM to LM, 28/4/57. MFC.
40 AM to LM, 30/4/57. MFC.
41 Miss Martha Gellhorn in an interview with the author, 12/1/88.
42 AM to LM, 7/12/57. MFC.
43 Ditto, 19/12/57. MFC.
44 William Shawn to AM, 1957. NLA.
45 Dick Waller in an interview with the author.
46 LM to AM, undated letter, 1959. NLA.
47 Martha Gellhorn to AM, 16/1/61. NLA.
48 AM to Phyllis Whitehead, undated letter, c. 1961. MFC.
49 Text of speech, undated. NLA.
50 Prof. Manning Clark in an interview with the author, 11/11/87.
51 AM's journal, 26/6/66. MFC.
52 *The Australian*, 23/8/66.
53 *The Age*, Melbourne, 11/11/66.
54 AM in article for *SR Magazine*, 8/10/66.
55 Dick Waller in an interview with the author, 1988.

Chapter XIV
1 Phyllis Whitehead in an interview with the author, 16/11/87.
2 LM to Dr. Andrew, 6/1/67.
3 Ditto, 25/7/67.
4 Ditto, 31/1/69.
5 Valerie Eaton Griffith in an interview with the author, 6/12/88.
6 Anthony Fry in an interview with the author, 8/11/88.
7 Caroline Moorehead in an interview with the author, 28/1/88.
8 John Moorehead in an interview with the author, 15/2/88.
9 LM to Dr. Andrew, 13/9/70.
10 Lord Bernstein in an interview with the author, 15/2/88.
11 LM to Dr. Andrew, 5/5/72.
12 Ditto, 14/8/78.
13 LM to William Pope, National Library of Australia, 21/2/78. NLA.
14 John Moorehead in an interview with the author, 15/2/88.
15 Douglas Brass in an interview with the author, 17/11/87.
16 Erl Gray in an interview with the author, 17/11/87.
17 John Moorehead in an interview with the author, 15/2/88.

Epilogue
1 Michael Charlton in an interview with the author, 25/1/88.

Index